W9-CIP-178

CARD GAMES

LITTLE GIANT® ENCYCLOPEDIA

CARD GAMES

THE DIAGRAM GROUP

STERLING INNOVATION
An imprint of Sterling Publishing Co., Inc.

New York / London
www.sterlingpublishing.com

STERLING, the Sterling logo, STERLING INNOVATION, and the
Sterling Innovation logo are registered trademarks of Sterling Publishing
Co., Inc.

Library of Congress Cataloging-in-Publication Data Available

10 9 8 7 6 5 4 3 2

Published in 2009 by Sterling Publishing Co., Inc.
387 Park Avenue South, New York, NY 10016
© 1995 by Diagram Visual Information Ltd.
Distributed in Canada by Sterling Publishing
c/o Canadian Manda Group, 165 Dufferin Street
Toronto, Ontario, Canada M6K 3H6
Distributed in the United Kingdom by GMC Distribution Services
Castle Place, 166 High Street, Lewes, East Sussex, England BN7 1XU
Distributed in Australia by Capricorn Link (Australia) Pty. Ltd.
P.O. Box 704, Windsor, NSW 2756, Australia

Printed in China
All rights reserved

Sterling ISBN 978-1-4027-6417-2

For information about custom editions, special sales, premium and
corporate purchases, please contact Sterling Special Sales Department
at 800-805-5489 or specialsales@sterlingpublishing.com.

Foreword

Card playing has been popular for more than 500 years, and the greatest variety of card games in existence today reflects both this long history and the tremendous potential of playing cards as a source of entertainment. This illustrated encyclopedia brings together more than 250 card games and variations – old and new, easy and difficult, familiar and unfamiliar. Detailed rules of play are given step-by-step for each game in clear, concise language complemented by explanatory diagrams

The first four sections of the book place card games in one of four categories: general games, children's games, gambling games, and solitaire games. Obviously these divisions are somewhat arbitrary: some general games may be played for money; some children's games are popular with adults; some gambling games require high levels of card-playing skill; and some solitaire games require two players.

The order in which the games appear within each of the first four sections is basically alphabetical. In the gambling games section, for example, the games run literally from a to z, from Ace-deuce-jack to Ziginette. Alphabetical ordering, however, has not been applied to variants of games; these are included under the same main heading as the parent game (although they are also listed separately in the index). Thus Gin Rummy, for example, appears under the main heading for Rummy, not between Forty-five and Grand. Similarly, although the names are quite different, Black Maria appears under the heading for Hearts.

Obviously an important consideration when choosing a card game is the number of players. In the title bar for each game, a number indicates the number of players who can enjoy the game to best advantage.

Further useful informaton on finding a suitable game is to be found in section 5. This includes cross-referenced lists of games for different numbers of players, a list of variations, a list of alternative names, and a comprehensive index.

Contents

Section 1
General card games

10 General rules	**76** Five hundred	**122** Piquet
18 All fives	**79** Forty-five	**130** Pope Joan
20 Auction pitch	**84** Grand	**136** Preference
22 Bezique	**88** Hearts	**138** Rummy
31 Boston	**94** Imperial	**143** Seven up
34 Bridge	**98** Kalabriasz	**146** Skat
48 Calabrasella	**104** Knaves	**154** Solo whist
50 Canasta	**106** Loo	**157** Spoil five
56 Casino	**109** Michigan	**161** Vint
62 Cribbage	**112** Napoleon	**164** Whist
70 Ecarté	**114** Oh hell	
72 Euchre	**116** Pinochle	

Section 2
Gambling games

170 Introduction
172 Ace-deuce-jack
175 Baccarat/Chemin de fer
188 Bango
191 Banker and broker
194 Blackjack
219 Blücher
222 Brag
230 Card craps
238 Card put-and-take

241 Chinese fan-tan
244 Faro
252 Hoggenheimer
255 Horse race
258 Injun
261 Kentucky derby
266 Lansquenet
269 Monte bank
279 Poker
314 Polish red dog
318 Red and black

320 Red dog
328 Skinball
332 Slippery Sam
335 Stuss
338 Thirty-five
341 Thirty-one
344 Trente et quarante
349 Yablon
352 Ziginette

Section 3
Solitaire card games

358 Procedure and terms
362 Accordion
364 Beleaguered castle
366 Bisley
368 Braid
370 Bristol
372 Calculation
374 Canfield
378 Clock
380 Crazy quilt
382 Eight away
384 Florentine
386 Flower garden
388 Friday the thirteenth
390 Frog
392 King Albert
395 Klondike
397 La belle Lucie
400 Leapfrog
402 Maze
404 Miss Milligan
406 Monte Carlo
408 Napoleon at St Helena
410 Poker solitaire
413 Puss in the corner
415 Pyramid
418 Royal cotillion
420 Russian bank
425 Scorpion
427 Spider
430 Spite and malice
433 Windmill

Section 4
Children's games

436 Introduction
438 Beggar my neighbour
440 Card dominoes
442 Cheat
444 Concentraion
446 Donkey
448 Give away
450 Go boom
453 Go fish
455 Knockout whist
458 Linger longer
461 Menagerie
463 My ship sails
464 Old maid
467 Play or pay
469 Racing demon
472 Rolling stone
474 Sequence
476 Slapjack
478 Snap
481 Snip-snap-snorem
484 Spit
487 Stealing bundles
489 War

Section 5
Finding a game

494 How many players?
504 Variations and alternative names
507 Index

Section 1

GENERAL CARD GAMES

GENERAL RULES

The origin of playing cards is a mystery. Chinese playing cards, it seems, grew out of a marriage between divinatory arrows and paper money. Such cards may have reached Europe via the Crusades or the China trade. Alternatively Western playing cards may have had a separate European origin – seeming to have appeared quite suddenly, around 1370, in almost their present form.

THE CARDS

The deck The standard international deck of playing cards consists of 52 cards, divided into four suits of 13 cards each. Many decks also contain two jokers, sometimes used as wild cards.

The suits are named hearts, diamonds, spades, and clubs, and each card of the suit bears the appropriate symbol, as shown. Hearts and diamonds bear red symbols, spades and clubs black symbols.

The cards in any one suit are all of different denominations: nine are numbered from 2 to 10; three are "face" cards (jack, queen, king); the remaining card is the "ace," which is the "1" but is often the most powerful card of the suit.

The denomination of numbered cards is shown both by numbers and by the appropriate number of suit symbols. The ace is shown by an "A" and a single large suit symbol. Face cards are shown by stylized drawings and by initial letters, which vary according to the country of origin of the deck. In English language countries these letters are "J" (for jack), "Q" (for queen), and "K" (for king).

The rank of cards is usually either:
2 (low), 3,4,5,6,7,8,9,10,j,q,k,a (high);
or a (low), 2,3,4,5,6,7,8,9,10,j,q,k (high).
In either list, a card beats any card listed before it.
These rankings are referred to in the text as "cards rank normally, ace high," and "cards rank normally, ace low."

A meld is a scoring combination of cards in certain games. It is usually either:

a three or more cards of the same denomination; or
b three or more cards in consecutive order of rank and of the same suit.

Trumps In games with tricks (see p 16), it is often ruled that certain cards are made trump cards (trumps). If so, any trump card ranks above any other card.

Usually, all the cards of one suit are chosen as trump cards (trump suit). But in some games only some cards of one suit are the trump cards; or in many other games there are other trump cards in addition to the trump suit.

Within a trump suit, cards rank in the standard order for the game being played.

Choice of trump suit The method depends on the game being played.

Some games use a permanent trump suit, chosen by agreement or convention at the beginning of the game. But usually a suit has the role of trump suit for only one deal at a

Complete deck of cards

Hearts

Diamonds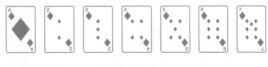

Spades

Clubs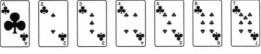

time. In this case, the trump suit for a deal is decided in one of the following ways, depending on the game being played:

a by competitive bidding among the players;

b by chance, ie turning a certain card face up, the suit revealed becomes trumps;

c by set order of rotation among the suits.

PREPARING AND DEALING

Choice of partners for partnership play is usually by an initial draw. Each of the four players draws one card from the deck; the two players with the highest ranking cards form one partnership and the other two players form the second.

Choice of the first dealer

a By high cut. Any agreed player acts as temporary dealer and shuffles the cards. Any other agreed player cuts them. Each player then cuts the deck, beginning with the player to the temporary dealer's left, going clockwise, and ending with the temporary dealer.

Each cut consists of lifting a section of cards from the top of the face-down deck. The card cut by the player is that at the bottom of this section.

The section is held up so all players can see this card.

After each cut, the two sections of cards are restacked in their original order, before passing to the next player.

The player cutting the highest denomination card becomes the first dealer. Cards rank normally; ace ranks high or low according to the game played. Players who cut equal-highest, cut again until a decision is reached between them.

b By deal of cards. Any agreed player acts as temporary dealer and shuffles the cards. Any other agreed player cuts them. The temporary dealer then deals one card face up to each player, including himself, beginning with the player to his left and going clockwise, until the first card of a specified denomination is dealt (eg the first ace). The player receiving this card becomes the first dealer.

Shuffle and cut are often required before every deal. The dealer shuffles. Any other player also has the right to shuffle, but the dealer has the right to shuffle last.

The procedure of shuffling is not governed by rules – providing that an adequate shuffle is given to the cards in some way. One simple and satisfactory procedure is illustrated here.

Shuffling

The player to the dealer's right is offered the cards to cut. If
he declines the player to his right is offered the cut, and so
on. If no player wishes to cut, the dealer must cut.

A cut consists of lifting a section of cards from the top of the
deck, placing it on the table, and placing the other section on
top of it.

Cards remain face down and unexposed throughout.

There must be at least five cards in each section.

The deal Unless otherwise stated, the dealer gives one card
at a time to each player, beginning with the player to his left
and going clockwise. This rotation is repeated until each
player has the required number of cards. The deal must be
from the top of a face down deck.

Deal in packets is a deal in which each player receives more
than one card at once. It is required for certain games.

On the deal, the dealer gives each player a specified number
of cards (eg three cards), before going on to the next player.
Otherwise the deal follows normal procedure.

Sometimes the number of cards specified changes during the
deal. For example, in solo whist:

when the dealer goes round the circle of players for the first,
second, and third times, he gives each player three cards
each time;

when he goes around the fourth (last) time, he gives each
player one card, as in a normal deal.

A widow is a batch of cards dealt in addition to the players'
hands. Its role varies from game to game.

The stock is, in certain games, the part of the deck which
remains undealt after the deal is complete but which
becomes available to players in the course of play.

ROTATION OF PLAY

Unless otherwise stated, play begins with the player to the
dealer's left, and continues with the other players in
clockwise rotation.

TRICKS

A trick signifies, in certain games, one round of cards during play – one card being contributed by each active hand. It also means the cards themselves when gathered together.

On each trick one player plays first ("has the lead"), and the other players follow in clockwise rotation.

Each player's action consists of taking one card from his hand and placing it face up in the center of the table.

The lead is held, in most games:

a on the first trick after the deal – by the player to the dealer's left;

b on the remaining tricks of a deal – by the player who won the previous trick.

Winning a trick

Trumps

Lead

King wins

Trump wins

Choice of cards The lead may play any card he wishes. The other players must "follow suit" if possible, ie each must play a card of the same suit as the lead card if he has one. If a player cannot follow suit, he may play any other card that he has.

A trick is won by the highest ranking card of the suit led–
providing that no trump is played. If one or more trump
cards are played, it is won by the highest ranking trump card.
A player may usually only play a trump card if he cannot
follow suit.

The player playing the winning card takes the trick: he
gathers the cards together, and places them face down on the
table, usually near his (or his partner's) position.

Revoking A player who has failed to follow suit when he in
fact had a card of the required suit is said to have "revoked."
Penalties for this vary from game to game.

IRREGULARITIES

Rules on irregularities in play vary from one game to
another. But the following rules are general.

A misdeal should be declared:

a if, during a deal, a card is found face-up in the deck; or

b if the rules of shuffling, cutting or dealing are broken.

Imperfect deck If the deck is found to have cards missing,
or added, or duplicated, the hand being played is
immediately abandoned. However, any scores made so far
on that hand are valid.

2-3   All fives

Rank

All fives is a similar game to seven up, but has a different scoring system. It is a game for two or three players.

Cards A standard deck of playing cards is used. Cards rank normally, with ace high.

Deal Players cut for the deal; highest card deals.

Each player is dealt six face down cards in packets of three. The next card is turned face up to denote trumps. The deal passes clockwise around the table.

Trumps If the player to the left of the dealer is happy to play with the trump suit designated by the face up card, he says "Stand" and play begins.

If the player to the dealer's left would prefer a different trump suit, he says "I beg". The dealer can then choose whether or not to change the trumps.

If the dealer chooses to keep trumps as they are, he says "Take one"; the player to his left then scores one point and play begins.

If the dealer agrees to change the trump suit, he sets aside the face-up card, deals three more cards to each player, and then turns the next card face up to denote trumps. If this card shows a different suit from the first face up card, play begins with this suit as trumps.

If the new face up card belongs to the same suit as the first face up card, the dealer gives another three cards to each player and turns up another face up card; this procedure is repeated until a new trump suit is determined. If the deck is used up before a new trump suit is found, the entire deck is shuffled and redealt.

Play Rules of play are as for whist.

Scoring At the end of each round the tricks are turned face up for scoring. Points are scored for trump cards in tricks won:

a ace of trumps, four points;
b king of trumps, three points;
c queen of trumps, two points;
d jack of trumps, one point;

e 10 of trumps, ten points;
f 5 of trumps, five points.
Game is 61 points.

2-7   Auction pitch

Rank

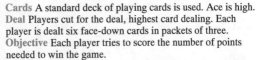

This game is derived from seven up and is especially popular in the United States. It is also called setback. It is a game for two to seven players.

Cards A standard deck of playing cards is used. Ace is high.

Deal Players cut for the deal, highest card dealing. Each player is dealt six face-down cards in packets of three.

Objective Each player tries to score the number of points needed to win the game.

Bidding Each player in turn, starting with the player to the dealer's left, makes a bid of one, two, three or four – or passes. A bid indicates the number of points the bidder intends to make. A bid of four is called "shoot the moon," "slam," or "smudge."

Each bid must be higher than the previous bid, except that the dealer may hold (ie take over) the previous bid if it is under four.

The highest bidder, or the dealer if he held a previous bid, is called the "pitcher."

Play The pitcher leads to the first trick and his card denotes trumps for the deal.

In a trump suit players must follow suit or, if they cannot, must discard one card. In a plain (non-trumps) suit, players may either follow suit or play a trump card – if they can do neither, they discard.

The winner of a trick leads to the next.

Scoring Players other than the pitcher score points exactly as in seven up, ie:

a "high," one point for the player dealt the highest trump;

b "low," one point for the player dealt the lowest trump;

c "jack," one point for the player who takes the jack of trumps in a trick;

d "game," one point for the player who takes the highest

total value of cards in tricks (for which purpose, cards are valued four for an ace, three for a king, two for a queen, one for a jack, ten for a 10).

The pitcher only scores if his score is equal to or greater than his bid. If he fails to make his contract, he is set back by (ie loses) the number of points he bid.

Game is usually seven points, but players can decide to play for 10,11 or 21 points.

If the pitcher ties with another player, the pitcher is the winner. For ties between other players, points are counted in the order: high, low, jack, and game.

AUCTION PITCH WITH JOKER

A joker is added to the deck for this version of auction pitch. It ranks as the lowest card of the trump suit in play.

If the pitcher leads the joker to the first trick, spades are trumps.

The player who takes the joker in a trick scores one point.

"Low" is scored by the player who is dealt the lowest trump card above the joker.

Game is 10 points. If there is a tie, the order for counting points is: high, low, jack, joker, and game.

2   Bezique

Rank

Bezique is a card game that originated in France, and is based on games played over 350 years ago. It became particularly popular in the mid-nineteenth century. The standard game is for two players, but there are variants for three or more players.

Pinochle is derived from bezique.

TWO-HANDED BEZIQUE

The deck comprises a double piquet deck, or two standard 52-card decks from which the 2s, 3s, 4s, 5s, and 6s have been removed – making a total of 64 cards in play.

The cards rank: a (high), 10,k,q,j,9,8,7.

The objective of the game is to make winning melds or declarations, and to take tricks containing certain scoring cards known as brisques.

Deal Players cut for deal. The dealer gives eight cards to each player, dealing three, two, and three cards at a time. The next (the seventeenth) card is placed face up on the table and indicates the trump suit for that hand. If this card is a 7, the dealer scores 10 points.

The remaining cards are turned face down in a pile, forming the "stock."

Play is in two stages.

The first stage lasts as long as there are cards in the stock.

Declarations

Trumps	a	b	c	d	e
	20 points	40 points	40 points	40 points	60 points

The non-dealer leads first; thereafter the winner of each trick leads to the next one.

After each trick the winner may make any declaration, and then both players draw cards from the stock to replenish their hands, the winner of the trick drawing first.

The winner of the last trick takes the last stock card, and the loser takes the exposed trump card.

During this stage the players are not obliged to follow suit. A trick is taken by the higher card of the suit led or by a trump card. If cards of equal value are played, the card that led takes the trick.

The second stage begins when the stock is exhausted.

The players must follow suit for these last eight tricks, except they may trump if they cannot follow suit. A player must win a trick if he is able to.

The winner of the last trick scores 10 points.

Declarations may be made after winning a trick.

The cards of each meld must be laid face up in front of the player, but they may be played to tricks as if they were still in the hand.

The possible declarations are as follows:

a common marriage: king and queen of the same suit, except trumps, 20 points;

b royal marriage: king and queen of the trump suit, 40 points;

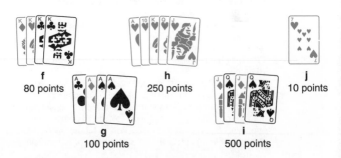

f
80 points

h
250 points

j
10 points

g
100 points

i
500 points

c bezique: queen of spades and jack of diamonds, 40 points (when spades or diamonds are trumps, some players prefer to make "bezique" the queen of clubs and jack of hearts);

d any four jacks, 40 points;

e any four queens, 60 points;

f any four kings, 80 points;

g any four aces, 100 points;

h sequence: a,10,k,q,j of the trump suit only, 250 points;

i double bezique: both queens of spades and both jacks of diamonds, 500 points;

j exchanging the 7 of trumps for the face-up card, 10 points (the holder of the other 7 of trumps scores 10 points when he plays it, which does not count as a declaration).

A player may make only one declaration after winning a trick. But if his exposed cards show a second possible declaration, he can announce that he will declare it when he next takes a trick. No card may form part of a second similar declaration. For example, a queen of spades in "four queens" cannot form part of a second declaration of "four queens," but can form part of a "bezique," "double bezique," "royal marriage," or "sequence."

The cards used to form a "bezique," can be used again to form part of a "double bezique," but neither card can be used with a fresh partner for a second "bezique."

Brisques are every ace and every 10 taken in tricks, and they count 10 points each.

The brisques are counted up by each player examining his tricks at the end of the game.

Game is either 1000 or 2000 points up.

Penalties If a player draws out of turn, his opponent scores 10 points.

If a player holds more than eight cards, his opponent scores 100 points provided he himself has the right number of cards. A player who plays to the next trick without having drawn a card during the first stage forfeits 10 points to his opponent. A player who revokes (fails to follow suit although able to) during the last eight tricks, or fails to take a

trick if he is able to do so forfeits all eight tricks to his opponent.
Scoring is most easily done using special bezique markers;
but it can also be done with pencil and paper, counters, or with
a cribbage board (each hole on the board counting as 10).

THREE-HANDED BEZIQUE

Three-handed bezique is the same as ordinary bezique except
that 96 cards (three piquet decks) are used. Each player plays
for himself. Triple bezique scores 1500 points.

RUBICON BEZIQUE

Rubicon bezique is a popular two-player variation of the
standard two-handed game. It is similar to standard bezique,
with the following differences.

The deck consists of 128 cards, or four piquet decks.

The deal consists of nine cards to each player, dealt either
singly or in threes.

Trumps are established by the first sequence or marriage
declared by either player. No stock cards are turned up, and
the 7 of trumps has no value.

Play is the same as for standard bezique, except that the last
trick counts 50 points.

Declarations are as in standard bezique, with the following
additions.

a Carte blanche: worth 50 points, and scored if either player
is dealt a hand not containing a face card. The hand must be
displayed. (See diagram overleaf.)

If, after drawing a further card, the player's hand still does not
contain a face card, carte blanche may be scored again, and
this continues until a face card is drawn.

Once a player has held a face card, carte blanche cannot be
scored.

b Ordinary sequence/back door: a sequence not of the trump
suit, 150 points.

c triple bezique: three queens of spades and three jacks of
diamonds, 1500 points.

d quadruple bezique: four queens of spades and four jacks of
diamonds, 4,500 points.

Cards may be reused to form the same combinations. For example, if "four queens" are declared and one queen is played, a fifth queen may be laid down to form "four queens" again. Two marriages of the same suit may be rearranged to form two more marriages.

Brisques are only counted if there is a tied score, or to save a player from being "rubiconed," ie failing to reach 1000 points. If one player chooses to count brisques, the other player's brisques are also scored.

Game is a single deal. The player with the higher score wins 500 points plus the difference between his and the loser's score. If the loser is rubiconed, the winner gets 1000 points, plus the sum of his and the loser's scores, plus 320 points for all his brisques.

(This applies even if the winner himself has scored fewer than 1000 points).

If the loser fails to score 100 points, the winner scores an extra 100 points.

Any fractions of 100 points may be ignored in scoring, except if the player's scores are very close.

Rubicon: declarations

Trumps

a
50 points

b
150 points

c
1500 points

d
4500 points

SIX-DECK BEZIQUE

Six-deck bezique, also known as Chinese bezique, is a variant of rubicon bezique. The rules are the same as for rubicon bezique, with the following changes.

The deck is 192 cards (six piquet decks shuffled together).

The deal is 12 cards to each player, dealt singly or in threes.

Trumps are indicated by the first declared marriage or sequence.

Brisques do not count at all.

Declarations can be made as in rubicon bezique, reusing cards in similar scoring combinations.

In six-deck bezique, carte blanche (**a**) is worth 250 points, as is winning the last trick. Declarations in addition to those in rubicon bezique are, in the trump suit only:

b four jacks, 400 points;

c four queens, 600 points;

d four kings, 800 points;

e four 10s, 900 points;

f four aces, 1000 points.

Bezique varies according to which suit is trumps, as follows: hearts, queen of hearts and jack of clubs;

Six-deck: declarations

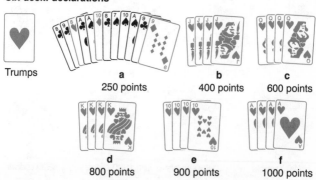

Trumps

a
250 points

b
400 points

c
600 points

d
800 points

e
900 points

f
1000 points

diamonds, queen of diamonds and jack of spades;
clubs, queen of clubs and jack of hearts;
spades, queen of spades and jack of diamonds.

Game is a single deal. Scores are calculated as for rubicon bezique, except that:
the winner gets a game bonus of 1000 points instead of 500;
and the rubicon point is 3000 instead of 1000.

EIGHT-DECK BEZIQUE

Eight-deck bezique is played like six-deck bezique, with the following variations.

The deck consists of 256 cards, or eight piquet decks.

The deal is 15 cards to each player.

Declarations are as in six-deck bezique, with the following changes and additions:

a bezique, 50 points;

b quintuple bezique, 9000 points.

Eight-deck declarations

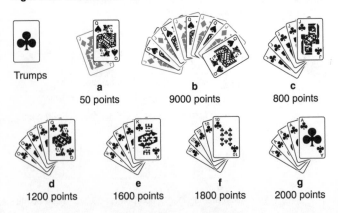

Trumps

a
50 points

b
9000 points

c
800 points

d
1200 points

e
1600 points

f
1800 points

g
2000 points

In the trump suit only:
c five jacks, 800 points;
d five queens, 1200 points;
e five kings, 1600 points;
f five 10s, 1800 points;
g five aces, 2000 points.
A player is rubiconed if he fails to score 5000 points.

FOUR-HANDED BEZIQUE

Four-handed bezique is similar to rubicon bezique, but the game is played with 192 cards (six piquet decks). The players play in partnership, two against two.

Four-handed declarations

Trumps

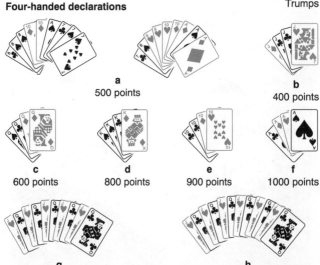

a
500 points

b
400 points

c
600 points

d
800 points

e
900 points

f
1000 points

g
13,500 points

h
40,500 points

The deal is nine cards to each player, the player on the dealer's left leads to the first trick.

Declarations may be made by any player after winning a trick; alternatively he may allow his partner to make the declaration. A player may use both his own cards and any of his partner's declared cards to make a declaration.

Scoring is as in rubicon bezique, with the following variations and additions:

a double carte blanche: both players in a partnership being dealt a hand without a face card, 500 points;

b any four jacks, 400 points;

c any four queens, 600 points;

d any four kings, 800 points;

e any four 10s, 900 points;

f any four aces, 1000 points;

g quintuple bezique, 13,500 points;

h sextuple bezique, 40,500 points.

Boston   4

This game developed from whist and is itself an ancestor of the now more popular solo whist. It was very popular at the time of the American Revolution.

Rank

Players The game is for four players, each player for himself.
Cards Two standard decks are used: one in play and the other for determining the "preference" and "color" suits. (If the preference and color suits are determined before the deal the game can be played with only one deck). Cards rank normally, with ace high.
Chips A large number of chips are required for scoring purposes. (To make settlement simpler, players sometimes use chips of different values).
Objective Each player tries to contract and fulfil a bid.
Choice of first dealer is by high cut, with ace low.
Pool Before each hand, each player pays 10 chips into a pool. If the pool exceeds 250 chips, the excess is put aside for the next pool.
Deal The dealer deals out all the playing deck, beginning with the player to his left and going clockwise. The cards are dealt three at a time, with a final round of single cards.
If there is a misdeal, the dealer must pay 10 chips into the pool. The deal then passes one player to the left.
Determining preference and color suits After the deal, the second deck is cut by the player sitting opposite the dealer. The top card of the bottom section is turned face up and denotes the preference suit. The other suit of the same color is called the color suit.
Bidding Each player in turn, beginning with the player to the dealer's left, may make a bid or pass.
The bids are ranked in the following order, with each outbidding the one before:

a "Boston," ie a bid to win five tricks with one of the plain suits as trumps;

b six tricks;

c seven tricks;

d "little misery," ie a bid to lose 12 tricks, playing with no trumps and after each player has discarded one card face down;

e eight tricks;

f nine tricks;

g "grand misery," ie a bid to lose every trick, playing with no trumps;

h 10 tricks;

i 11 tricks;

j "little spread," ie a bid to lose 12 tricks, playing with no trumps and the hand exposed;

k 12 tricks;

l "grand spread," ie a bid to lose every trick, playing with no trumps and the hand exposed;

m "grand slam," ie a bid to win all 13 tricks.

Trumps There are no trumps for misery and spread bids. For other bids the player chooses his own trump suit, usually stating what it is only when his bid has been accepted. However, if two or more players wish to make a bid for the same number of tricks, the bids are ranked as follows according to the proposed trump suit: preference suit (high), color suit, plain suits (low).

No bid hands If all players pass, each one throws in his cards and pays 10 chips into the pool. The deal then passes one player to the left.

Play The player to the left of the dealer leads to the first trick. Play is as for whist (p 164).

A player who revokes loses the hand and must pay 40 chips into the pool.

Settlement If a player fulfils his bid he receives chips from each of the other players, and if his bid was for seven tricks or higher, he also receives the chips in the pool.

If a player fails to fulfil the bid he pays to each of the other players and must also double the chips in the pool.

For misery and spread bids the bidder pays or receives chips as follows: 20 for a little misery; 40 for grand misery; 80 for little spread; 160 for grand spread.

If a player fulfils any other bid he is paid according to table A.

If a player fails to fulfil any other bid he pays according to the number of tricks by which he fails – as given in table B. A player is said to be "put in for" the number of tricks by which he fails.

Table A

Tricks bid	5	6	7	8	9	10	11	12	13
Payment	10	15	20	25	35	45	65	105	170

Table B

Tricks bid	Number put in for												
	1	2	3	4	5	6	7	8	9	10	11	12	13
	Payment												
5	10	20	30	40	50								
6	15	25	35	45	55	65							
7	20	30	40	50	60	70	80						
8	25	35	45	55	70	85	100	115					
9	35	45	55	65	80	95	110	125	140				
10	45	55	70	80	95	110	125	140	155	170			
11	70	80	95	110	125	140	155	170	185	200	220		
12	120	130	145	160	180	200	220	240	260	280	300	320	
13	180	200	220	240	260	280	300	320	340	360	390	420	450

4　　Bridge

Rank

For many people bridge is the most fascinating of card games: it is played in homes, clubs, and tournaments throughout the world. Its origins can be traced back some 400 years to the development of whist in England, but it was only in 1896 that the game of bridge itself evolved.

CONTRACT BRIDGE
This form of bridge was developed in 1925, and within a few years had become by far the most popular form of the game.

General rules
Cards A standard deck of 52 cards is used. By convention a second deck with contrasting backs is also used, so that while one player deals another can shuffle in readiness for the next deal.

The cards rank: ace (high) through 2 (low). The 2 is commonly called a "deuce," and the 3 a "trey."

Players As in whist, there are four players, each pair forming a partnership. Partners sit opposite each other. One partnership is usually called North–South, the other East-West.

Objective Each partnership aims to win a "rubber," by winning the most points in the best of three games.

A game is won by scoring 100 points, earned by taking tricks that have been contracted for.

Honors are the high-ranking cards in the trump suit, from the ace down through and including the 10. In "no trump" games, the four aces are honors.

Suits For the purpose of bidding, the suits are ranked as follows: spades (highest), hearts, diamonds, clubs (lowest).

The draw At the beginning of a bridge game, one deck is spread face down on the table, and each player draws one card from the deck.

The two players who draw the highest cards form one partnership; the other two players form the second. The player with the highest card becomes the first dealer and chooses his seating position; his partner sits opposite him. If cards of the same denomination appear on the draw, they are ranked according to suit, as for bidding.

Shuffle and cut The player to the left of the dealer shuffles the deck; the player to the dealer's right cuts the deck. As the cards are being dealt, the alternate deck is shuffled by the dealer's partner.

The deal begins with the player to the dealer's left. The cards are dealt in a clockwise direction, one at a time and face down, until each player including the dealer has 13 cards.

Rank of suits

♠
♥
♦
♣

Honors

Bidding

The auction begins once players have had a chance to study their cards. It opens with the dealer and continues in clockwise rotation. Each player, according to his hand, makes a "call," which may be a bid, pass, double, or redouble.

If a player passes, he may still make another call at a later stage in the bidding. But when a bid, double, or redouble is followed by three passes in succession, the auction ends.

If there are four passes at the opening of bidding, one from each player, the cards are "thrown in" to the center of the table and shuffled. A new hand is then dealt by the next dealer.

A pass indicates that a player does not choose to make any other call at that time in the bidding.

A bid is a statement of a number and a trump suit, eg "three clubs," or "five no trumps." It offers an undertaking that if that suit is trumps (or if there are "no trumps") the bidding player's partnership will take a number of tricks.

Bidding refers to the number of "odd" (ie additional) tricks that a bidder undertakes to make over six tricks.

A bid of "one club," for instance, means that a player thinks that his partnership can make seven tricks in all, if clubs are trumps.

A bid of "four no trumps" offers the undertaking to make ten tricks in all, if no suit is trumps.

Continuing the bidding As the auction continues, each successive bid must be higher than the preceding bid – either by calling a greater number of tricks or by naming a higher ranking suit.

For instance, a bid of "two spades" is higher than two hearts, diamonds, or clubs.

A no trump call ranks above all suits. So, for example, a bid of "two no trumps" is higher than two spades. The next player to bid would have to bid at least "three clubs."

Sample deal and bidding

♠ 8 6
♥ J 10 7 6
♦ A Q 9 8 6 4 3
♣

Deal by South

♠ A 5 4 3
♥ 8 5
♦ J 10
♣ K 8 7 6 5

♠ K Q J 9 7 2
♥ 3 2
♦ 5 2
♣ 10 9 4

♠ 10
♥ A K Q 9 4
♦ K 7
♣ A Q J 3 2

Bidding

S	W	N	E
1 ♣	double	1 ♦	1 ♠
2 ♥	2 ♠	3 ♦	double
3 ♥	pass	pass	3 ♠
4 ♥	pass	pass	pass

The contract is four hearts: North-South have bought the contract and South is declarer.

The contract The highest bid of the auction becomes the "contract." The players in the partnership making that bid must, in play, make as many tricks as they have contracted for, or more. Their opponents have only to prevent them from doing this – it does not matter what they themselves have bid

The first six tricks taken by the contracted bidders are commonly referred to as "making the book."

Slam The maximum number of tricks in any played hand is 13. This gives a maximum bid of "seven," when one side believes it can take all the tricks: the book (of six), plus seven odd tricks. If a side succeeds in bidding and winning 13 tricks, this is known as a "grand slam."

A "small slam" occurs if a side bids and wins a total of 12 tricks.

Doubling If a player says "Double" after any of his opponents' bids, it means that he believes he could prevent them from making their bid, if it became the contract.

A bid that has been doubled need not become the contract: it can be overbid in the usual way, by either partnership. If, however, it does become the contract and succeeds, the contracting players' score is doubled. Should the bidders "go down" (ie not make their contract) the side that doubled gets at least twice the score that it would otherwise have had.

Redoubling If a bid has been doubled either player of the bidding partnership may say "Redouble." This confirms his confidence in the bid, and – as in doubling – the scoring is affected whether or not the contract is made (see the section on scoring p 41).

A bid that has been redoubled can be overbid in the usual way.

The declarer The player in the contracting side who first made a bid in the trump suit of the contract (spades, hearts, diamonds, clubs, or no trumps), is referred to as the "declarer." He plays both hands of the contracting partnership's game.

Beginning the play

Dummy

South dealt and also made the contract (p 37). West leads. North (dummy) then lays out his hand.

Play

A trick consists of four cards, one played from each player's hand, in clockwise rotation. The player who must play first is called the "lead."

The lead The opening lead is held by the player to the dealer's left. He plays the first card after the bidding ends. After this, the winner of each trick makes the next lead.

A player may lead any card, and the other three players must follow suit if possible. If a player cannot follow suit, he may play any other card in his hand.

Winning the trick If none of the four cards is a trump, the trick is won by the highest card played in the suit led. If one or more of the four cards is a trump, the trick is won by the highest trump.

No trump When a "no trump" bid becomes the contract, all suits have equal rank and the highest card in the suit led always wins the trick.

Dummy As soon as the opening lead has been made, declarer's partner lays down his cards face up on the table, sorted out by suit, with trumps to his right.

The exposed cards, and declarer's partner himself, are referred to as "dummy" for that hand.

Only declarer can choose the cards to play for the dummy hand. The dummy partner may not participate in that hand, other than physically to play a specified card at declarer's request. Plays from a dummy must be in correct order of rotation, ie following a card played by the player to declarer's left.

Declarer must play a card in dummy that he touches (except when rearranging the cards or touching a card next to the one to be played).

Gathering won tricks is done by either player of the side winning the trick.

The four cards are gathered together and placed face down on the table.

All declarer's and dummy's tricks are placed in front of declarer; all the opponents tricks' are placed in front of one opponent.

The arrangement of gathered tricks must show clearly how many tricks have been won and in which order. Common procedure is to bunch the first six of the declarer's tricks into one group, so that it is clear how many odd tricks have been made.

A trick may be inspected by the declarer or by either opponent, until a player of the inspecting side has led or played to the following trick.

Scoring

It is important to master the scoring in contract bridge as this strongly affects the game's strategy.

Both sides should keep score in case of disagreement.

A scoring pad has a central vertical line dividing "we" (one partnership) from "they" (its opponents).

A horizontal line is initially drawn across the scoring pad, and a partnership can score points either "below the line" or "above the line."

Trick points are entered below the line. Only declarer's side can score trick points on a hand, and only if the contract is made. Only the odd tricks contracted for can be scored below the line. Trick points show each side's progress toward winning the current game.

Premium points are scored above the line, and may be scored by both sides in any hand. They are won for:

a overtricks;

b successful doubling or redoubling;

c bidding and making a slam;

d having a certain number of honors cards in one hand in the deal or;

e winning the final game of a rubber.

Undertricks If declarer's side fails to make the contract, the number of tricks it has failed by are known as "undertricks." These are credited to the opponents' premium points and scored above the line.

Vulnerable A partnership is "vulnerable" if it has won its first game towards the rubber. (It is therefore possible for both partnerships to be vulnerable).

Winning a game The first side to reach a score of 100 or more, either in one or several hands, wins the game.

A horizontal line is then drawn below the trick scores of both sides. Trick scores for the next game are entered below this line, both sides beginning again from zero.

Winning the rubber When one side has won two games, the rubber ends.

This side earns 700 premium points if its opponents have won no game, and 500 premium points if its opponents have won one game.

All trick and premium points are then totalled, and the side with the higher total wins the rubber.

The back score indicates an individual player's standing. It is used in any competition in which partners rotate.

After a rubber, the difference between the two sides' final scores is calculated by subtracting the lower from the higher. This difference is rounded to the nearest 100 (50 and above become 100), and divided by 100. For example, 753 becomes 800, giving 8. Each player of the winning partnership is then given a score of plus 8 and each opponent a score of minus 8. In subsequent rubbers, with different partnerships, the same procedure is followed. The player with the highest plus score at the end is the overall winner.

Scoring

a	
WE	THEY
70	

b	
WE	THEY
150	
70	
30	

c	
WE	THEY
150	200
70	
30	

d	
WE	THEY
	150
150	200
70	
30	
	60

Explanation of scoring diagrams

a "We" score 70 trick points.

b "We" score 30 trick points and 150 premium points. "We" win first game and are now vulnerable.

c "We" go under by two tricks. "They" score 200 undertrick points.

d "They" score 60 trick points and 150 premium points.

Contract bridge scoring table

Trick score: scored by declarer below the line

	♣	♦	♥	♠	NT
First trick over six bid and made	20	20	30	30	40
Subsequent tricks bid and made	20	20	30	30	30
Doubling doubles trick score					
Redoubling doubles doubled score					

Premium score: scored by declarer above the line

	Not vulnerable	Vulnerable
Small slam	500	750
Grand slam	1000	1500
Each overtrick undoubled	Trick value	Trick value
Each overtrick doubled	100	200
Each overtrick redoubled	200	400
Making a doubled or redoubled contract	50	50

Rubber, game, and partscore: scored above the line

	Points
For winning rubber, if opponents have won no game	700
For winning rubber, if opponents have won one game	500
For having won one game in an unfinished rubber	300
For having the only partscore in an unfinished rubber	50

Honors: scored by either side above the line

	Points
Four trump honors in one hand	100
Five trump honors in one hand	150
Four aces in one hand, no trump contract	150

Undertricks: scored by opponents above the line

	Undoubled	Doubled	Redoubled
First trick, not vulnerable	50	100	200
Subsequent tricks	50	200	400
First trick, vulnerable	100	200	400
Subsequent tricks	100	300	600

DUPLICATE CONTRACT BRIDGE

Duplicate contract bridge is very popular among advanced bridge players. It is the only form played in international tournaments. All groups of players are presented, in turn, with the same deal of cards. In this way, the game relies more on skill than on luck of the deal.

Equipment:

1 one table for every four players in the tournament;

2 the same number of duplicate boards or trays as tables;

3 one deck of cards for each board.

Players Competing units may be individuals, pairs, or teams of four or six, depending on the nature of the tournament. In individual events, partnerships change during the tournament; in team events, partnerships change at half-time; and in pairs matches, the same partnerships are preserved throughout.

A duplicate board is used at each table. Each board has four pockets, an arrow or label indicating North's side, and markers indicating the dealer and the vulnerability or otherwise of partnerships.

Before the tournament the boards are arranged so that a quarter have North-South vulnerable, a quarter East-West vulnerable, a quarter both pairs vulnerable, and a quarter neither pair vulnerable.

Within each category, the position of dealer is distributed equally between the pairs.

Basic procedure Each board maintains the same deal of cards throughout the tournament.

The boards and players move from table to table in a specified way.

The tournament ends, according to the system used, either:

a when all North-South players have met all East-West players; or

b when all players have played with and against all other players.

Deal For the first hand at each board, the designated dealer shuffles and deals the cards in the usual way.

Thereafter, following each hand, this original deal is preserved. Each player's cards are placed in the appropriate board pocket, in readiness for the next set of players.

The auction for any hand takes place in the usual way, commencing with the player indicated as dealer. If all players pass there is no redeal.

Play on any hand proceeds as in contract bridge, except that after each trick is completed the cards are not gathered together.

Each player takes back his card, and turns it face down on the table in front of him. He points the card lengthwise toward the partners who won the trick; this allows players to keep track of the number of tricks won by each side.

Scoring a hand No points are given for winning a rubber. If a side bids and makes a contract that gives it a game (100 trick points), it gets 500 premium points if vulnerable, 300 if not. Additional premium points for making a grand slam are 1500 if vulnerable, 1000 if not; and for a small slam, 750 if vulnerable, 500 if not.

If a side bids and makes a contract less than game, it gets 50 premium points.

A score made on one board cannot be carried forward to affect scoring on the next.

Unless cumulative tournament scoring is used, no premium points are given for holding honors in one hand.

Scoring the tournament

a Match point procedure is always used if the competing units are individuals. It can also be used for pairs.

The comparison is between scores made at the same board, ie success in playing the same deal.

Each score is given two points for each lower score made in the same position on that board, and one point for each exactly equal score.

Each individual in an individual event receives points for the score made by his partnership.

The individual or pair with the highest number of match points wins the competition.

b International match point (imp) scoring is usually used for teams. Each partnership's surplus (or deficit) of points over its opponents is calculated for each hand, and added together at the end to give a team total. This is then converted into match points on the basis of an established scale.

c Cumulative (total point) scoring is still sometimes used for team competitions.

AUCTION BRIDGE

A forerunner of contract bridge, auction bridge evolved from the game of whist.

Except for the scoring – which greatly affects the strategy of the game – its rules are as for contract bridge.

Major differences The two major differences in scoring are as follows:

1 In auction bridge there is no concept of vulnerability. If one partnership has won a game there is no extra penalty (as in contract bridge) for failure to make a contract.

2 All odd tricks, whether contracted for or not, are scored "below the line." They contribute to winning the game, provided that declarer has succeeded in making the minimum number of tricks named in the contract.

Trick points	♣	♦	♥	♠	NT
Undoubled	6	7	8	9	10
Doubled	12	14	16	18	20
Redoubled	24	28	32	36	40

Game The first side to score 30 points below the line wins a game. A horizontal line is drawn across the scoring pad, as in contract bridge, to indicate that a game has been completed.

Rubber The first side to win two games out of three wins the rubber and is awarded an additional 250 points.

Honors If either side has three or more honors in the trump suit (or aces and no trumps) then – whether or not that side is declarer – the following scores are given above the line:

three honors or aces, 30 points;

four honors or aces, divided, 40 points;

five honors, divided, 50 points;

four honors, one hand, 80 points;

five honors, divided four to one, 90 points;

four aces, one hand, 100 points;

five honors, one hand, 100 points.

Bonuses 50 points are given above the line if a doubled contract is bid for and made. In addition, declarer's side gets 50 points for each trick in excess of the contract.

If declarer succeeds in making a redoubled contract, both the bonuses mentioned above are raised to 100 points each.

Undertricks If declarer's side fails to make contract, the opponents are given the following points (above the line) for each undertrick:

undoubled contract, 50;

doubled contract, 100;

redoubled contract, 200.

Slams If either side makes a small slam (12 tricks), it receives 50 points above the line – regardless of the bidded contract. If a grand slam (13 tricks) is won, 100 points are awarded.

3   Calabrasella

Calabrasella is an interesting and fast-moving card game for
three players. Its characteristic features are a stripped deck,
unusual rankings of cards, and the absence of a trump suit.

Rank

Cards A standard deck of playing cards with the 8s, 9s, and
10s removed is used.
The cards rank 3 (high), 2, a, k, q, 7, 6,5,4 (low).
Players This is a game for three.
Objective Each player tries to take certain tricks.
Deal Players cut for the deal and the lowest card deals.
The dealer gives each player 12 face-down cards in packets
of four. The four remaining cards are placed face down in a
pile in the center of the table as the widow (extra hand).
Bidding Starting with the player to the left of the dealer,
each player in turn may choose either to play or pass.
The first player to choose to play is opposed by the other two
players in partnership for that round.
If none of the three players wishes to play, the hand is
thrown in and the cards are redealt.
Widow The player who decides to play may discard, face
down, up to four of his cards and replace them with cards
from the widow, turned face up. The discarded cards, if any,
and any remaining widow cards are then placed face down in
a pile. These four cards will go to the winner of the last trick.

Play The player to the left of the dealer leads to the first trick with any card he likes. In turn, each of the other players must follow suit if possible, or discard if not.

The winner of each trick leads to the next.

Scoring Players score for taking cards in tricks as follows: aces, three points each;

3s, 2s, ks, qs and js, one point each.

The player who takes the last trick scores an extra three points, and also scores for the four spare (widow or discard) cards.

Thus the maximum possible score is 35 points.

Each side totals its score, and the difference between them is the final score for the hand.

Payoff If the single player wins, each of the opponents pays him the final score in counters or points.

If he loses, he pays each opponent the final score.

If one side scores the maximum of 35 points, the payoff is 70 points or counters.

Game is 100 points. Alternatively, play can continue until one player has lost all his counters.

4 Canasta

Canasta is a partnership game of the rummy family. Originating in Uruguay, it reached the United States in 1949 and in the early 1950s became one of the biggest fads in the history of card playing.

Cards Two standard decks of 52 cards and four jokers are used, shuffled together.

The cards are not ranked.

There are 12 wild cards: the four jokers and all eight deuces (2s). Wild cards can be given any denomination that the holder wishes.

Players In the standard game there are four players divided into two partnerships.

The objective is to be the first side to score 5000 points over a series of hands. Points are mainly scored by making melds.

A meld is a set of at least three cards of the same denomination. They can be all natural cards, or a mixture of natural and wild cards. But whatever the size of the meld, there must be at least two natural cards and not more than three wild cards.

Melds score according to the cards they contain (see table A, p 55).

Cutting for partners Each player cuts a card from the deck, and the two who cut the highest cards play against the other two. For this purpose, cards rank normally (ace high) and suits rank spades (high), hearts, diamonds, clubs (low).

Players cutting a joker or exactly equal cards cut again.

Player cutting highest becomes first dealer and has choice of seats.

Shuffle and cut are normal.

The deal begins with the player to the dealer's left.

The cards are dealt one at a time and face down in a clockwise direction until each player including the dealer has

11 cards. The remaining cards are then placed face down on the table as the stock. The top card of the stock is turned face up alongside to start the discard pile.

Play starts with the players to the dealer's left.

In a normal turn a player first takes the top card of the stock. He then makes any melds that he can, or adds to those that he or his partner have already laid out on the table.

Finally he discards by placing one card from his hand face up on the discard pile.

The initial meld of a partnership after each deal must total at least a certain number of points – how many depends on their score so far (see table B, p 55).

Once either partner has made this first meld, both partners can make new melds of any value and can add to melds that they have already laid out on the table.

A player may add to either his own or his partner's melds.

Wild cards

Melds

Natural   Mixed   Canasta

A canasta is a meld of seven cards.

A natural canasta consists of seven cards of the same rank and has a bonus value of 500 points on top of the card score. A mixed canasta has natural cards and one to three wild cards, and has a bonus value of 300 points.

Once a canasta is completed, the cards are gathered into a pile.

A natural canasta has a red card placed on top for identification, and a mixed canasta has a black card.

Further cards may be added to a canasta. But a mixed canasta may not receive a fourth wild card and a natural canasta loses its value if a wild card is added.

Taking the discard pile In place of taking the top card from the stock, a player may in his turn take the upcard from the discard pile – but only if he has in his hand at least two natural cards of the same denomination.

He must lay the appropriate hand cards face up on the table and meld the upcard with them.

He then also takes all the remainder of the discard pile, and immediately uses as many cards as possible by adding to existing melds or laying out new ones. Any cards that he cannot use become part of his hand.

The player ends his turn by discarding one card to start a new discard pile.

Provided it is not "frozen", a player may also take the discard pile:

a if he can meld the upcard with one card of the same denomination and one wild card; or

b if the upcard matches an existing meld of his partnership.

Frozen discard pile The discard pile is frozen as follows.

1 It is frozen for a partnership that has not made its initial meld.

2 It is frozen for a player if a black 3 is the upcard. In this case it is no longer frozen after the player has drawn from the stock and discarded.

3 It is frozen for all players if the discard pile contains a red 3 or a wild card. In this case further discards are placed

crosswise on top of the freezing card. The discard pile remains frozen until one player unfreezes it by melding the upcard or wild card with two natural cards from his hand.
Red 3s are bonus cards counting 100 points each (**a**). They cannot be melded.
If a player draws a red 3 from the stock, he must lay it face up on the table and draw another card from the stock.
If he is dealt a red 3 he must lay it face up on the table and draw a card from the stock in addition to his regular draw.
If a red 3 is taken as part of the discard pile, it must be laid face up on the table without any extra card being drawn from the stock.
If a partnership holds all four red 3s, these cards count 200 points each, ie 800 points in all (**b**).
All red 3 points count against a partnership if it has not made an initial meld when the play ends.

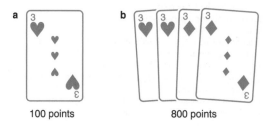

a 100 points

b 800 points

Black 3s may only be melded when a player is going out. They can never be melded with wild cards. Their main use is as "stop cards" to freeze the discard pile.
Going out occurs when a player is able to meld all his cards, providing that when he has gone out his side has made at least one canasta. A player can go out without discarding if he wishes.

Concealed going out occurs when a player melds all his cards when he has not previously melded any cards.

Note that a player must always meld a canasta unless his partner has already melded one.

Permission is usually asked to go out, in the form of "May I go out, partner?" A yes or no answer is required and is binding. This procedure is generally used as a warning to a partner to meld as many cards as possible, so that the requesting player can go out in his next turn.

Scoring Each partnership receives the total of all bonus points earned in the hand (see table C), plus the total point value of all melded cards, less the value of any cards remaining in the hands of either player in the partnership at the end of play.

(Note that the low bonuses for going out make the completion of high-scoring melds more significant than being first to go out).

If one partnership has failed to meld at all, the value of any red 3s it has laid down count against it.

It is possible for a partnership to make a minus score on a hand.

Hands continue until one side has made a total of 5000 points and wins the game.

For each successive hand the deal passes clockwise.

Variant rules The following variations on the standard rules are widely accepted.

1 Even if the discard pile is not frozen, a player may not take the upcard to add it to a completed canasta of his own side.

2 When taking the upcard from the discard pile to make a new meld, a player must always have a natural pair to match it (ie not a matching card and a wild card).

Table A

Card	Points for each card in meld
Joker	50
Deuce (2)	20
Ace	20
8,9,10,j,q,k	10
4,5,6,7 5	
Black 3	5
Red 3	see text (p 53)

Table B

Accumulated score of partnership	Value required for initial meld
Any minus score	15
0-1495	50
1500-2995	90
3000 or more	120

Table C

	Bonus points
Natural canasta	500
Mixed canasta	300
Going out	100
Concealed going out	100 extra
Red 3s	See text (p 53)

2-4   Casino

Casino can be traced back to the fifteenth-century gambling games of France. In the United States, its era of greatest popularity was eclipsed by the gin rummy boom of the 1930s.

Although appearing comparatively simple, casino is in fact a game of considerable mathematical skill.

CASINO: BASIC GAME

Players The game can be played by two, three, or four players.
A deck of standard playing cards is used.
Face cards have no numerical value; aces count 1; and other cards count their face value.

Objective Each player tries to "capture" certain cards during play and to score the most points.

Deal Players cut for the deal and the lowest card deals. If there are two players, two cards are dealt face down to the nondealer, then two cards face up to the center of the table, then two cards to the dealer. This procedure is repeated so that each player has four cards and there are four face-up cards in the center of the table.

If there are three or four players, the dealer deals two cards to each player including himself, two face-up cards to the center of the table, two more cards to each of the players, and then two more cards to the center.

Each time the players have played the cards in their hands, they are dealt a further four cards in packets of two – no more cards are dealt to the center.

Players take turns to deal the whole deck.

Play Beginning with the player to the left of the dealer, players take turns to play one card. Each player may "capture," "build," or "trail" with each card.

Capturing Cards are captured in the following ways. (See diagram overleaf.)

a Pairs: if a face up card has the same numerical value as a player's card, the player may capture the face up card. He does this by placing his card face down on the face up card, and then moving the pair toward him. For example, a 7 of spades may capture a 7 of diamonds.

If two or more face up cards match a single card in the player's hand, he may capture them all at the same time.

b Groups: if the combined value of two or more face up cards is equal to the numerical value of a player's card, the player may capture all the face up cards involved. He puts the face up cards in a pile in front of him and places his own

Capturing

a

b

c

card face down on top of them. For example, a 9 could
capture a 2, 3 and 4 from the center.
If one of the player's cards has the same numerical value as
both a single face up card and a group of face-up cards, he
may capture all the cards involved at the same time. For

example, a 9 of spades could capture both a 9 of diamonds and a group of cards (eg 2,3 and 4) totalling 9.

c Court cards: if a player holds a face card he may either capture one matching face up face card, or alternatively three matching face up face cards if he holds the fourth.

This means that if, for example, he holds a queen and there are two face-up queens, he can only capture one of them in a turn (but had there been three face-up queens, he could have captured all of them in turn).

Building may be in either one of two ways: single or multiple.

Single build A player may build a card face up onto a central face up card provided;

a the combined numerical value of the cards does not exceed ten; and

b he holds another card that is of equal value to the build he is making, so that in his next turn he would be able to take that build.

For example, if a player holds a 4 and a 7, he may build the 4 onto a face up 3 (ie 4 + 3 = 7) and say "Building 7."

A build may be increased by either player with a card from his hand, provided that the total of all the cards in the build still does not exceed ten, and that he holds a card equal in value to the build he is making.

For example, if the opponent holds an ace and an 8, he may build the ace onto an existing build of 7, saying "Building 8."

Multiple build A single build can be changed to a multiple build by duplicating the single-build value with other cards.

For example, a player may add an ace from his hand to a build of 7 in order to make a build of 8 (ie 3 + 4 + 1 = 8), and add to that build another build of 8 (ie 2 + 6) and say "Building 8s."

Once a multiple build has been established, its stated value cannot be altered.

A multiple build is captured by a card equal in value to its stated value (8 in the example above).

Next turn If a player makes or adds to a build, unless his opponent plays to the build immediately, he must in his next turn either;

a capture it himself (placing the captured build face down in front of him):

b make a new build; or

c add to a build.

Trailing If in his turn a player cannot build or capture, he simply places one card from his hand face up on the table.

End of a round When all the cards have been dealt out, the last player to capture cards takes all the remaining face up cards for scoring.

Scoring Points are scored for capturing cards as follows:

one point for the 2 of spades ("little casino");

two points for the 10 of diamonds ("big casino");

one point for each ace;

one point for seven or more spades;

three points for 27 or more cards.

In addition, one point is scored for capturing all the center face-up cards in any single turn during the course of play; this is known as "making a sweep."

Game Players may either: count each deal as a separate game (the player with the most points being the winner), or end the game as soon as one player (the winner) has made a set number of points (usually 21).

ROYAL CASINO

This differs from casino in that the court cards are given numerical values and can be included in builds and captured in tricks like other cards.

A jack counts 11, a queen 12, and a king 13. Aces may count either 1 or 14 as the player chooses.

DRAW CASINO

In draw casino only the first 12 cards are dealt. Thereafter, each player draws a card from the stock every time he plays a card.

Otherwise, play is the same as casino.

SPADE CASINO
Spade casino is played like the basic game, but has
additional scoring as follows:
jack of spades, two points;
2 of spades, two points;
other spades, one point each.
Game is 61 points

Single build

 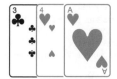

Multiple build

2   **Cribbage**

Cribbage is reputed to have been invented by Sir John
Suckling, an English poet and courtier who lived in the early
1600s. Six-card cribbage for two players is the most popular
form of the game today, but there are also five -and seven-
card forms as well as adaptations for three and four players.

Cards All forms of cribbage are played with one single
standard deck of 52 cards.
Card values Face cards count 10 each, and all other cards
count their face value.
Cribbage board The score can be kept with pencil and
paper, but it is easier to use a special cribbage board.
Most cribbage boards are made of wood and measure about
10in by 3in.
There are four rows of 30 holes, two rows for each player,
and additional game holes at one or both ends of the board.
Each player has two pegs, usually red or black for one player
and white for the other.
When there are four game holes, the players usually put their
pegs in them for the start of play.
A player marks his score by moving his pegs first along his
outer row and then back along his inner row of holes.

Cribbage board

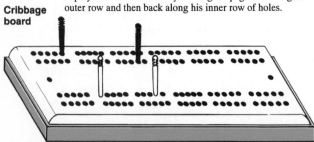

Moving pegs Both pegs are used to score in the following way:

a a player marks his first score by moving one peg that number of holes from the start;

b his second score is marked by placing his second peg that number of holes beyond his first peg;

c his third score is marked by placing his first peg that number of holes beyond his second peg;

d scoring continues in this way until a player's forward peg has passed all the scoring holes to end in one of the game holes.

Moving pegs

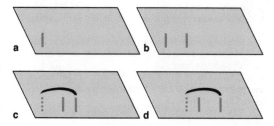

SIX-CARD CRIBBAGE

Players The basic game is for two players.

Objective The game is won by the first player to score 121 points, ie to go "twice around the board."

The deal Players cut for deal. The player with the lowest cut (with ace low) deals first, and then the deal alternates between players.

The deal is six cards, one at a time, to each player. The remaining cards are placed face down to one side.

The crib is an extra hand scored by the dealer. It is formed by each of the players discarding two cards and placing them, face down, to the dealer's right. Each player is thus left with a hand of four cards.

The cut After the discards the nondealer cuts the deck, and the dealer turns up the top card of the remaining stack. This card is placed face up on the stack for the rest of the game.

It is known as the "start" or "starter."

If the start is a jack, the dealer scores "two for his heels."

Scoring Points are scored both during the playing of a hand and when the hands are shown after play.

Combinations of cards score as follows:

a A pair, two cards of the same rank, scores two points.

b A pair royal, three cards of the same rank, scores six points (two points for each of the possible pairs to be made).

c A double pair royal, four cards of the same rank, scores 12 points.

d A sequence or run is a series of cards in face order (ace low) and scores one point for each card. The cards do not have to be of the same suit.

e A flush is four or five cards of the same suit and scores one point for each card. If a flush is also a run, points are scored for both features.

f Fifteen is any combination of cards with a face value totalling that number. It scores two points.

Scoring

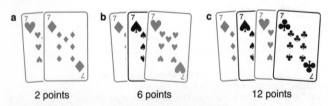

a   2 points   b   6 points   c   12 points

Play begins with the nondealer. He places a card face upward in front of him and calls out its face value as he does so. Face cards are called as 10.

The dealer then places one of his cards face upward in front of himself and calls out its value.

Whenever a pair, pair royal, double pair royal, sequence or fifteen (but not a flush) is formed during play, the player putting down the card that forms it scores the appropriate points.

If the nondealer lays down a 5 and the dealer follows it with another 5, the dealer would say "ten for a pair" and score two points. If a third 5 is played, the nondealer would say "fifteen for eight," the eight points being made up of fifteen and a pair royal.

A sequence of cards scores regardless of the order in which it is played. Thus if cards are played in the order ace, 2,5,4,3, the player putting out the 3 can count on a run of five cards. Should the second player be able to add a 6 he can score a run of six cards, and so on.

When the count during play reaches 31, the cards are turned face down and the player whose card brought the total to 31 scores two points.

If a player at his turn is unable to play a card that is within the limit of 31, he says "Go." His opponent then plays any of his cards that are low enough to be within the limit. If they make 31 he scores two points; if less than 31 he scores one point and also says "Go."

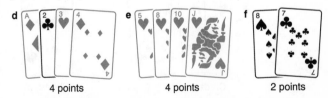

d   4 points   e   4 points   f   2 points

Play then resumes with the remaining cards in hand, and proceeds until all the cards are played or 31 is again reached. Playing the last card of a hand scores "one for the last."

The show After all the cards have been played, each player picks up his own cards from in front of him.

The nondealer shows and scores his hand first, which gives him an advantage if he is very near reaching 121. The start is taken into the reckoning as part of each hand.

A card may be ranked for scoring in any number of different combinations. Thus two 10s and two 5s would give a score of eight points for fifteens plus four points for pairs – giving a total of 12 points. The combination 4,4,5,6,6 scores eight points for fifteens, four points for pairs, and 12 points for sequences – giving a total of 24 points (see illustration).

If a player holds a jack of the same suit as the start, he scores "one for his nob."

A flush of four cards in a hand scores four points. If the start is of the same suit the player scores five points, but a flush of four cards including the start scores nothing.

After the nondealer has declared his score, the dealer shows and scores his own hand. After which he shows and also scores for the crib.

The crib is scored in the same way as the hands, except that the only flush allowed is a five-card one.

Sample show

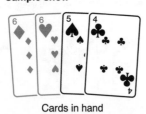

Cards in hand

The "start"

Scoring of sample show

Total score: 24 points

8 points
for fifteens

4 points
for pairs

12 points for
sequences

Muggins If a player overlooks a score, whether in his hand or in play, his opponent may call "Muggins" and claim the score for himself. (This rule may be dropped).

Lurch If a player reaches 121 before his opponent is half-way around the board he scores a lurch and counts two games instead of one.

Errors If an error in dealing is noticed during the deal, there should be a redeal.

If an error in dealing is found after play has started, the non-dealer scores two points and the error is rectified either by a redeal or by drawing additional cards from the stack.

If after "Go" is called a player fails to play his additional cards, he may not subsequently play those cards and his opponent scores two points. Errors in counting during play are not penalized.

FIVE-CARD CRIBBAGE
This is an earlier form of the game than six-card cribbage. Except as specified, the rules are as for the six-card game.
Objective Game is 61 points.
The deal is five cards to each player.
The crib consists of two cards from each player.
Play Nondealer pegs three points before play begins, to compensate for not having the crib.
Hands are not played out after 31 is reached or "Go" is called.
Hands are shown and scored; then there is a new deal.

SEVEN-CARD CRIBBAGE
This version is played in the same way as six-card cribbage, except that:
a game is 181 points;
b the deal is seven cards each (of which two go to the crib).

THREE-HANDED CRIBBAGE
The game is adapted as follows for three-handed play.
Game is 61 points.
The deal is five cards to each player and one to the crib.

Each player then gives one card to the crib.

Play begins with the player to the left of the dealer, and passes to the left. The player who leads also has the first show.

FOUR-HANDED CRIBBAGE

This is a partnership form of the game. Partners sit opposite each other, and play begins with the player to the dealer's left.

Game is 121 points.

The deal is usually five cards to each player (of which one goes to the crib).

2 Ecarté

Ecarté is a card game for two players that first became popular in France in the early 1800s. Its name is the French word for "discarded."

Rank

Deck A 32-card deck is used: a standard 52-card deck with 6s,5s,4s,3s, and 2s removed.

Cards rank: k (high), q,j,a,10,9,8,7.

Objective Each player tries to take tricks and to score points.

Deal Players cut for deal, highest card dealing first (the cards rank as in play). The dealer gives each player five face-down cards, in packets of either two then three, or three then two. Whichever system is used must be kept throughout the game. The deal passes clockwise around the table.

Trumps The eleventh card is placed face up beside the stock and indicates trumps.

Exchanging cards The nondealer may propose an exchange of cards. To do this he says "Cards."

If the dealer accepts, the nondealer exchanges as many cards as he wishes for cards drawn from the stock. The dealer may then do likewise.

The nondealer may repeat the proposal, and players go on exchanging cards until the stock is exhausted.

But if the dealer refuses at any time by saying "Play," there is no more exchanging.

If the nondealer does not wish to exchange at any time, he says "I play."

The dealer cannot propose an exchange.

Deal

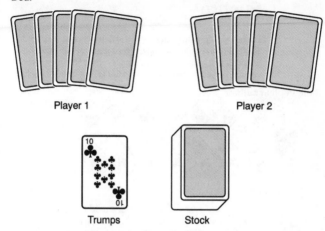

Player 1   Player 2

Trumps   Stock

Play The nondealer leads first. Players must follow suit if they can and may trump if they cannot.

A player must always take a trick if he can. The winner of a trick leads to the next trick.

Scoring is as follows:

a "point" or "the trick" (three tricks won), scores one point;

b "the vole" (all five tricks won), scores two points;

c king turned up to indicate trumps, scores one point for the dealer; and

d king of trumps held in the hand, scores one point if it is declared before the holder plays his first card.

Game is five points.

Penalties If a player has refused to exchange and fails to make at least three tricks (point), his opponent scores an extra point if he makes a point.

There is no penalty if the opponent scores vole.

2-6 Euchre

Euchre is a derivative of ecarté and dates back at least to the
1800s. For a time it was the national game of the United
States. It is a game for two to six players depending on the
version played; perhaps most popular is four-handed euchre.

Rank in plain suits

Rank in trumps

FOUR-HANDED EUCHRE

Four people play in partnerships of two. Each player sits
opposite his partner.

Deck A 32-card deck is used: a standard deck with the
6s,5s,4s,3s, and 2s removed. Ace ranks high, and 7 low.

Trumps The jack of trumps, called the "right bower," ranks
as the highest trump. The other jack of the same color, called
the "left bower," ranks second. For example, if diamonds are
trumps, the jack of hearts is the left bower.

Thus the trump suit ranks: rb (high), lb,a,k,q,10,9,8,7 (low).

Objective Each partnership tries to win the most tricks.

Deal Players draw for first deal, lowest card dealing.
Each player is dealt five face-down cards, in packets of three
and two. The dealer then turns the next card face up to
indicate trumps. The deal passes clockwise around the table.

Nominating trumps Each player, beginning with the player
to the dealer's left, has the option of accepting the suit of the
face-up card as trumps, or refusing it in the hope of
nominating a different suit.

To accept, the dealer's opponents say "I order it up": the
dealer's partner says "I assist"; and the dealer says nothing
but indicates his acceptance by discarding one card and
adding the face up card to his hand.

To refuse, the nondealer says "I pass," and the dealer puts
the face-up card under the stock.

Once one player has accepted, play begins.

If all four players refuse, there is a second round in which
each player in turn has the right to nominate the trump suit or
pass. Once a player has nominated a suit, play begins.

If all players pass, the hands are thrown in and the cards are
dealt by the next dealer.

Play The player who nominated trumps is called the
"maker." Before play begins, he may decide to play the hand
without his partner, in which case he says "I play alone."
His partner then lays his hand face down on the table.
Although he does not play the hand, he shares in any stakes.
Rules of play are the same as in whist.

Scoring If the maker and his partner win all five tricks, this
constitutes a "march," and scores two points. If the maker is
playing alone, he scores four points for a march.

If the maker and his partner win four or three tricks, they
score one point; if they win fewer than three tricks they are
said to be "euchred," and their opponents score two points.

Players may use counters to keep the score, but it is
customary to use a 3 or a 4 from the unused cards as
markers, one card being face up, the other face down, as
illustrated overleaf:

a the 3 exposed with the other card across it signifies one point;
b the 4 exposed with the other card across it is two points;
c the 3 on top of the other card is three points;
d the 4 on top is four points.

Game is generally five points, but some players prefer to set a target of seven or ten.

Keeping the score

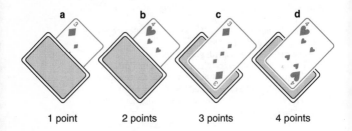

a	b	c	d
1 point	2 points	3 points	4 points

RAILROAD EUCHRE

In this variation of four-handed euchre, the joker is used as an additional trump, ranking above the right bower.

TWO-HANDED EUCHRE

The deck is reduced to 24 cards by discarding the 8s and 7s. Rules are the same as for four-handed euchre, except that there is no need for a declaration to play alone.

THREE-HANDED EUCHRE

In three-handed euchre (also called cutthroat euchre) the maker plays on his own, with the other two players in partnership against him. The maker scores three points for march; otherwise scoring is as in the four-handed game.

CALL ACE EUCHRE

This is a version for four, five, or six players, each playing for himself. The rules are as in four-handed euchre, with the following differences.

Calling The maker has the right to decide whether to play on his own or with a partner. To choose a partner he says "I call on the ace of..." and nominates a suit. If a player holds the ace named, he plays as the maker's partner, but does not declare his partnership until he plays the ace. As the ace may in fact not have been dealt, the maker may find he is playing alone!

Scoring A lone maker wins points as follows:

a march, as many points as there are players;

b four or three tricks, one point.

A partnership wins points as follows:

a march, two points for each player if there are three or four players, and three points for each player if there are five or six;

b four or three tricks, each partner scores one point.

If the maker, with or without partner, is euchred, the other players score two points each.

3   Five hundred

Five hundred is related to euchre and also has certain
similarities to bridge and whist. The basic game is for three
players.

THREE-HANDED FIVE HUNDRED
Deck 33 cards are used: a standard deck excluding the
6s,5s,4s,3s and 2s; plus a joker. Ace ranks high, and 7 low.
In the trump suit cards rank, in descending order, as follows:
joker, right bower (jack of the trump suit), left bower (other
jack of the same color), a,k,q,10,9,8,7.
In no-trump hands, there are no right and left bowers. The
holder of the joker may then nominate it to represent any suit
he pleases; the joker automatically ranks as the highest card
of that suit and takes any trick to which it is led or played.
Objective Each player aims to make a contract by bidding
and to win enough tricks to fulfill it.

Rank in plain suits

Rank in trumps

Deal Players cut for the deal (king ranks high, ace low, and joker lowest): lowest card deals.

Ten face-down cards are dealt to each player, in packets of either three, two, three, two; or three, three, three, one.

The remaining packet of three cards constitutes the "widow" and is placed face upward on the table.

The deal passes clockwise around the table.

Scoring table for five hundred

Tricks bid	♠	♣	♦	♥	no trumps
6	40	60	80	100	120
7	140	160	180	200	220
8	240	260	280	300	320
9	340	360	380	400	420
10	440	460	480	500	520

Bidding Each player in turn makes a bid, starting with the player to the dealer's left. Each player specifies the number of tricks he intends to take and his choice of trumps.

The lowest number of tricks that can be bid is six, and the highest ten. For bidding the calls are ranked: no-trumps (highest), hearts, diamonds, clubs, spades (lowest).

Any player who passes cannot make a further bid in that round of play.

Widow The player who wins the contract adds the three widow cards to his hand and discards face down any three cards of his choice.

Play Rules of play are the same as in whist.

If a player leads the joker in a no-trump hand, he cannot nominate it to a suit in which he has either declared himself void or that he has failed to follow when able.

The winner of the trick leads to the next trick.

Scoring The players opposing the contract play as partners, but each always scores ten points for each trick he makes.

The bidder scores points according to the table, provided he has made his contract.

If he fails to score sufficient tricks, he loses the value of the contract.

Bonuses There are no bonuses for overtricks (ie tricks over the number bid).

However, a player who has made a contract of less than eight clubs but has scored "grand slam" (all ten tricks), receives a total of 250 points.

(There is an optional system for when grand slam is scored after a bid of eight clubs or better. In this system, the successful player scores a bonus equal to the contract.

For example, a bid of eight diamonds that results in a grand slam is worth 280 points plus a bonus of 280.)

Players losing contracts may well find their scores going into minus figures.

Game is 500 points. If two players reach this total in the same deal, the player who reached 500 first wins.

TWO-HANDED FIVE HUNDRED

This is played in the same way as the three-handed game, except that a third hand, known as a "dead-hand," is dealt. It remains face down throughout the game, and adds a degree of uncertainty to the bidding and play.

FOUR-HANDED FIVE HUNDRED

This game is also played like the three-handed game, but facing players act as partners. The deck is increased to 43 cards by adding the 6s, 5s and two 4s – one of each color.

Forty five

This game is related to loo and spoil five. Cards have the same unusual ranking as in spoil five, but in forty-five there is a different scoring system and no pool. It is a game for two, four, or six players, divided into two equal and opposing sides.

Cards A standard deck of playing cards is used. The cards are ranked, in descending order, as follows. (See diagrams overleaf.)

Spades and clubs
Plain suits (ie non-trump): k,q,j,a,2,3,4,5,6,7,8,9,10.
Trump suits: 5,j,a of hearts, a of spades or clubs,
k,q,2,3,4,6,7,8,9,10.

Hearts
Plain suit: k,q,j,10,9,8,7,6,5,4,3,2.
Trump suit: 5,j,a,k,q,10,9,8,7,6,4,3,2.

Diamonds
Plain suit: k,q,j,10,9,8,7,6,5,4,3,2,a.
Trump suit: 5,j,a of hearts, a of diamonds,
k,q,10,9,8,7,6,4,3,2.

Objective Players try to win tricks and to prevent their opponents from doing so.

Deal Players draw for deal, using standard ranking with ace high and 2 low. The player drawing the lowest card deals. Five face-down cards are dealt to each player in packets of two then three, or vice versa. The next card is turned face up to indicate trumps. The deal passes clockwise around the table.

Exchanging If the face-up card denoting the trump is an ace, the dealer may, before the first card is led, exchange this face-up card for any card in his hand.

Any player who has been dealt the ace of trumps has the option of exchanging any card in his hand for the face up card. If he does not exchange a card, he must announce that

Rank in plain suits

Spades   Hearts   Diamonds
and clubs

Rank in trumps

Spades and clubs	Hearts	Diamonds

he has the ace at his first turn of play. Failure to announce that he has the ace of trumps means that this card becomes the lowest trump for the round.

Play Rules of play are as in whist, except as follows.

If a card of a plain suit is led, a player may choose either to trump or to follow suit; he may discard another plain suit card only if he can neither follow suit nor trump.

If a card of the trump suit is led, a player must usually follow suit; he is not, however, obliged to play any of the top three trumps if the leading card was a lower trump.

Scoring Points are scored by the winning player or partnership. According to one scoring system, 5 points are scored for making three or four tricks and 10 points for making five tricks. An alternative scoring system gives 5 points for three tricks, 15 points for four tricks, and 25 points for five tricks.

Whichever scoring system is used, the game is won by the first side to score 45 points – a fact that gives the game its name.

AUCTION FORTY-FIVE

Auction forty-five is very popular in parts of Canada. Its basic rules are the same as for spoil five, with the following variations.

Players Four or six people play in partnerships of two or three respectively. Each player sits between two players of the opposing side.

Bidding The player to the left of the dealer bids first, followed by each player in turn to his left.

The bids, indicating the number of points each side is contracted to make, are 5,10,15,20,25, and 30. Each bid must outbid the previous bid.

The dealer has the option of "holding," ie outbidding, the previous bid without increasing it. Each of the other players who bid may then bid again; but the dealer has the option of holding a second time.

Trumps are nominated by the highest bidder.

Discards Each player may exchange as many cards as he
likes for cards drawn from the top of the stock.

Play The player to the left of the highest bidder leads first.

Scoring Each trick counts five points, and the highest trump
in play scores five extra points for whichever side takes it.

If a side fulfills its contract it scores the number of points bid
plus the points scored with its tricks.

If it fails, it loses the number of points bid.

The side that did not make the contract scores all the points it
makes in play.

Game is 120 points.

4   Grand

Grand is a combination of whist, euchre, and hearts. Each hand is played like one of these three games or according to rules for a fourth – "grand" – option, depending on the choice of the bidder.

Players Four people play, in partnerships of two.
Deck A standard deck of playing cards is used. The rank of the cards depends on the type of game being played.
Objective Each partnership aims to make and fulfil a contract.
Deal Players cut for the deal (ace ranks low), and highest card deals. Cards are dealt in a clockwise direction, one at a time and face down, until each player has 13 cards.
Bidding Each player in turn, starting with the player to the left of the dealer, has one chance to either bid or pass.
The bids are five and multiples of five, and indicate the number of points the bidder expects to score in that hand if he is the highest bidder.
At the end of bidding the highest bidder names which game (whist, grand, euchre, or hearts) will be played for that round. If the first three players pass, the dealer must make a bid.
General play Unlike whist, euchre, and hearts, the bidder always leads to the first trick.

Whist
If whist is chosen, the bidder names the trump suit. Play is the same as in whist.
Scoring Each trick more than six counts five points. For example, on a bid of 25 the bidding partnership needs to take 11 tricks to score.
If the bidding partnership makes a grand slam (winning all 13 tricks), it scores for all 13 tricks, making 65 points.

No points are scored for honors.

Setbacks If the bidding partnership fails to make its bid, the entire amount of its bid is deducted from its previous score. In addition, the opposing partnership wins five points for each trick that it takes above six tricks.

Grand

If grand is chosen, play is the same as in whist, except that there are no trumps.

Scoring Each trick more than six scores nine points.

A grand slam also scores 40 points for the first six tricks, making a total of 103 points. If either partnership makes a grand slam, it wins the game – regardless of its score.

Setbacks are scored in the same way as in the whist option, except that each trick counts nine points.

The opponents also win nine points for each trick they take over six tricks.

Euchre

Euchre can only be chosen on a bid of 25 or less. The bidder names the trump suit. Each player then discards eight cards face down – he may not keep any trumps lower than 8.

Play is the same as in euchre with the following differences. If the bidder calls less than 20 he cannot play alone. If he bids 20, he may choose whether or not to play alone. If he bids 25, he must play alone.

If playing alone, the bidder may exchange any one of his cards for the best card in his partner's hand. The bidder's partner puts his cards face down on the table.

Scoring Points are scored by either partnership as follows:
three tricks, 5 points;
four tricks, 10 points;
five tricks if made in partnership, 20 points;
five tricks if made by lone hand, 25 points.

Setbacks If the bidding partnership fails to make its bid, the amount bid plus 20 points is subtracted from its score. If a lone hand fails to make his bid, he loses twice the amount bid.

Hearts

Hearts is only allowed on a bid of 50 or less. Play is as in hearts.

Scoring If the bidding partnership does not take any tricks containing hearts, it wins 50 points.

Setbacks If the partners do take tricks containing hearts, the amount bid plus one point for each heart taken is subtracted from their score. The opponents are set back one point for each heart they take.

Heart bid option If the first bidder passes when the dealer's partnership has a score of less then 70, it is generally regarded as an indication that he is prepared to play hearts. If the dealer's side has 70 or more points, the first bidder may determine that hearts are played by leading a heart and saying "Hearts."

Game is 100 points, but the game may finish at the end of a time limit or after a set number of rounds. The scores at the end of play are used to calculate the final result.

1 The difference between 100 and the lowest score at the end of play stands as a separate score for the side with the highest score at the end of play.

2 The difference between the number of times each side has been set back is multiplied by ten. This stands as a separate score for the side with the fewer setbacks.

3 The result of this final scoring indicates the winner.

For example, if at the end of play side A has a score of 80 with seven setbacks and side B has a score of 60 with five setbacks, then the final result is calculated as follows:

1 100 – 60 = 40 (awarded to side A):

2 (7 – 5) x 10 = 20 (awarded to side B):

3 so side A wins with a total of 40 against side B's total of 20.

3-7 Hearts

Hearts is one of the avoidance games – meaning that it is
based on the principle of not taking penalty cards rather than
of winning tricks. It evolved in the nineteenth century, since
when many interesting variants have appeared.

Penalty cards

HEARTS: BASIC GAME

Players Three to seven people can play. There are no
partnerships.

Cards A standard deck of 52 playing cards is used.
2s are discarded as follows:
one 2 with three players;
none with four players;
two with five players;
three with seven players.
If possible, the 2 of hearts is not discarded.
The cards rank normally, with ace high. There are no trumps.

Choice of first dealer is by low cut.

Deal The dealer deals out all the cards one at a time and face
down, beginning with the player to his left and going
clockwise.

Play The player to the dealer's left leads to the first trick.
Thereafter the winner of one trick leads to the next. Each
player after the lead must follow suit if he can. If he cannot,
he may play any card he likes.
A hand ends when all the hearts suit has appeared in play.

Revoking If a player fails to follow suit when he is able to, he may correct his mistake without penalty if he does so before the trick is picked up.

Otherwise he scores 13 penalty points and the hand ends. No other players can score penalty points on that hand.

Scoring Each player scores one penalty point for each card of the hearts suit contained in tricks taken by him.

Continuing play After each hand, the deal passes one player to the left.

The winner is the player with the fewest penalty points after an agreed number of hands.

Alternatively, the winner is the player with the fewest penalty points when one player reaches a set number of points (eg 50 points).

SPOT HEARTS

Also called chip hearts, this game is played in the same way as basic hearts except that each heart card counts as many penalty points as its face value. The king counts 13, the queen 12, and the jack 11.
(Almost any hearts variant can be scored in this way).

BLACK LADY HEARTS

In this popular version the queen of spades is an extra penalty card, scoring 13 penalty points. Each heart card counts one penalty point.

Sometimes it is ruled that a player must take the first possible opportunity to discard the queen of spades.

13 points

GREEK HEARTS

In this variant the penalties are the same as for black lady hearts, but play and scoring differ in the following ways.

Exchanging Before play begins, each player, after looking at his cards, passes three cards of his choice face down to the player to his right. No player may look at the cards he is receiving until after he has passed on his own cards.

Scoring Each heart is scored as in spot hearts, and the queen of hearts counts 50 penalty points, except that if one player

50 points

takes all the penalty cards he does not score at all for this
hand and instead all the other players score 150 penalty
points each.

DOMINO HEARTS

The penalty values are as in the basic hearts game, but play
varies as follows.

Deal Six cards are dealt to each player, and the remainder
are placed face down to form the stock.

Play If a player cannot follow suit he draws cards one at a
time from the top of the stock until he can follow suit.
Drawn cards of other suits remain in his hand to be played
later. When the stock is exhausted players may discard as in
the basic hearts game.

Each player drops out when he has played all his cards. The
last player left in scores one penalty point for each heart card
left in his hand as well as for those in his tricks.

If a player wins a trick with his last card, the lead passes to the next player to the left.

The winner is the player with the lowest score when one player reaches 31 points.

JOKER HEARTS

In this hearts game, the 2 of hearts is discarded and a joker used.

5 points

The joker ranks between the 10 and jack of hearts, and wins any trick in which it is played, regardless of the suit led, unless a higher heart has also appeared in that trick – in which case the higher heart takes the trick.

A high heart played when the joker is not played is a discard as usual, unless hearts were led.

The joker counts five penalty points.

HEARTSETTE

In this variant of hearts a widow hand is dealt face down in the center of the table.

The 2 of spades is not used if there are three or four players.

The size of the widow depends on the number of players:

with three or four players, three cards;

with five players, two cards;

with six players, four cards.

All other cards are dealt out to the players.

Play and penalties are as in the basic hearts game except that the winner of the first trick adds the widow to it and scores penalty points for any penalty cards it contains.

TWO-HANDED HEARTS

This is an adaptation of the basic game for two players.

It is played like basic hearts except that 13 cards are dealt to each player and the remainder are placed face down to form a stock.

After each trick the winner takes the top card from the stock and the loser takes the next card.

The game continues until all the cards have been played.

BLACK MARIA

This very popular version of hearts is also known as **Slippery Anne**.

Play is as for basic hearts except as follows.

Penalty cards As well as hearts (one point for each card), there are three penalty cards:

The queen of spades (Black Maria), 13 points;

the king of spades, 10 points;

the ace of spades, seven points.

Exchanging occurs before play as in Greek hearts.

Each hand ends when all penalty cards have been played.

13 points

10 points

7 points

2   Imperial

This game resembles piquet, but there is a trump suit and the cards rank differently. It is a game for two players.

Cards A 32-card "piquet" deck is used – a standard deck with the 2s, 3s, 4s, 5s, and 6s removed.
Cards rank k (high), q,j,a,10,9,8,7 (low).
"Honors" are the k,q,j,a, and 7 of trumps.

Rank

Chips are used for scoring: 12 white chips and eight red. One red chip is worth six white. At the beginning of the game all chips are placed together in a central pool.
Objective The aim is to be the first to win five red chips.
Shuffle is normal.
Cut is by the nondealer. There need be only two cards in each section. Otherwise the cut is normal.
The deal is in packets of three cards, face down. When both players have 12 cards each, the 25th card is placed face up in the center of the table to denote trumps for the hand. The undealt part of the deck is placed to one side, out of use for the remainder of the hand.
Scoring procedure Scoring occurs before, during, and after each hand of play.
Whenever a player scores, he takes the appropriate chip or chips from the central pool. Whenever a player has collected

six white chips, he exchanges them immediately for one red chip from the pool.

Whenever a player gains a red chip in any way, his opponent must put back into the pool any white chips that he holds.

Scoring before play occurs in the following order:

1 the dealer scores one white chip if the turned up (25th) card is an honor card;

2 either player scores one red chip if he has been dealt carte blanche, ie a hand containing no king, queen or jack;

3 players declare and score for combinations – point, sequences, and melds – held in their hands;

4 players declare and score for sequences and melds that use the turned up card in addition to cards in their hands.

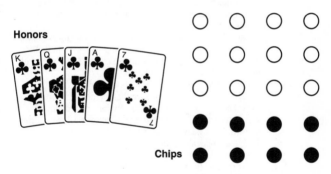

Honors

Chips

Declarations Combinations are declared in the order: point, sequences, melds. A player may include any card in more than one combination.

To avoid revealing more information than necessary, players use the same formal dialogue used in piquet (see Announcing the declarations, p 125). In imperial, all winning combinations must be declared and shown.

Point This term refers to a player's longest suit (ie the suit of which he holds most cards).

The player with the longest suit scores the point and takes one white chip for each card that he holds in that suit.

If players have suits of equal length, the point goes to the player whose relevant cards have the highest face value (counting ace 11, court cards 10 each, and other cards at their numerical face value). If players still tie, the nondealer scores.

Sequences These are consecutive cards belonging to the same suit. These may be of three or four cards but may contain only kings, queens, jacks, and aces. A four-card sequence beats a three-card sequence. Three-card sequences rank according to the top card. The player with the best sequence scores one red chip. If the players tie, the nondealer scores.

Melds These are cards of the same rank. Only fours of kings, queens, jacks, aces and 7s are counted – ranking in that order, with king high. Threes do not count. The player with the best meld scores one red chip.

Combinations using the turned up card

1 Players declare any sequence that includes the turned up card. The higher ranking sequence wins one red chip.

2 A player declares if he has a meld of four using the turned up card. If so, he wins one red chip.

Play The nondealer leads to the first trick; thereafter the winner of each trick leads to the next one.

In every case, the second player to a trick must take it if he can. He must follow suit if possible. If he cannot follow suit he must use a trump if he has one; only if he has no trump may he discard.

Cards are not collected in tricks. Each player puts the cards he has played face up in front of him, and is free to examine them at any time.

Scoring during play

1 A player taking the jack of trumps by leading the king or queen wins one red chip.

2 A player taking the ace also wins one red chip.

3 A player takes one white chip for each trump honor contained in tricks that he wins.

Scoring after play If one player takes more tricks in a hand than his opponent, he wins one white chip for every trick in excess of his opponent's total.

Thus if a player wins all 12 tricks – referred to as "capot" – he wins two red chips.

The winner is the first player to win five red chips. Hands continue until one player does this, with the deal alternating between players.

If a player gains five red chips in the middle of a hand, the hand is abandoned at once.

2   Kalabriasz

This excellent game is also known as klaberjass, clab, and clobber. It is essentially the same as the French game, belote.

Players The basic game is for two players.
Cards Play is with a standard deck of cards from which the 2s,3s,4s,5s, and 6s have been removed.
The cards rank as follows:
a in plain suits, a (high), 10, k,q,j,9,8,7 (low).
b in the trump suit, j (high), 9,a,10,k,q,8,7 (low).
Objective Players aim to meld sequences and to take certain scoring cards in tricks.
Choice of dealer for the first hand is by high cut, with ace low.
First deal The dealer gives each player six cards face down in packets of three. He then places the next card face up in the center of the table, and places the rest of the deck – the stock – face down in a pile beside it.
Determining trumps Players make bids to determine the trump suit.
1 The nondealer opens with a bid of "Accept," "Schmeiss," or "Pass."
If he bids to accept, the suit of the central face up card becomes trumps for the hand.

**Rank in
plain suits**

Rank in trumps

A bid of schmeiss is a proposal for a new deal. The dealer then has the opportunity of agreeing to a new deal or of accepting the suit of the central face up card as the trump suit.

If the nondealer says "Pass," the dealer has a turn at bidding.

2 The dealer may now either: accept the suit of the central face up card as trumps; bid "Schmeiss," in which case the nondealer must agree to the new deal or accept the suit of the face up card as trumps; or pass, in which case there is a second round of bidding.

3 If both players pass in the first round of bidding, the nondealer may then either: nominate any trump suit that he wishes, in which case play will be with this suit as trumps; or pass, in which case the dealer may nominate trumps, or pass. If both players pass in the second round of bidding, the cards are thrown in and a new first deal made.

The player who actually determines the trump suit is called "maker."

Second deal Once the trump suit has been established, each player is dealt three more cards, one at a time, and face down.

The dealer then takes the bottom card of the stock and places if face up on top of the stock.

If the suit of the central face up card was accepted as trumps, a player holding the 7 of that suit may exchange it for the central face up card if he wishes. The 7 of trumps is called the "dix."

Declaring sequences usually takes place before play begins, but may be after the nondealer has led to the first trick. By their declarations players establish who holds the highest sequence.

Sequences All cards in a sequence must be consecutive and of the same suit. There are two kinds of sequence:

a a sequence of three cards, worth 20 points; and

b a sequence of four or more cards, worth 50 points.

For sequences cards rank in the order a (high), k,q,j,10,9,8,7 (low).

Sequences of equal value are ranked according to their highest card. Note that a sequence of four cards beats a longer sequence provided that the four-card sequence is headed by the highest card.

If sequences are of equal value and are headed by cards of the same rank, a sequence in the trump suit is higher.

If equal sequences headed by cards of the same rank are both in plain suits, some versions of the game rule that the nondealer's sequence is higher while others rule that the sequences are equal and neither player may score.

Sequences

20 points

50 points

Declaration procedure The nondealer begins by announcing "Sequence of 50" if he has a sequence of four or more cards, or "Sequence of 20" if he has a three-card sequence.

The dealer then replies "Good" if he cannot beat it, "Not good" if he can beat it, or "How high?" if he has a sequence with the same points value.

If the dealer replies "How high?" the nondealer states the rank of the card that heads his sequence, and then the dealer replies "Good" if he cannot beat it, or "Not good" if he can.

Scoring of sequences Only the player with the highest sequence scores any points at this stage of the game. He scores for his highest sequence after first showing it to his opponent. He also scores for any other sequences that he is prepared to show.

Play Nondealer leads to the first trick.

Players must follow suit if they are able, and if they cannot follow suit must play a trump if they have one. If a trump is led the opposing player must take the trick if he can.

The winner of a trick places it face down in front of him and leads to the next trick.

Bella is a meld comprising the king and queen of trumps. It is worth 20 points to any player who holds it, and is scored automatically when the second of these cards is played.

Scoring during play Players score points as follows for cards taken in tricks: (See diagram overleaf)

a "jasz" (jack of trumps), 20 points;

b "menel" (9 of trumps), 14 points;

c each ace, 11 points;

d each 10, 10 points;

e each king, four points;

f each queen, three points;

g each jack but jasz, two points.

The player who takes the last trick scores a further 10 points.

The final score for each hand is calculated as follows.

a If the player who determined the trump suit (the maker) has a points total higher than his opponent, each player scores his own total.

b If the opposing player has a higher total, he scores both his own points total and that of the maker. This is called "going bate."

c If the players have an equal number of points, the maker scores no points and his opponent scores his own points total. The maker's opponent is said to have gone "half bate." **Game** is usually 500 points. If both players reach the agreed game total in the same hand, the one with the most points wins.

Scoring during play

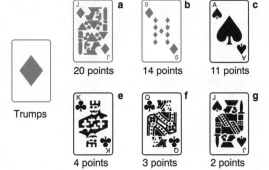

Trumps

a 20 points	**b** 14 points	**c** 11 points	**d** 10 points
e 4 points	**f** 3 points	**g** 2 points	

THREE-HANDED KALABRIASZ

In the three-handed game turns pass clockwise around the table. The maker must score more than both his opponents together, or go bate. Players score their own sequences and points won in play, but opponents share the maker's points if he goes bate.

PARTNERSHIP KALABRIASZ

This differs from the basic game as follows.

All but the last card are dealt out so that the dealer has seven cards and the other players eight each.

The last card becomes the central face up card. Before play, the player with the dix exchanges it for a face up card and the dealer takes the dix to complete his hand.

After one player has established the highest sequence, his
partner may also score for any sequences.
Partners keep their tricks together and score as a side.

3 Knaves

Penalty cards

4 points

3 points

2 points

1 point

This game combines the principles of trick-taking and of avoidance games. Players score points for taking tricks, but must then subtract points for any tricks containing jacks.

Players Knaves is a game for three players.
Cards A standard deck of 52 cards is used.
Object Each player tries to win tricks without taking any jacks.
Deal and play are as for whist (p 164).
Tactics Each player plays for himself, but if one player is winning, the other two often act as a temporary partnership to try to reduce his lead.
Scoring At the end of each hand, each player scores one point for each trick he has taken.
If he has taken any jacks, he then subtracts points as follows:

a jack of hearts, four points;
b jack of diamonds, three;
c jack of clubs, two;
d jack of spades, one.

A player may have a minus score.
The winner is the first to reach 20 plus points.

POLIGNAC

This game is a French version of knaves. Players must avoid taking tricks containing jacks, especially jack of spades, which is given the name Polignac.
Players Four to six can play.
Cards For four players a standard deck without the 2s,3s,4s,5s, and 6s is used.
For five or six players the two black 7s are also removed.
Deal and play are as in whist (p 164), but without trumps.

Scoring At the end of each hand, each player scores penalty points for each jack he has taken, as follows:
one point each for the jack of hearts, diamonds, and clubs;
two points for the jack of spades (Polignac).

"General" A player may decide to try and take all the tricks in a hand. This is known as general, and the player must announce his intention before the lead to the first trick.
If he succeeds, all the other players score five penalty points.
If he fails, he scores five penalty points and the jacks score penalty points in the usual way against the players who take them.

The winner is the player with the fewest points after an agreed number of hands.

3-6   Loo

Rank

Loo, or lanternloo as it is sometimes called, was once one of the most widely played games in Europe. It has several variations but is always played for stakes.

THREE-CARD LOO

Players Three or more people can play, but about six is best.

Deck A standard 52-card deck is used. Ace ranks high.

Objective Each player tries to win at least one trick.

Deal Players cut for deal, lowest card dealing.

Each player is dealt three face down cards, one at a time. An extra hand known as a "miss" is also dealt, as either the first or last hand of each deal. The top card of the remaining cards is turned face up and denotes trumps.

The deal passes clockwise around the table.

Pool In an optional opening deal called a "single," no miss is dealt, and only the dealer puts three counters into a pool. In subsequent deals, or if no single has been played, a miss is dealt and each player contributes three counters to the pool.

The choice Beginning with the player to the dealer's left, each player in turn chooses one of the following:

a to play with the cards he holds;

b to throw in his own cards and play with the miss; or

c to pass.

To indicate their choice, players say "I play," "I take the miss," or "I pass," as appropriate.

If a player passes, he throws in his cards and takes no further part in that deal. If everyone passes, the dealer takes the pool.

If only one player decides to play but has not taken the miss, the dealer must play him, using the cards in the miss. If the dealer loses, he does not pay, nor is he paid if he wins.

If only one player decides to play and has taken the miss, the dealer may either play him with standard scoring, or just let him take the pool.

Play The first player to choose to play leads to the first trick, with his highest trump if he has one.

Each player who did not pass plays a card to each trick. He must follow suit if he can, and if possible must play a higher card than any already played to that trick.

If a player cannot follow suit, he should trump the trick with a higher trump than any already played to that trick; if he cannot do this, he may discard.

The winner of a trick must lead with a trump if possible.

Scoring The winner of each trick takes one third of the pool.

Looing A player who has not won a trick is said to be "looed."

In limited loo, a looed player pays an agreed amount (usually three counters) into the pool.

In unlimited loo, he pays as many counters as there were in the pool at the beginning of the hand.

Penalties A player is also looed for:

a playing out of turn;

b looking at the miss without taking it;

c failing to take a trick when possible; and

d failing to lead the ace of trumps when holding it.

Variations

a The trump card is not turned up until a player cannot follow suit.

b If a player is dealt three trumps, he collects the pool. The hands are thrown in, and the cards are shuffled and dealt for the next round.

FIVE-CARD LOO

This variant is played in the same way as three-card loo, except for the following changes.

Deal Each player receives five cards.

Pool Contributions to the pool are five not three counters.

Miss is never dealt.

Exchanges Each player may exchange up to five cards for the same number of cards drawn from the stock. A player who exchanges must then play his hand.

Pam The jack of clubs, called "pam," ranks as the highest trump regardless of suit. If a player leads the ace of trumps and says "Pam be civil," the pam cannot be played to that trick.

Flushes are five cards of the same suit, or four of the same suit plus pam. The holder of a flush exposes it before play and wins the pool. Each of the other players is then looed unless he also holds a flush or flush with pam.

If there is more than one flush, a trump flush wins over one in a plain suit, and if there is a clash between plain suit flushes, the highest card wins. If two or more plain suit flushes are equal, the pool is divided.

Blaze This is an optional winning hand, entirely made up of face cards. The same rules of precedence apply as with flushes, and a blaze outranks a flush.

IRISH LOO

This is played like three-card loo, with the following changes.

a Miss is not dealt.

b Exchanging is carried out in the same way as in the five-card game.

c "Club law": if clubs are trumps every player must enter the game.

Michigan 3-8

Michigan is a popular and fast-moving game usually played for low stakes. It is easy to learn but can also be a challenging game for the experienced player. Other games by which Michigan is known are boodle, Newmarket, Chicago, and Saratoga.

Boodle cards

Players Any number from three to eight can play.

Cards In addition to one standard deck of playing cards, an ace, king, queen and jack – each in a different suit – from a second deck of cards are used. The four cards are called "boodle" cards and are placed face up in the center of the table.

Cards rank normally, with ace high.

Chips Each player is given a supply of betting chips or counters.

Objective Each player tries to play certain cards, thereby collecting chips, and to be the first to get rid of all his cards.

Ante Before each hand is dealt, every player must ante by putting one chip on each of the four boodle cards.

Deal Players cut for the deal, highest card dealing.

The dealer gives one face down card at a time to each player and an extra hand (widow) to the dealer's left.

Each player must have the same number of cards. Any card or cards left over at the end of the deal are placed face down on the table.

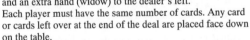

Auction Before the start of play the dealer has the right to exchange his hand for the widow. If he does so, he discards his hand face down.

If the dealer chooses not to take the widow, the other players may bid for it. The highest bidder pays the dealer in chips, discards his hand face down and takes the widow.

If no player wants the widow, it is left face down without being seen by any player.

Play begins with the player to the dealer's left. He places his lowest card in any suit face up in front of him.

The player with the next card higher in that suit (ie either the same or another player) plays it face up. This continues with cards played in sequence until either the ace is reached or nobody has the next card in the sequence.

Usually, players announce the rank and suit of cards as they play them.

Each player forms a pile of face up cards in front of him. Once a card is covered, it cannot be inspected.

Stopped play At the end of a sequence play is said to be "stopped." The last person to have played a card starts a new sequence with his lowest card in any other suit. If he cannot do this, the next player to his left able to lead with another suit does so.

If none of the other players can lead another suit, the first player may lead with his lowest card in the same suit as the previous sequence.

Boodle winnings Whenever a player lays down a card that matches one of the four boodle cards, he wins all the chips on that card.

If no player claims the chips on a boodle card during a hand, the chips remain on the card and carry over to the next deal. Before each hand, each player antes one chip on each boodle card.

Play ends as soon as one player has got rid of all his cards. Every other player must then pay him one chip for each card still in his hand.

Penalty If a player fails to play a card in sequence when able to do so, he must pay one chip to each of the other players. If by failing to play a card he prevented another player from winning boodle chips, he must make up the loss to the dispossessed player with his own chips. The chips on the boodle card remain and are carried over to the next deal.

The winner of a game is either:
a the first person to win an agreed number of chips; or
b the player with the most chips at the end of a set number
of deals or on the expiration of a time limit.

2-7   **Napoleon**

Also called nap, this game is in some ways similar to euchre.
Any number of players from two to seven may take part.
There are no partnerships.

Rank

Deck A standard 52-card deck is used; ace ranks high.
Objective Each player aims to contract a bid and take tricks
to fulfil it.
Deal Players cut for deal, highest card dealing first. Each
player is dealt five face down cards, one at a time. The stock
is then placed face down on the table.
The deal passes in clockwise rotation.
Bidding Beginning with the player to the dealer's left, each
player can either pass or bid two, three, four, or "Napoleon"
– indicating the number of tricks he intends to win.
(Napoleon signifies five tricks).
Each bid must be higher than the previous bid, and the player
with the highest bid becomes the bidder.
There is only one round of bidding.
Trumps The bidder leads to the first trick, and the suit of his
opening card denotes trumps.
Play is the same as in whist.
Scoring Napoleon is played for stakes, the usual ones being:
two units for a bid of two;

three units for three;

four units for four; and

ten for Napoleon.

If the bidder wins his contract, each of the other players pays him the stake. If he fails to win his contract, he pays each of the other players the stake. If he fails on a bid of Napoleon, he pays only half the stake.

Optional bids The following optional bids are sometimes used.

a "Wellington" is a declaration to win all five tricks at double stakes. It cannot be called unless Napoleon has already been called.

b "Blücher" overcalls Wellington, and is for five tricks at triple stakes.

c "Misère" or "misery" is a declaration to lose every trick. In the bidding it ranks between three and four, and carries the same stakes as three. There are no trumps in this bid.

PURCHASE NAP

The rules of purchase nap are the same as for Napoleon, except that each player may exchange any number of cards for fresh ones from the stock, on payment of one unit for each card.

The payments are put in a kitty, won by the first player to make a bid of Napoleon.

SEVEN-CARD NAP

In seven-card nap, each player receives seven cards. Play is the same as for Napoleon, but bids of Wellington and Blücher are not permitted.

The order of bids with their stakes are as follows:

three bids, a stake of three;

four, a stake of four;

nap and misère (optional), stake of 10;

six, stake of 18; and

seven, stake of 24.

Players losing nap, misère, six, or seven pay half stakes.

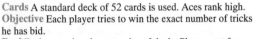

3+   **Oh Hell**

Rank

Also known as blackout, this game has many features in common with whist. It is a game for three or more players, each playing for himself.

Cards A standard deck of 52 cards is used. Aces rank high.
Objective Each player tries to win the exact number of tricks he has bid.
Deal Each game involves a series of deals. Players cut for the first deal (highest card deals) and thereafter the deal passes in a clockwise direction around the table.
In the first deal, each player is dealt one card; in subsequent deals, the number of cards dealt to each player is increased each time by one card. When the size of the hand can no longer be increased by one card per player, the game is finished. Thus with four players, the cards will be dealt 13 times, and with five players ten times.
At the end of each deal, the dealer turns the top card of the stock face up to denote trumps. If in the final deal there is no spare card to turn face up, the hand is played without trumps.
Bidding Starting with the dealer, each player in turn bids the number of tricks he expects to win, or "nullo" if he expects to lose every trick.
In the first deal, possible bids are one or nullo; the number of possible bids increases with the size of each hand.
Play is opened by the player to the dealer's left. He leads with any card, and the other players must follow suit; if unable to do so they may trump or discard. The winner of a trick leads to the next.
Scoring Every player who fulfils his bid exactly scores one point for each trick of his bid and a ten point bonus.
There is no standard score for making nullo; sometimes ten points are awarded, sometimes five, or five points plus the number of tricks in the deal. If a player wins more or fewer

tricks than the number he bid, he neither scores nor pays a penalty.

Optional scoring A successful bid of small slam – winning all but one of the tricks in the hand – with a hand of more than five cards earns a 25 point bonus. Similarly, a successful bid of grand slam – winning all the tricks in the hand – earns a 50 point bonus.

The winner is the player with the highest cumulative score after all the deals have been played.

2 Pinochle

Rank

This game is derived from bezique and is widely played in North America. Its name is also spelled pinocle and sometimes penuchle.

Players The basic game is for two players.

Cards A 48-card deck is used: made from two standard decks excluding all the 2s,3s,4s,5s,6s,7s, and 8s. Cards rank a (high), 10,k,q,j,9 (low).

Objective Each player aims to take tricks containing certain cards, and to make melds.

Choice of first dealer is by high cut. Thereafter the deal alternates.

Shuffle and cut are normal (see p 14), except that the nondealer must cut.

Deal The dealer gives 12 cards to each player in packets of three or four.

The thirteenth card is then turned face up on the table, and its suit becomes trumps for that hand.

The rest of the deck, the "stock," is then placed face down on the table, half covering the trump card.

First stage of play This lasts as long as there are any cards in the stock.

The nondealer leads to the first trick. Thereafter the winner of one trick leads to the next.

In this stage, players may play any card to a trick. This includes playing a trump when holding a card of a plain suit led. Each trick is won by the highest trump, or, if no trumps appear, by the highest card of the suit led. If two cards of the same denomination and suit appear, the one played first wins. The winner of a trick places it face down in front of him. After each trick, the winner may make one meld (see the section on melding). Then, whether or not a meld has been made, the winner draws the top card from the stock and the loser draws the next card.

The winner then leads to the next trick.

Drawing after tricks continues until all the stock and the exposed trump card have been drawn. (It is often ruled that the player who draws the last face down card must also expose it.)

Melding After each trick in the first stage, the winner of the trick may claim one meld.

A meld is claimed by placing the cards involved face up on the table, and stating the score.

A player can only score for one meld in a turn – even if the cards he exposes for that meld have also given him another scoring combination.

Each card melded can also be used later to form another meld of a different class (see the section on melds) or one of a higher score in the same class. However, each new meld formed in this way requires a new turn and the addition of at least one card from the player's hand.

Any card that a player uses in a meld may still be played to a later trick, but once a card has been played to a trick it cannot then be used in further melds.

Melds There are three classes of meld. Points are scored as follows when the melds are put on the table. (See diagram overleaf)

Class A:

"sequence" (or "flush") – a,10,k,q,j of trumps – 150 points;

"royal marriage" – k and q of trumps – 40 points;

"marriage" – k and q of any plain suit – 20 points.

Class B:

"pinochle" – q of spades and j of diamonds – 40 points;

Class C:

four aces, 100 points;

four kings, 80 points;

four queens, 60 points;

four jacks, 40 points;

(Note that all "fours" must contain one card of each suit.)

Melds
Class A

150 points

40 points

20 points

Class B

40 points

Trumps

Class C

100 points

80 points

60 points

40 points

The second stage of play, or "play out," begins with each player taking back into his hand any cards that he has melded. The players then play for the remaining 12 tricks to use up the cards in their hands. The winner of the last trick in the first stage leads to the first trick in the second.

In this stage a player must follow suit if he can, and may only trump if he cannot.

If a trump is led, the following player must play a higher trump if he can. (Usually it is made a general rule for this stage that a following player must win any trick he can.) Tricks are won as in the first stage, and the winner of one trick leads to the next. No melds are made in this stage.

The "dix" is the name given to the 9 of trumps.

If the card turned up to decide trumps is a 9, the dealer scores 10 points immediately.

If a player holds a dix during the first stage of play, he can declare it and win 10 points by placing it face up on the table after winning the trick. (Most players rule that a meld can also be made in the same turn).

The "dix"

10 points

If the first dix to appear is one declared by a player, it is not left face up in front of him but is exchanged for the exposed trump card at the bottom of the stock pile. The player takes that trump card into his hand and puts the dix in its place.

Scoring of tricks Points for cards taken in tricks are scored at the end of each hand. Cards are scored as follows:

a each ace, 11 points;   **d** each queen, three points;
b each 10, 10 points;   **e** each jack, two points.
c each king, four points;

Scoring of tricks

a 11 points   b 10 points   c 4 points   d 3 points   e 2 points

The winner of the last trick in the second stage scores a further 10 points.

Points for tricks are rounded to multiples of 10 (only 7, 8, or 9 being rounded up) before being added to the players total score.

Game is usually 1000 points. If both players reach 1000 or more after the same hand, play continues until one player reaches 1250. If the same happens again, play continues to 1500, etc.

AUCTION PINOCHLE

In this version, players bid on how many points they expect to score. Chips are collected by successful players.

Players Three people play. Usually the game is played at tables of four, with the dealer taking no active part.

Cards The deck and rank of cards are as in basic pinochle.

Deal 15 cards are dealt to each player in five packets of three. After each player has been dealt one packet, a widow of three cards is dealt face down.

Bidding Each player in turn, starting with the player to the dealer's left, may make a bid as to the number of points he expects to score.

Bidding must start at an agreed minimum (usually 300) and must rise 10 points at a time.

A player must bid or pass. If he passes, he may bid again in that hand. Bidding ends when two players have passed. The other player is then the "bidder," and his highest bid is his contract.

The other two players together try to prevent him making his contract.

Melding The bidder takes up the widow cards, shows them to the other players, and then adds them to his hand.

He then names the trump suit and lays down his melds. No other player is allowed to make melds at any time.

Melds and their scores are as in basic pinochle, except that the dix counts as a Class A meld scoring 10 points, and is scored only if the bidder places it on the table with his other melds.

Starting play The bidder begins by discarding three cards face down from those still in his hand. He then picks up his meld cards and leads to the first trick.

He may change his mind about his melds, discards, or

trumps at any time before he actually leads to the first trick. But if he discards a meld card that he has scored for, he forfeits the game unless he corrects the mistake before leading to the first trick.

Tricks are won as in basic pinochle. Each player must follow suit if he can; and, if trumps are led, must try to win the trick if he can.

If a player cannot follow suit he must trump rather than discard. This still applies after a trick has been trumped, but he need not trump higher if he does not wish to.

The winner of each trick leads to the next.

Scoring of tricks may be as in basic pinochle.

Alternatives are:

a 10 points for each ace or 10, and 5 points for each king or queen; or

b 10 points for each ace, 10, or king.

Whatever the points system, the bidder scores for any scoring cards contained in the three cards he discards, and there is a bonus of 10 points to the bidder if he wins the last trick.

Game Each hand is a complete game. If the bidder makes or exceeds his contract, he wins chips from each player.

Typical amounts are:

a 300-340 bid, three chips; **e** 500-540 bid, 20 chips;
b 350-390 bid, five chips; **f** 550-590 bid, 25 chips;
c 400-440 bid, 10 chips; **g** 600 or more, 30 chips.
d 450-490 bid, 15 chips;

These amounts are doubled if spades are trumps.

A kitty usually features in auction pinochle. The following are typical rules.

1 Each player must put three chips into the kitty before play begins.

2 If all players pass on a deal, all pay three chips into the kitty.

3 If a bidder makes, or fails on, a contract of 350 or more, he collects from, or pays to, the kitty, as well as each other player. Amounts are the same as for settlements between players.

2   Piquet

Rank

Piquet is a card game for two players that allows great opportunities for skill. It has been known, under various names, since the middle of the fifteenth century. The present French name and terminology were adopted in English during the reign of Charles I of England, as a compliment to his French wife, Henrietta Maria.

Players The game is for two.
Objective Each player aims to score points, both with certain combinations of cards in his hand and by playing for tricks.
Cards A deck of 32 playing cards is used, commonly called a piquet deck. This is a standard 52-card deck from which all the 2s,3s,4s,5s, and 6s have been removed.
Usually two decks are used alternately, one being shuffled in readiness for the next hand while the other is being dealt into play.
The cards rank normally, from 7 low to ace high.
Choice of first dealer is by low cut (see p 13). The first dealer also has choice of seats.
Shuffle is normal (see p 14).
Cut is by the nondealer.
There need be only two cards in each section. Otherwise the cut is normal.
The deal is in packets of two cards, face down. The dealer gives two cards to his opponents, then two to himself, until each has 12 cards.
The remaining eight cards form the stock, which is placed face down in the center of the table. The stock is divided so that the upper five cards rest at an angle to the lower three.
Discards The dealer has the chance to discard first. Under American rules, he need not discard; under English rules, he must discard at least one card. In either case, the most cards he can discard is five.

If he is discarding, he places the discards face down beside him, and draws an equal number from the stock. (Players must draw cards in the order in which they are stacked in the stock. Even if the dealer does not draw, or does not draw all five, he may look at the cards that he could have drawn, and then replace them without showing them to his opponent. Then the nondealer discards at least one card and at most as many cards as remain in the stock.

He places his discards face down beside him and draws an equal number of stock cards, beginning with any left by the dealer. The nondealer may look at any cards in the stock that remain undrawn. But in this case the dealer may turn these cards face up for himself to see also. (Sometimes it is ruled that the dealer may do this only after leading to the first trick).

A player may inspect his own discards during play.

Scoring Points are scored in two ways. Some points are scored by "declaration," which occurs immediately after discarding and before play. Other points are scored during play.

Declarations Each player declares certain combinations of cards held in his hand, and scores points if his declaration ranks higher than his opponent's.

A player does not have to declare a potentially winning combination if he prefers not to – but he cannot then score points for it. This is called "sinking."

A player may include any card in more than one combination.

Scoring combinations

Point The player with the most cards of one suit scores one point for each card he holds in that suit.

If both players have long suits of the same length, the better point is the one with the higher face value. (Face value is calculated by counting the ace as 11, face cards as 10 each, and other cards as their numerical face value). If the players tie, neither scores.

A player can only score for one point – even if he has more
than one suit longer than his opponent's longest.

Sequences The player with the most cards in rank order in
one suit scores as follows:

tierce (three cards), three points;

quart (four cards), four points;

quint (five cards), 15 points;

sextet or sixième (six cards), 16 points;

septet or septième (seven cards), 17 points;

octet or huitième (eight cards), 18 points.

The holder of the highest sequence can also score for any
other sequences he holds.

If players tie for the longest sequence, the sequence with the
higher top card wins. If both sequences have the same top
card, neither scores for any sequences.

Sequence

Meld The player with the highest ranking meld, of three or
four cards of a kind, scores as follows:

trio or "three" (three cards of the same denomination), three
points;

quatorze or "fourteen" (four cards of the same denomination),
14 points.

But only aces, kings, queens, jacks, or 10s may be declared
for melds (and sometimes it is ruled that 10s only count if a
quatorze is held).

If both players have sets of equal length, the one with the
higher ranking cards wins.

The winner also scores for any other melds he holds.

Meld

Announcing the declarations is by a formal dialogue,
designed to reveal no more information than necessary.
The nondealer makes the first declaration in each category of
combination, following the order point, sequence, meld.
Declaring a point Nondealer says "A point of _____ ,"
stating whatever number of cards he holds in his longest suit.
Dealer replies:
"Good," if he concedes the point;
"Not good," if he holds a longer suit – stating its length;
"How many?" if he holds a suit of equal length.
If the reply is "How many?" the nondealer must then declare
the face value of his point. The dealer then replies "Good,"
"Not good" (stating the value of his point), or "Equal" (in
which case no one scores).
Whoever has won the point then states the length of his point
again (adding the face value if that also had to be declared),
and announces his score.
Declaring a sequence Nondealer says "A sequence
of _____ ," (or "A tierce," etc), stating the number of
cards in his longest sequence.
The procedure then follows as in declaring a point – except
that when the dealer holds a sequence of equal length his
reply is "How high?" The nondealer then declares the top
card of his sequence, and the dealer states "Good," "Not
good," or "Equal."

Declaring a meld nondealer says "A three (or fourteen) of _____ ," naming the denomination. (Alternatively he can use the words "trio" or "quatorze.") The dealer cannot hold a meld of the same length and denomination, and so must reply "Good" or "Not good."

A sample declaration

nondealer: "A point of five."

Dealer: "Good."

Nondealer: "A point of five. I score five". Then he names his best sequence: "A sequence of four" (or "A quart").

Dealer: "How high?"

Nondealer: "Queen."

Dealer: "Not good. Ace. Also a tierce. I score seven."

Nondealer (naming his best meld): "Three kings" (or "A trio of kings").

Dealer: "Not good. Fourteen queens" (or "quatorze of queens". I score 14. I start with 21."

Nondealer (playing the lead to the first trick and automatically adding one point to his score – see next page): " I start with six."

English style declaration

In this, the dealer only names his combinations after the Nondealer has led to the first trick. For example:

Nondealer: "A point of five."

Dealer: "Good."

Nondealer: "A point of five. I score five. A quart."

Dealer: "How high?"

Nondealer: "Queen."

Dealer: "Not good."

Nondealer: "A trio of kings."

Dealer: "Not good."

Nondealer (playing first card): " I start with six."

Dealer: "A quart to the ace. Also a tierce. Seven And a quatorze of queens: 14. I start with 21."

Showing combinations Sometimes it is ruled that all winning combinations must be shown before they score. More usually, winning combinations are shown only at the opponent's request. A combination that is shown is replaced in the holder's hand as soon as the opponent has seen it.

Play The nondealer leads to the first trick. Each player must follow suit to a lead if he can. If not he may discard any card. The winner of a trick leads to the next.

Scoring during play A player scores for tricks; also players may score additional points in various ways.

Scoring for tricks Each player scores as follows:

a one point for leading to a trick;

b one point for taking a trick that his opponent led to;

c one point for taking the last trick; and

d 10 points for taking seven or more tricks.

Each time a player scores he announces his total score so far.

Variation Sometimes it is played that:

a a player scores for leading to a trick only if the card led is higher than a 9;

b a player scores for winning a trick only if the winning card is higher than a 9.

Additional scoring Points may also be scored in the following ways.

a Carte blanche is a hand devoid of face cards, and scores 10 points. It must be claimed by a player immediately before he discards after the deal. (Under English rules, it must be claimed before either player discards.)

b Pique is scored by the nondealer if he scores 30 points before the dealer scores anything. It scores 30 bonus points.

c Repique is scored by either player if he scores 30 points on declaration, ie before the lead to the first trick. It is worth 60 bonus points.

d Capot is scored by either player if he captures all 12 tricks in play. It is worth 40 bonus points, but the 10 standard points for taking a majority of tricks are not scored.

A game is known as a partie. It consists usually of six deals, though some players prefer to have a partie of four deals, with scores for the first and fourth deals counting double. The turn to deal alternates between the two players.

Scoring the partie

a The scores for the individual deals are added together to give a total for each player.

The procedure then depends on whether these totals exceed the "rubicon" of 100 points.

b If both players have 100 or more points, the player with the higher total wins by the difference between the two totals plus 100 points bonus for the partie.

For example, if the dealer has totalled 120 and the nondealer 108, the dealer wins and scores 112 points (120–108+100).

c If either or both players have less than 100 points, the player with the lower total is said to be "rubiconed." The player with the higher total wins by the sum of the totals plus 100 points bonus.

For example, if the scores are 125 and 92, the player with 125 wins and scores 317 (125+92+100); if the scores are 98 and 92, the player with 98 wins and scores 290 (98+92+100).

PIQUET AU CENT

This version has different final scoring. Deals continue until one player totals 100 points or more. At the end of the deal, the player with the higher total scores the difference between his own and his opponent's totals – or double that difference if his opponent's total was below 50.

AUCTION PIQUET

This piquet variation puts more emphasis on the play of the hands.

Bidding takes place before the discard. The nondealer bids or passes first. If both pass, the cards are dealt again by the same player. Once a bid has been made, bidding continues until one player passes.

The minimum bid is seven. A bid may be either "plus" (winning the stated number of tricks) or " minus" (losing that number). Plus and minus bids rank equally: to continue the bidding a player must bid a greater number of tricks.

The final bid is the "contract" as in contract bridge.

Other rules are as for basic piquet, with the following exceptions.

Discards Players need not discard at all.

Declarations may be made in any order.

Sinking is not allowed on minus contracts.

Pique is scored after 29 points in plus contracts and 21 points in minus ones.

Repique is scored after 30 points in plus contracts and 21 points in minus ones.

Scoring for tricks Each player scores one point for each trick that he takes (whoever led to that trick).

Players do not score for leading to a trick or for taking the last trick.

Scoring the contract If the contracted player exceeds his contract, he scores 10 points for every trick won (on plus contracts) or lost (on minus contracts) in excess of his contract. If he fails to make his contract, every trick by which he fell short scores 10 points for his opponent.

Doubling and redoubling are allowed, as in bridge, but affect only the scores for overtricks or undertricks.

Scoring the partie Rubicon is 150 points, and bonus for the partie is also 150 points.

3+ **Pope Joan**

Pope Joan is a card game for three or more players and was
invented by combining two earlier games, commit and
matrimony. Contestants try to play their cards in such a way
as to win as many counters as possible.

Cards A standard deck of 52 cards is used, but with the 8 of
diamonds removed.
The cards are referred to in the usual way, except for the 9 of
diamonds which is called Pope Joan. Aces count low.
Counters At the start of a game, each player should have an
equal number of counters.
Betting layout A board or other betting layout is required
for the game.
Layouts are usually circular or square, and are divided into
sections labelled ace, jack, intrigue, queen, matrimony, king,
Pope Joan, and game. Some traditional Pope Joan boards
comprise a circular tray revolving on a central stand.
A layout can easily be drawn on a sheet of plain paper or
material. Each section should be large enough to hold at least
20 counters.
Objective Each player aims to win as many counters as
possible by playing certain cards. Counters are also won by
the first contestant to use all his cards.
Bet and deal Players decide upon a dealer.
Each player, including the dealer, then places counters in the
different sections of the betting layout. This may be done in
one of two ways, either:
a each player, including the dealer, puts out the same agreed
number of counters, dividing them equally between the
different sections; or
b each player, including the dealer, puts four counters in the
pope section, two in matrimony, two in intrigue, and one in
each of the other sections.

Layout

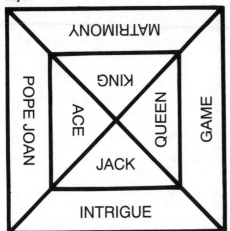

Betting

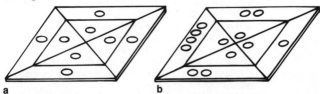

a   b

The dealer then deals one hand to each player including himself, and one extra hand.

He deals by giving one card to each player in a clockwise direction, beginning with the player to his left. The card for the extra hand is dealt just before he deals to himself.

All cards are dealt face down. The deal continues in this way until all the cards but one have been dealt; this card is placed face upward on top of the extra hand.

Pope Joan

The exposed card If the card dealt face upward is Pope Joan (the 9 of diamonds), the dealer wins all the counters in the pope and the game sections. (In an alternative version of play the dealer wins all counters on the layout.)

The round ends and the player to the dealer's left becomes the new dealer.

If any other card is dealt, its suit determines trumps for that hand. If the card dealt face upward is an ace or a face card, the dealer wins the counters on the section with the same name.

Play Each player examines his own hand, but no player may look at the extra hand.

The player to the dealer's left begins. He plays any one card from his hand face up onto the middle of the playing area and says its name, eg "3 of hearts."

The player with the 4 of hearts then plays it, followed by the player with the 5, the 6, and so on.

This continues until no player can add to the sequence because either:

a the sequence has been completed by reaching the king;

b the next card needed is the 8 of diamonds; or

c the next card needed is hidden in the extra hand or has already been played.

At this point the cards already played in the sequence are turned face down, and whoever played the last card begins a new sequence by playing any card of his choice.

Claiming counters Anyone who plays the ace, jack, queen, or king of trumps receives all the counters in the section marked with the same name (**a**).

If a player plays the jack and queen of trumps in sequence, he wins all the counters in the intrigue section, as well as those on jack and queen (**b**).

If anyone plays the queen and king of trumps in sequence, he receives all the counters in the matrimony section, as well as those on queen and king (**c**).

Claiming counters

a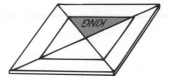

Trumps

b

c

d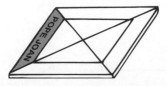

A player putting out Pope Joan wins all the counters on that section (**d**).

It should be noted that these cards only win counters when played in the correct way, ie by starting or adding to a sequence. They win nothing if they are still unplayed at the end of a round.

Ending the round The round continues until any one player has played all his cards, when he may take all the counters in the game section.

All the other players have to give him one counter for every card still in their hand, with the exception of any one holding the unplayed Pope Joan, who is exempted from paying for the cards left in his hand.

Unclaimed counters Any counters that are not won in a round remain on the betting layout until won in subsequent rounds. New counters are added as usual to all sections at the beginning of each round.

Any counters left at the end of a game are distributed by redealing the cards, face up, without an extra hand.

The players who receive the ace, jack, and queen of diamonds take any remaining counters in those divisions. And counters in the matrimony section are divided between the holders of the king and queen, and those in the intrigue section between the holders of the queen and jack.

3   Preference

This is a fairly straightforward game usually played for small stakes. Three players take part, each playing for himself.

Cards A standard deck with all the 2s,3s,4s,5s, and 6s removed is used.
The cards are ranked: ace (high), k,q,j,10,9,8,7 (low).
The suits, in descending order, rank: hearts (known as "preference"), diamonds, clubs, spades.

Rank

Objective Each player tries to be the highest bidder and to fulfil the contract.

Preliminaries Before the start of play, each player puts an equal agreed number of chips into the pool.
Players must also decide:
a how much a successful bidder should receive from the pool, depending on the rank of the trump suit; and
b the payment to be made into the pool by an unsuccessful bidder.

Deal Any player may deal the first hand; thereafter the deal passes clockwise around the table.
The dealer gives ten face-down cards to each player, and also deals two cards face down in the center of the table as the "widow," making the deal as follows.

He first deals a packet of three cards to each player, then he deals the widow, then another packet of four cards to each player, and finally a packet of three cards to each player.

Bidding Each player in turn, beginning with the player to the dealer's left, either bids a suit or passes.

By bidding a suit, the player indicates that he intends to win at least six tricks of the possible ten, with the named suit as trumps.

Each player is permitted one bid only, and each bid must be in a higher ranking suit than the previous bid.

If all three players pass in the first round of bidding, there is a second round in which each player can either pass or put chips into the pool. The player putting most chips into the pool then wins the right to name the trump suit; he may also discard any two of his cards and take the widow into his hand.

If a player bids in the first round, the widow is not used.

Play The player to the left of the successful bidder leads to the first trick.

Every other player must follow suit if he can; if he cannot he may play a trump card or discard any card.

The highest card in the suit led or the highest trump played takes the trick.

The winner of a trick leads to the next trick, and the game continues until all ten tricks have been taken.

Settlement If the bidder fulfils his bid (takes at least six of the ten tricks) he wins the agreed number of chips from the pool, depending on the rank of the trump suit. If the bidder fails in his contract, he pays the agreed number of chips into the pool.

2-6 Rummy

Rummy is one of the most commonly played of all card games, second only to poker in popularity. Formerly known as rum poker, rummy developed in the saloons and gambling houses of late nineteenth-century America. Although its rules are easily learned, it nonetheless offers plenty of scope for skilful play.

RUMMY: BASIC GAME
Cards A standard deck of 52 cards is used.
In play, the cards rank normally with ace low.
For scoring, the jack, queen, and king are each worth 10 points; all other cards are worth their face value.
Players Two to six may play. There are no partnerships.
Objective Each player attempts to be the first to go out through having "melded" all his cards. Cards are melded in either groups or sequences.
A group is three or four cards of the same rank (eg 4 of hearts, 4 of spades, and 4 of clubs).
A sequence is three or more cards of the same suit falling in numerical order (eg 9, 10, and jack of diamonds).

Group   **Sequence**

Starting the game The player with the lowest cut or draw becomes dealer. The dealer shuffles, and the player to his

right cuts the deck. The cards are dealt in a clockwise
direction. The number of cards dealt varies according to the
number of players:

two players, 10 cards each;

three to four players, seven cards each;

five to six players, six cards each.

After the deal, the remaining cards are turned face down to
form the stock. The top card from the stock is turned face up
beside it to start the discard pile (this card is called the
upcard).

Play Players take their turns in a clockwise direction,
beginning with the player to the dealer's left.

The player starts his turn by drawing the top card from either
the stock or the discard pile. He may then meld a group or a
sequence face up on the table.

He may also "lay off" (add) as many cards as possible to any
matched sets already melded on the table, whether the
original melds were his own or an opponent's.

He ends his turn by rejecting one card from his hand and
placing it face up on the discard pile. If he began his turn by
drawing a card from the discard pile, he is not permitted to
end the turn by discarding that same card.

If the stock is used up before any player goes out, the discard
pile is turned face down (unshuffled) to form a new stock.

Going out A player goes out – and wins the hand – if he
succeeds in getting rid of all his cards, with or without a final
discard.

Going rummy A player "goes rummy" if he goes out by
melding all his cards in one turn without having previously
melded or laid off any cards.

Scoring If a player goes out, the numerical value of all the
cards then left in his opponents' hands is totalled to give the
winner's score for the round. This score is doubled if the
player went rummy.

Continuing play The deal passes to the next player to the
left if there are more than two players. If there are two
players, the winner of one round deals the next.

Game The first player to reach a previously agreed total wins the game.

GIN RUMMY

This is probably the most popular of all rummy variations.

Cards Two standard decks of 52 cards are used. While one player deals, the other shuffles the second deck ready for the next deal.

The cards rank normally, with ace low. They are valued as for basic rummy.

Players Basic gin rummy is for two players. It can be adapted for any larger even number by dividing players into two equal sides, and holding separate but simultaneous games between pairs of players.

Objective As in rummy each player tries to meld his cards in groups or sequences. Unlike basic rummy, however, it is possible for a player to win a hand without melding all his cards.

Choice of first dealer The player cutting the higher card has the choice of seat, deck of cards, and whether he wants first deal.

Shuffle and cut are normal.

Deal The dealer deals 10 face down cards to each player, beginning with his opponent and dealing one card at a time. The twenty-first card is then turned face up and becomes the first card on the discard pile (the upcard).

The remaining cards are played face down on the table alongside the upcard to form the stock.

Start of play The nondealer then decides whether or not he wants the upcard. If he decides not to take it, the dealer has the option of taking it.

If the dealer does not want it, then the nondealer must draw the top stock card.

Whichever player takes a card must then discard one.

Turn of play In subsequent turns a player takes the top card from either the discard pile or the stock, and then discards.

Players do not lay melds on the table until one player ends the hand by "going gin" or "knocking."

Going gin A player goes gin if he can meld all 10 of his cards in matched sets. He declares this when it is his turn, and lays all his cards face up on the table.

His opponent may then lay down his own melds, but he may not lay off any cards on to the winner's melds.

Knocking is an alternative way of going out. It may be done if the unmatched cards – deadwood – in a player's hand add up to 10 points or less.

A player can knock only when it is his turn. He draws a card in the usual way, knocks on the table, and discards one card face down. He then lays out all his remaining cards face up on the table, grouping them into melds and unmatched cards.

His opponent must then, without drawing, lay out his cards on the table. Cards should be grouped into melds and unmatched cards, but the player also has the opportunity of laying off cards onto the knocker's melds.

Each player's deadwood cards are then totalled, and the totals compared.

Scoring a hand

1 If a player goes gin he gets a 25 point bonus in addition to the value of his opponent's deadwood.

2 If a player knocks and his deadwood count is less than his opponent's the knocker wins the hand and his score is the difference between the two counts.

3 If a player knocks and his opponent's deadwood count is lower than or the same as his own, the opponent has "undercut" the knocker and wins the hand. For this he scores a 25 point bonus as well as any difference between the dead-wood counts.

"No game" The last two cards in the stock may not be drawn. If the player who draws the fiftieth card is unable to go gin or knock, the hand is a tie and no points are scored. The same dealer deals for the next hand.

Box (or line) A running total is kept of each player's score.
When a player wins a hand, a horizontal line called a box (or
line) is drawn under his score.

Game score The first player to score 100 or more points
ends the game and has 100 points added to his score.
If his opponent has failed to win a hand, the winner then
doubles his score (including the 100 point bonus).
Finally, for every hand a player has won – as shown by the
boxes in his running score – he receives an additional 25
point bonus.

Seven up

Seven up is a card game for two or three players and
originated in England in the seventeenth century. Other
names by which it is known are all fours, high-low-jack, and
old sledge.

SEVEN UP: BASIC GAME

Deck A standard deck of cards is used. Ace ranks high.

Objective Each player tries to score seven points and so win
the game.

Deal Players cut for the deal, highest card dealing. Each
player is dealt six face down cards in packets of three.
The next card is turned face up and denotes trumps, and if it
is a jack the dealer scores one point.
The deal passes clockwise around the table.

Trumps If the player to the dealer's left is happy to play
with the trump suit shown, he says "Stand" and play begins.
Should he prefer to play another trump suit he says "I beg,"
and the dealer can choose whether or not to change trumps.
If the dealer chooses to keep the same trump suit he says
"Take one" to the player, who scores one point. Play then
starts. If the dealer agrees to change the trump suit, he sets
aside the face up card, deals a further three cards to each
player, and turns the next card face up to denote trumps.
If this card shows a different suit from the first face up card,
play begins with this suit as trumps – and if it is a jack, the
dealer scores one point.
Should the face up card be the same suit again, however,
another three cards are dealt to each player and a third card is
turned face up.
This procedure is repeated until a new trump suit is
determined, and the dealer scores one point for each jack that
is turned up, provided it is not of the same suit as the suit
initially rejected.

If the deck is exhausted before a new trump suit is turned up, the entire deck is shuffled and redealt.

Discarding If the trump suit has been changed, each player discards face down a sufficient number of cards to reduce his hand to six.

Play is the same as in whist.

Scoring At the end of each round the tricks are turned face up for scoring. Points are scored as follows:

"high," one point for the player dealt the highest trump;

"low," one point for the player dealt the lowest trump;

"jack," one point for the player who takes the jack of trumps in a trick;

"game," one point for the player who takes the highest total value of cards in tricks. The cards are valued as follows:

four for each ace;

three for each king;

two for each queen;

one for each jack;

ten for each 10.

Game The first player to make seven points wins the game. If more than one player reaches seven points in the same hand, the points are counted in the following order so as to determine the winner: high, low, jack, game.

FOUR- HANDED SEVEN UP

In this version four people play in partnerships of two. Each player sits opposite his partner.

Play is the same as in the basic game, except that the two players to the right of the dealer do not look at their cards until after trumps has been determined.

CALIFORNIA JACK

This variant of seven up is sometimes called draw seven or California loo. It is played by two people and differs from seven up in the following ways.

Trumps The first card turned face up denotes trumps. After each trick, first the winner and then the loser of that trick take a card from the top of the stock. The next card of the stock is then turned face up and denotes trumps for the next trick. When the stock is exhausted, each player's remaining cards are played out using the last trump suit, and with the winner of each trick leading to the next.

Scoring One point is scored for taking each of the following in tricks: the highest trump, the lowest trump, and the jack of trumps. The first player to make 10 points wins.

3-5   **Skat**

Skat developed in Germany in the early 1800s and its rules were codified in 1896. It has since flourished on both sides of the Atlantic, being one of the most skilful of all card games. The simplified variant described here – Rauber Skat – is gradually replacing the original game.

Players Three to five people can play, but only three play on any one deal.

With four players, the dealer sit out. With five, the dealer and the third player to his left sits out: the first, second, and fourth play.

The first player to the dealer's left is called "forehand," the next "middlehand," and the last player with cards "endhand."

Cards Skat is played with a standard deck from which all the 2s,3s,4s,5s, and 6s have been removed.

Rank of cards Most contracts require trumps.

The highest trumps are always the four jacks, which rank in the order clubs (high), spades, hearts, diamonds (low).

In addition there may also be a trump suit. If so, the rest of that suit rank below the lowest jack, in the order
a (high),10,k,q,9,8,7 (low).

When play is with trumps, cards in plain suits also rank
a (high),10,k,q,9,8,7 (low).

When there are no trumps, all suits rank a (high),
k,q,j,10,9,8,7 (low).

Rank with no trumps

All suits

Rank with trumps

Trump suit

Trumps   Plain suits

Objective Each player tries to win the right to choose the game that will be played, and then successfully to complete that game.

Choice of first dealer is by high cut. Thereafter the deal passes one player to the left after each game.

Deal A packet of three cards is dealt to each active player. Then a "skat" of two face-down cards is set aside. A packet of four is next dealt to each active player, and finally a further packet of three.

This gives three hands of ten cards each, and two cards in the skat.

Bidding The player who makes the highest bid wins the
right to name the game. He then tries to fulfil his bid and the
other two players try to prevent him.

A bid states only the number of game points that the player
believes he can make if he wins the right to choose the game.
The lowest permitted bid is 18; the highest practicable bid is
about 100.

Bidding follows the deal.

Middlehand bids first, or passes.

If middlehand bids, forehand must reply. He must state
either "Pass" or "Hold."

"Hold" means that he makes the same bid as middleman.
By bidding hold, he retains the right to name the game,
because a player cannot lose this to a player to his left unless
that player has bid higher.

This continues with forehand holding bids and middlehand
raising bids until either player passes.

Then endhand must either raise the bid or pass; and if he
bids, the survivor of the first pair replies by passing or
holding. This continues as between the first pair, until one
bidder gives in.

If both middlehand and endhand pass without bidding,
forehand may make a bid or may pass. Once a player has
passed, he may not make a bid.

The player who survives in the bidding will now be referred
to as the "bidder."

The skat The bidder begins by deciding whether or not to
pick up the two cards that form the skat.

If he picks up the skat, he must then discard any two cards
from his hand. These discards will eventually count toward
his final score.

If he does not pick up, this is referred to as "handplay." The
skat is then set aside for the duration of play. At the end of
the hand, the fate of the skat depends on the game that has
been played.

If the bidder chooses to pick up the skat, this limits his
choice of game for the hand (since for certain games it is

ruled that the skat may not be picked up).

The games The bidder then chooses which game will be played in that hand. His choice is between "suits," "grand," "simple null," "open null," and "reject."

(A bidder who has picked up the skat is not permitted to choose simple null, open null, or reject.)

To fulfil his bid, he must not only successfully complete the game he chooses (for example, by making sufficient trick points if that is required), but must also score sufficient "game" points to equal or exceed his bid.

Suits In this option, the bidder names a suit. All the cards in that suit become trumps, together with the jacks.

The bidder's aim is to make at least 61 trick points by taking tricks containing scoring cards.

Grand Only the four jacks are trumps. The bidder's aim is as in suits.

Simple null There are no trumps. The bidder aims to lose every trick.

Open null As in simple null, but the bidder must play with all his cards exposed. He lays them face up on the table before the opening lead.

Reject This game may only be chosen by forehand, and he may choose it only if middlehand and endhand have both passed without a bid. He does not make a numerical bid, but simply states "Reject."

Only the four jacks are trumps.

Each player tries to take fewer trick points than any other player.

Open If the bidder has opted for handplay, and names suits or grand, he may increase the value of his game by declaring "Open."

The bidder must then play with all his cards exposed, laying them face up on the table before the opening lead.

Schneider or schwarz If the bidder has named suits or grand, he may, before the opening lead, declare:

a "Schneider," ie he aims to win at least 91 trick points; or
b "Schwarz," ie he aims to take every trick.

He need not declare either – in which case his goal remains 61 trick points.

Play Forehand leads to the first trick. Thereafter the winner of one trick leads to the next.

Other players must follow suit if possible. If unable to follow suit they may trump (if there are trumps in the game) or they may discard.

The highest trump played, or the highest card of the suit led if no trumps appear, wins the trick.

Scoring of trick points Cards taken in tricks score as follows:

each ace, 11 points;
each 10, 10 points;
each king, four points;
each queen, three points;
each jack, two points.

Scoring the skat After the last trick has been taken, the skat is allocated as follows:

a at suits or grand, to the bidder (if he took the skat before play, he is given the cards he discarded);

b at reject, to the winner of the last trick;

c at null, to no one – the skat is discarded.

Whoever receives the skat (or discards) counts trick points for any scoring cards it contains.

Making the game Except at reject (see separate section on reject play, p 152), the bidder makes the game if he achieves that game's object (ie 61 trick points, 91 trick points, all tricks, or no tricks.)

He must, however, then consider if he has made the number of game points that he bid.

Making the bid Except at reject, a bid is made if the bidder's game score equals or exceeds the number of game points stated in his bid. Game points are scored as follows:

a At null games, the game value is fixed: 23 game points for making simple null, and 24 for making open null. Provided that the player's bid was not higher than this, he makes his bid.

b At suits or grand, the game value has to be calculated – by multiplying a base game value by various multipliers. A player does not know how many multipliers he will qualify for until after play ends. The player makes his bid if the total game value (base x all multipliers) equals or exceeds his bid.

Base values for the games are:

diamonds, nine game points;

hearts, 10 game points;

spades, 11 game points;

clubs, 12 game points;

grand, 20 game points.

The multipliers are as follows:

a automatic multiplier for having made game, one;

b for holding "matadors" (see separate section), the multiplier varies but is at least one;

c for choosing handplay, one;

d for making schneider or schwarz (see separate section), the multiplier varies but is at least one.

The player adds all his multipliers together. The total will be between two and 14. He then multiplies the base value for his game by this total.

Matadors The jack of clubs and all other trumps in unbroken sequence in the bidder's hand (including the skat, whether or not it is used in play) are called matadors.

When the bidder holds the jack of clubs, his hand is said to be "with" a number of matadors.

When he does not hold the jack of clubs, his hand is said to be "without" a number of matadors.

The multiplier is the number of matadors that the bidder is with or without (it does not matter which).

Two examples are shown (right).

a Spades are trumps, the player is with three matadors (the missing jack of diamonds breaks the sequence before the ace of spades). The multiplier is three.

b Hearts are trumps, the player is without two matadors (the top two trumps are missing). The multiplier is two.

Multipliers for schneider and schwarz The bidder may only count one of the following multipliers:

a schneider made but not predicted, one;

b schwarz made but not predicted, two;

c schneider predicted and made, three;

d schneider predicted and schwarz made, four;

e schwarz predicted and made, five.

Scoring Except when reject is played (see separate section), scoring is as follows. Only the bidder scores.

If he has made his bid, he scores the total of his game points (which may be higher than his bid).

If he has not made his bid:

a at suits or grand, he loses the amount of his bid at handplay – or twice that amount if he took the skat;

b at null, he loses the absolute game value.

Scoring of reject In this game, there is no bidder and no bid. Normally the player who makes the fewest trick points scores 10. But:

a if he takes no tricks he scores 20;

b if two players tie for fewest trick points, the one who did not take the last trick receives the score of 10;

c if one player takes all the tricks, he loses 30 and the others score nothing;

d if all players tie with 40 trick points, forehand alone scores 10 for naming the game.

Winning The scores are recorded on a piece of paper and totalled at the end of a session.

The winner is the player with the highest score.

Often, an average score is worked out - players above the average then collect money accordingly, while players whose score is below average must make the payments.

Matadors

Cards in hand   Trumps

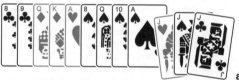

Three matadors: the
multiplier is three

Two matadors: the
multiplier is two

4 Solo whist

Rank

Temporary partnerships are formed in solo whist, but each player scores for himself. Basically play is as for whist, but the game has its own bidding and scoring systems.

Players Solo whist is a game for four players. At the start of each hand each player is on his own.

Cards A standard deck of 52 playing cards is used. Cards rank normally, with ace high.

Objective Each player tries to contract and fulfil a bid.

Choice of first dealer is by high cut, with ace low.

Shuffle and cut are normal.

Deal The dealer deals out all the cards, beginning with the player to his left and going clockwise. The cards are dealt three at a time, with a final round of single cards. All but the last card are dealt face down; the last card, dealt to the dealer, is dealt face up and indicates trumps for some bids. Rules for misdeals are the same as for whist.

Bidding Each player in turn, beginning with the player to the dealer's left, may make a bid or pass without making a bid. In certain circumstances players may have a second chance to bid.

The bids are ranked in the following order, with each outbidding the one before.

a Proposal and acceptance, or "prop and cop," involves a temporary partnership of two players. A call of "I propose" or "Prop" indicates that the player will try to win eight tricks in partnership with any of the others. Play is with the trump suit indicated at the deal. In his turn, a subsequent bidder may call "Accept" or "Cop" to become the partner.

b "Solo" is a bid to take five tricks playing alone against the other three. Play is with the trump suit indicated at the deal.

c "Misère" or "nullo" indicates that the player will try to lose every trick, playing with no trump suit.

d "Abondance" is a bid to take nine tricks, playing with
trump suit nominated by the bidder. He does not announce
the trump suit until all the remaining players have passed.

e "Royal abondance" or "abondance in trumps," is a bid to
take nine tricks, playing with the trump suit indicated at the
deal.

f "Misère ouverte" or "spread" indicates that a player will
try to lose every trick, playing with no trumps and turning
his remaining cards face up on the table after the first trick
has been taken.

g "Abondance declarée" is a bid to take 13 tricks, playing
with no trump suit.

Second bids may be made in the following cases:

a by the player to the left of the dealer to accept a proposal;

b by any player who has been overbid and wishes to make a
higher bid;

c by a proposer who has not been accepted and wishes to
amend his proposal to a higher bid.

No bid hands If all players pass, the cards are thrown in and
the deal passes to the left.

Play The player to the dealer's left leads first, unless the bid
is abondance declarée in which case the bidder leads.

The rules for making tricks and trumping are as for whist.
It is not always necessary to play a hand right out. For
example, after a misère bid the hand ends once the bidder
takes a trick.

Revoke A revoke (see p 166) loses or wins three tricks
depending on the bid and on which player made the error. A
hand is always played out after a revoke, and a bidder who
revokes must pay for the three tricks even if he makes his bid
without them.

Scoring Chips are usually used for scoring: red ones worth
five points each and white ones worth one point.
Alternatively a written record may be kept.

Scores are as follows. For a successful proposal and
acceptance bid, one partner receives five points from one

Rank in three-handed solo

opponent, and the other partner the same from the other opponent. For an unsuccessful bid, partners pay instead of receiving the points. For all other bids, the bidder receives points from each of the other players if successful, or pays each of them if unsuccessful.

The number of points varies with the bids:

solo, 10 points;

misère, 15 points;

abondance, 20 points;

royal abondance, 20 points;

misère ouverte, 30 points;

abondance declarée, 40 points.

In addition, for bids other than misère, misère ouverte, or abondance declarée, one extra point changes hands at each payment for each overtrick (trick in excess of the bid) or undertrick (trick fewer than the bid.)

THREE-HANDED SOLO

The game can be adapted for three-handed play as follows.

Cards There are two alternative changes:

1 A 40-card deck is used – obtained by stripping the 2s,3s, and 4s from a standard deck. 39 cards are dealt out and the 40th indicates the trump suit.

2 A 39-card deck is used – obtained by stripping out the whole of one suit. The trump suit is indicated by the last card dealt.

Bids There is no proposal and acceptance bid. Misère overbids abondance, and misère ouverte overbids abondance declarée.

Scoring Misère is worth 20 points, abondance 15 points, misère ouverte 40 points, and abondance declarée 30 points.

Spoil five

2-6

Spoil five is similar to loo but has an unusual and complex ranking system. It is especially popular in the Republic of Ireland.

Players Two or more people can play, but the game is best played with five or six. Each person plays for himself.

Deck A standard deck of playing cards is used. The cards are ranked, in descending order, as follows. (See diagrams overleaf.)

Spades and clubs
Plain suits (ie non trump): k,q,j,a,2,3,4,5,6,7,8,9,10.
Trump suits: 5,j, a of hearts, a of spades or clubs, k,q,2,3,4,6, 7,8,9,10.

Diamonds
Plain suit: k,q,j,10,9,8,7,6,5,4,3,2,a.
Trump suit: 5,j,a of hearts, a of diamonds, k,q,10,9,8,7,6,4,3,2

Hearts
Plain suit: k,q,j,10,9,8,7,6,5,4,3,2.
Trump suit: 5,j,a,k,q,10,9,8,7,6,4,3,2.

Note that the ace of hearts is always the third-best trump, regardless of suit; the 5 of the trump suit is highest; and the jack of the trump suit is second-highest.

Objective Each player tries to win three tricks and to prevent anyone else from doing so.

Deal Players draw for deal, using standard ranking with ace high and 2 low. Lowest card deals.

Five face-down cards are dealt to each player in packets of two then three, or vice versa. The next card is turned face up to indicate trumps.

The deal passes clockwise around the table.

Pool Each player puts an agreed number of counters into the pool. It is won by a player taking three tricks in one hand.

Exchanging If the face-up card denoting the trump suit is an ace, the dealer may exchange it for a card in his hand before the first card is led. This is called "robbing."

Rank in trumps

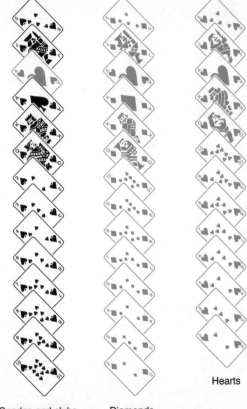

Spades and clubs   Diamonds   Hearts

**Rank in
plain suits**

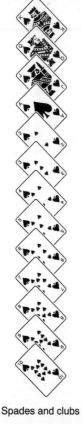

Spades and clubs

Diamonds

Hearts

If a player has been dealt the ace of trumps he may, if he wishes, exchange any card in his hand for the face-up card. If he does not exchange a card, he must announce that he has the ace at his first turn of play – otherwise the ace becomes the lowest-ranking trump for that round, even if it is an ace of hearts.

Play The player to the left of the dealer leads to the first trick and the winner of each trick leads to the next.

Rules of play are the same as for whist, with the following differences.

If a card of a plain suit is led, a player may either trump or follow suit. He may discard another plain suit card only if he can neither follow suit nor trump.

If a card of the trump suit is led, a player must follow suit if he can. He need not play any of the top three trumps if the leading card was a lower trump – holding back a card in this way is called "reneging."

Jinxing A player who wins three tricks may take the pool, and the hand ends.

Alternatively, he may call "Jinx," implying that he will try to win the remaining two tricks. Play continues, and if he wins the extra two tricks he takes the pool, plus a sum from each player equal to his original contribution to the pot. If he does not make both tricks he loses the pool and the hand counts as a "spoil."

Spoil is when nobody wins three tricks, or a winner fails to win all five after jinxing. The cards are dealt for a new hand but only the new dealer contributes to the pot. Only when the pot is won do all the players contribute to a new pot.

Vint   4

A member of the whist family, vint is a game for four
players playing in partnerships of two.

**Rank of
cards**

Cards A standard deck of cards is used. The cards rank
normally, with ace high. The suits rank no trumps (highest),
hearts, diamonds, clubs, and spades (lowest).

Objective Each partnership aims to make and fulfil a bid by
taking tricks.

Deal The entire deck is dealt out, one face-down card at a
time to each player. The deal passes clockwise around the
table with each round of play.

Bidding Starting with the dealer, each player in turn bids or
passes.

Each bid indicates the intention to take six tricks plus the
number called, in the suit name or with no trumps. Thus the
lowest bid is one spade (ie taking seven tricks with spades as
trumps); and the highest is seven no trumps (ie taking
thirteen tricks).

A bid is overcalled by a bid of more tricks in the same suit,
or the same number of tricks in a higher ranking suit or no
trumps. When a player is overcalled he may call higher when
his turn comes round again, even if the only other bidder is
his partner.

Play is opened by the player to the left of the highest bidder,
and proceeds in a clockwise direction around the table. Each
player must follow suit if able to do so; if he cannot, he
either plays a trump or discards. The winner of a trick leads
to the next trick.

Scoring Each partnership records its score on a scorepad or
piece of paper divided into two sections by a horizontal line
(as in bridge, p 42).

Game points are entered below the line. Each partnership
scores for each trick taken – whether or not the bid is

fulfilled. However, the number of tricks bid determines the value of each trick, ranging from ten points per trick for a bid of one, 20 points per trick for a bid of two, and so on up to 70 points per trick for a bid of seven.

The first partnership to score 500 game points wins the game – even if it reaches this score part way through a hand, and regardless of whether or not it won the bidding.

Bonus points are entered above the line. They are scored as follows:

a winning a game, 1000 points;

b winning a rubber (two out of three games), 2000 points;

c "little slam" (12 tricks) made but not bid, 1000 points;

d little slam bid and made, 6000 points;

e "grand slam" (13 tricks) made but not bid, 2000 points;

f grand slam bid and made, 12,000 points.

Honor points are scored above the line and comprise the a,k,q,j, and 10 of trumps and the other aces. In a trump suit, the ace is counted twice, both as an honor and as an ace. When playing no trumps, only the four aces are honors. The partnership holding the most honors scores ten times the trick value for each honor held in trumps, or 25 times the trick value for each honor (ace) held when playing no trumps.

For example, if the final bid is three trumps, each trick is worth 30 points and therefore each honor is worth 300 points (10x3=300).

If one partnership has a majority of aces and the other a majority of honors, those two majorities are compared, and the partnership that has the bigger majority scores for the difference.

For example, if side A has two honors and one ace, but side B has one honor and three aces, the two honors are deducted from the three aces and side B scores for one honor, worth ten times the trick value.

But if side A has three honors and one ace, and side B has one honor and three aces, neither side scores, as the three honors and the three aces cancel each other out.

If both sides hold two aces: at no trumps, neither side scores; at trumps, the side that wins most tricks scores for its honors.

Coronet Any player holding three aces or a sequence of three cards in a plain suit – known as a "coronet" – scores 500 points, entered above the line.

If a player holds the fourth ace, he scores a further 500 points; and each extra card in a sequence also scores a further 500 points.

If the sequence is in the trump suit, or in any suit when no trumps has been declared, coronet is worth double.

Unfulfilled bids If a partnership fails to make its bid, it is penalized for each undertrick by 100 times the value of each trick (entered above the line); but it also scores game points below the line for the number of tricks it took.

For example, if the bidding partnership made a bid of five no trumps (ie 11 tricks) and took only eight tricks (ie it failed by three tricks), scoring would be as follows:

a 3x50x100=15,000 penalty points;

b 8x50=400 game points;

c the opponents score game points in the usual way for the number of tricks they took, ie 5x50=250 game points.

Rank of suits

4   Whist

Whist evolved in the eighteenth century from an earlier
game called triumph. It has since given rise to a whole
family of games, including the popular contract bridge and
solo whist. The rules are comparatively simple, but a great
deal of skill is needed to play really well.

Rank

Players Whist is a game for four players, two playing against
two as partners. Partnerships are decided by draw (see p 12).
Players sit around a table, with partners facing each other.
By convention, players are referred to by the points of the
compass, with North and South playing against East and
West.

Cards A standard deck of 52 playing cards is used. Cards
rank normally, with ace high.

The suits are not ranked, except that one suit is designated
the trump suit for each hand. A card of the trump suit beats
any card from any other suit.

Objective Players aim to win tricks. A trick consists of four
cards, one played by each player.

Choice of first dealer is by high cut, with ace ranking low.

Shuffle and cut Any player has the right to shuffle, but the
dealer has the right to shuffle last. The player to the right of
the dealer cuts the cards and passes them to the dealer.

Deal Beginning with the player to his left and going
clockwise, the dealer deals out all but one of the cards, face
down and one at a time.

The remaining card is placed face up on the table and its suit indicates the trump suit. The dealer adds it to his hand when it is his turn to play.

Misdeal It is a misdeal if:

a more or fewer than 13 cards are dealt to any player; or

b any card other than the last one is exposed.

It is not a misdeal if a player is dealt two or more successive cards and the dealer rectifies the error at once.

If there has been a misdeal, players may agree to accept the deal after the error has been rectified.

Any player, however, has the right to demand a new deal until the first trick is completed. After that the deal must stand. If there is to be a redeal, players throw in their cards and the deal passes one player to the left.

Play The player to the dealer's left leads by placing any one of his cards face up in the center of the table.

Each of the other players in turn plays a card to the center of the table.

If a player has a card of the same suit as the card led, he must play this card. This is called "following suit," and failure to do so is penalized (see the section below on revoking). If he does not have a card of the suit led he may play any other card.

The trick is won:

a by the player of the highest trump card, or

b if no trump cards have been played, by the player of the highest card of the suit led.

The winner of one trick leads to the next. Play continues in this way until all 13 tricks of a hand have been played.

The deal passes to the next player in a clockwise direction. The cards are reshuffled and cut for the new deal.

Revoking is failing to follow suit when able to do so.

A player is not penalized if he corrects his error before the trick is turned over, and the partner of a player who fails to follow suit may caution him by asking if he does not have any cards of the suit led.

Once the trick has been turned over but before play to the next trick has begun, the opposing partnership may challenge and claim a revoke.

Points penalties for revoking vary with the different scoring systems for the game.

A partnership cannot win the game in any hand in which it revokes. If both partnerships revoke in the same hand, all cards are thrown in and a new deal is made.

Calling If a player exposes a card, other than when playing it to a trick, he must leave it face up on the table until one of his opponents "calls" on him to play it to a trick where it will not cause a revoke.

Scoring There are a number of ways of scoring, but the following systems are most common.

English whist uses a five-point game, including the scoring of honors. Games are grouped into rubbers.

There are three ways of scoring game points.

1 The first six tricks do not score. From the seventh trick onward, one game point is scored for each trick taken.

2 The honors are a,k,q, and j of trumps. A partnership scores four game points if it is dealt all four honors, and three game points if dealt any three.

However, if both pairs reach five game points in the same deal, the trick points from that deal take precedence over the honors points. At least one trick must be taken in the last deal before declaring game. After game, the losers' honors score, if any, is no longer counted in their game points total.

3 There are three alternative rulings concerning the penalties for revoking:

a the revoking pair loses three game points;

b the revoking pair transfers three game points to its opponents; or

c the opponents gain three game points.

After each game, additional points are scored by the winners as follows:

a three points if the opponents had no game points;

b two points if the opponents had one or two game points; and

c one point if the opponents had three or four game points.

A rubber consists of three games.

The winners of two out of three games score two extra points for the rubber. All points are then totalled, and the partnership with the highest score wins.

If the first two games of a rubber are won by the same pair, a third game is not played.

In America a seven-point game is usual, with two ways of scoring game points.

1 The first six tricks played do not score. Thereafter, each trick taken scores one game point.

2 Revoking also provides game points, as the pair that failed to follow suit transfers two of its game points to the other pair.

The first pair to get seven game points scores the difference between seven and the losers' score.

TERMS USED IN WHIST

Finessing consists of playing the third-best card of a suit when also holding the best – trusting that the opponents do not hold the second best.

Forcing is playing a suit in which another player is void.

Long trumps are the remaining trump or trumps left in a hand after all other trumps in the deck have been played.

Loose card is a card of no value.

Quarte is any four cards of the same suit in sequence.

Quarte major is a sequence of a,k,q,j, in the same suit.

Quinte is any five cards of the same suit in sequence.

See-saw occurs when each member of a partnership is trumping a suit, and each plays these suits to the other for that purpose.

Slam is winning every trick.

Tenace consists of holding the cards immediately above and below the opposing side's best in suit, for example ace and queen when the opponents hold the king.

Section 2
GAMBLING GAMES

INTRODUCTION
Included in this section are card games that are played
primarily for gambling. This is not to suggest that some of
them are any less interesting or demanding to play than some
of the games included as general card games in section 1 of
this book. Indeed, blackjack and poker in particular both call
for high levels of skill from their players. A number of the
games included here are professional games rarely found
outside casinos and gambling clubs. Others are private
games suitable for more general play.

Casino and gambling club games Depending on the game
being played, betting in casinos and gambling clubs may be
either against the house management acting as banker or
against other players. As well as winning money by acting as
banker in some games, managements charge players for the
services of their officials and also take a percentage cut when
money changes hands between players. Casino and gambling
club games described in this section are: baccarat/chemin de
fer, blackjack, card craps, faro, monte bank, poker, skinball,
trente et quarante, and ziginette. Some of these games are
also suitable for playing at home.

Private banking games In these games one player acts as
banker, taking on the bets of all the others. He also has a
different role from the other players in play. But unlike in
casino banking games no one person is banker continuously.
Instead, to equalize players' chances, the role of banker
moves around – often after every hand. Private banking
games included in this section are: ace-deuce-jack, banker

and broker, Blücher, card put-and-take, Chinese fan-tan, hoggenheimer, horse race, lansquenet, monte bank (private version), Polish red dog, red and black, red dog (banking version), and slippery Sam.

Pool games In these private gambling games there is no banker. Instead all players' bets take the form of contributions to a central pool. In many games the entire pool is then won by a single player – usually at the end of every hand – but in other games the pool acts as a reservoir of chips, from which payments are made to players according to their success. Pool games included here are: bango, brag, injun, Kentucky derby, red dog, thirty-five, thirty-one, and yablon.

NOTES ON BETTING

Betting chips When playing private gambling games, any counters, matchsticks, or other agreed objects may be used.
An ante is a contribution to a central betting pool made before a deal. It may be required from all the players or sometimes only from the dealer.
Odds The recognized forms in which payment odds are stated are:
a "x to y" (eg 30 to 1, also written as 30-1), in which case the player's stake is returned in addition to the win payment (giving a player who staked one chip at 30 to 1 a return of 31 chips); or
b "x for y" (eg 30 for 1), in which case the player's stake is returned as part of the win payment (giving a player a total return of 30 chips in our example).

<table>
<tr><td>2+</td><td># Ace-deuce-jack</td></tr>
</table>

The odds in this game are so heavily loaded that it is found
only as a hustler's game. The hustler simply has to ensure
that the sucker is on the wrong side of the particular version
being played – in which case the sucker will on average lose
his money in nearly 60 plays out of 100.

Equipment
1 one standard deck of 52 cards;
2 money for betting.
Players Two or more can play. One player is banker.

WITH THE HUSTLER AS BANKER
Objective Players bet that none of the three cards exposed in
play will be an ace, deuce (2), or jack.
Betting limits are agreed beforehand.
Shuffle and cut The banker shuffles. Any player has the
right to shuffle but the banker has the right to shuffle last.
Any player other than the banker then cuts the deck.
Preparation
1 The banker takes three cards face down from the bottom
of the deck, making sure that no one sees their denominations.
These three cards are ruled "dead," and are put to one side.
2 The banker then cuts two groups of cards from the deck,
taking care that no one sees the bottom of each cut. He
places each group face down alongside the deck, so that
there are now three groups of cards on the table.
Bet and play Each player but the banker may place a bet.
The banker then turns the three sections face up, exposing
the bottom card of each section.
Settlement If any one of the three cards is an ace, deuce, or
jack, the banker takes all bets. If none of the cards is one of
these denominations, the banker pays 1 to 1 on all bets.

Continuing play All cards in the deck are collected, shuffled, and then cut for the next turn of play.

Deal

Show

WITH THE SUCKER AS BANKER

Sometimes the sucker wants to be banker. The hustler then suggests the following version, in which players bet on which denomination will appear. "You bank, and we'll do the guessing too," says the hustler. "You can't help but win." On a big hustle, with a planned victim, the hustler may set up this version from the beginning.

Objective Players bet that one of the three cards exposed in play will be one of three specified denominations.

Betting limits are agreed beforehand.

Shuffle, cut, and preparation are as for the version with the hustler as banker.

Betting Each player but the banker may place a bet.
Sometimes the betting denominations are as in the first
version, ie ace, deuce, jack.

But usually the three denominations change for each hand,
and are chosen by the players as they place their bets.

This "guessing" process gives the banker the impression that
the odds are with him.

Play The banker turns the three sections face up, exposing
the bottom card of each section.

Settlement If none of the three cards is one of the three
denominations bet on, the banker takes all bets. But if any
one or more of the denominations appear, the banker pays 1
to 1 on all bets. (Note that he pays only 1 to 1 even if two or
three denominations appear).

Continuing play is as in the first version.

Baccarat/Chemin de fer

2+

Games of the baccarat and chemin de fer family originated in the baccarat that became popular in French casinos in the 1830s. In the present century they have travelled from Europe to the United States, from the United States back to Europe, and from both points to casinos throughout the world. This process has resulted in wide variations in playing rules, and what is called "baccarat" in one casino may more nearly resemble the "chemin de fer" of another. Three basic forms of play are described here.

Players: At least two, but usually seven or more. Often persons without seats may also bet.

Croupier The casino provides a croupier, who assists players in making and settling bets, advises on rules and odds, and takes the casino's cut. The croupier also plays the "bank" hand when the game is banked by the casino. The casino makes an hourly charge for the croupier and his assistants, and for supervising the game.

The objective is to bet on a winning hand, ie on a hand with a higher point value than the other hand(s).

Hands are of two or three cards.

Cards score as follows:

a face (court) cards and 10s, zero;
b aces, one point;
c any other card, its numerical value.

Card values

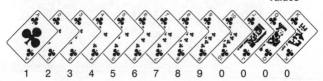

1 2 3 4 5 6 7 8 9 0 0 0 0

When scoring a hand tens are ignored – eg five plus seven counts as two not 12. Hence the highest possible score for a hand is nine.

The basic sequence of play is:

1 placing of bets;

2 dealing of hands;

3 receipt of another card on request;

4 comparison of hands and settlement of bets.

Equipment Several standard decks of playing cards are used. Other equipment is:

a a heavy table, padded and covered with green baize, and marked with a layout for 9 or 12 players;

b a card-holding box or "shoe," from which the cards are dealt one at a time;

c a discard box, positioned beneath a slot in the table;
d wooden palettes for distributing cards and payments to the players.

CHEMIN DE FER

The distinctive features of the "chemin de fer" game are that:
the role of banker rotates rapidly among the players;
only a bank hand and one non-bank hand are dealt;
bets can only be placed against the bank.
Cards Six or eight standard decks of cards are used.
The shuffle;
1 The croupier places the decks face down on the table.
2 Players and croupier take groups of cards and shuffle them, and then shuffle the groups of cards into each other.

Chemin de fer layout

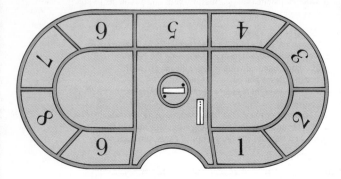

3 The croupier gathers the cards, gives them a final shuffle in large groups, gathers them all into a single deck, and cuts the deck several times.

4 The croupier asks one of the players to make a final cut. (Often the croupier makes the actual cut, after the player has inserted an indicator (a blank or advertising) card at the point where the cut should be made).

5 Often the croupier then inserts a second indicator card into the deck, around eight or ten cards from the bottom, to give warning of the end of the shuffled cards.

6 The croupier places the deck face down in the shoe.

7 The croupier deals three or four cards from the shoe, shows them, and discards them.

First choice of banker is either:

a by lot;

b by auction, with the players bidding the amounts they are prepared to put forward as the "bank";

c by acceptance, the bank being offered first to the first player to the croupier's left or right (according to house rules), and then on around the table clockwise or counterclockwise, until a player accepts the bank.

The croupier passes the shoe to the first banker.

Amount of the bank On the first play of a turn as banker, the bank is:

a what the player bid for it if the bank was gained by auction;

b any figure the banker wishes to put at risk if he gained the bank by lot or acceptance.

On all subsequent plays of a turn as banker, the bank is the amount stated on the first play plus subsequent winnings.

Betting takes place before any cards are dealt.

Players can only place bets against the bank – ie they bet that the bank will lose.

The total of bets on a single play is limited to the amount of the bank – the banker is never liable for payment of bets in excess of this.

The player to the banker's right (or left, according to house rules) has first bet. Any amount of the bank he does not "fade" (bet against), may be bet against by the next player in turn. Betting passes around the table until the entire bank is covered by several bets, someone has called "Banco," or everyone has bet who wishes to. Bystanders may bet if there is part of the bank left to cover or if one of them calls "Banco."

If the bank is not completely covered, the amount not faded is safe for the hand and is kept by the banker whether he wins or loses.

"Banco" A player or bystander who wishes to bet against the entire bank makes this known by calling "Banco."

A call of "Banco" makes all other bets void.

When two or more wish to banco, a player who bancoed on the preceding hand has precedence over all others.

Otherwise, a seated player has precedence over a bystander and the order of priority among players belongs to the player who is earliest in the betting order.

Play is as follows.

1 The banker deals two hands of two cards each. The cards are dealt singly and face down, alternately to the table and to the banker himself. The "table" hand represents all players betting against the bank. It is played by whoever made the highest bet against the bank. If there are two equal bets, the player nearer the banker in the betting order has priority.

2 The player and banker examine their hands without showing them.

3 If the player's hand totals eight or nine, it is a "natural," and is immediately declared and turned face up. If it is an eight hand, the player calls "La petite"; if a nine he calls "La grande."

4 If the player's hand is a natural, the banker shows his own cards. If only the player's hand is a natural, all bets against

Natural 8s

Natural 9s

the bank win. If both hands are naturals, a nine beats an eight. If both hands are naturals of the same number, it is a "stand-off" and all bets are returned.

5 If the player's hand does not contain a natural, he says "Pass." The banker then examines his own hand, and if it contains a natural he declares it immediately and wins all bets.

6 If both hands have been examined, and neither contains a natural, the player may "draw" (request another card, face up) or "stay" (not request another card). His decision must be based on the rules of mathematical advisability (see table overleaf), except that in some games a player who has bancoed is allowed to ignore these rules.

7 Whether the banker then draws another card or stays depends on the card that he has just given to the player (see table overleaf), except that in some games the banker is allowed the option when holding a five hand and having given a four. If a player has bancoed and is allowed to use his judgment, the banker may also ignore the rules for drawing or staying.

8 The hands are shown. If there has been any error, the banker must reconstruct the play as it should have been.

Winning The hand totalling nine or nearest nine wins.

a If the totals are the same, all bets are returned.

b If the banker has won, he collects all bets less any casino levy. In most countries the casino levies a percentage (usually 5%) on bankers' winnings. Sometimes the winnings on a player's first hand as banker are exempt from the levy. (In countries where a percentage levy is illegal, all casino profits come from the hourly rate charged by the casino).

c If the banker has lost, each player collects the amount of the bank that he had covered.

Keeping the bank If the banker has won a hand, he may keep the bank for the next hand.

In this case, the new bank comprises the original bank plus the winnings after any levy.

A player who keeps the bank is not permitted to remove any of his winnings between hands.

If the original bank plus winnings exceeds the house limit on bets, the excess is not at stake.

Passing the bank If the banker has won a hand but chooses not to keep the bank, he may take his winnings and pass the bank.

In this case:

a the bank is offered to the players in turn until one of them accepts it, after which the new banker decides the amount of his bank; or

b the house croupier holds an informal auction, and the bank passes to a player who will put up a bank equal to the one that has just been passed.

Losing the bank If the banker loses a hand, the bank is offered to the players in turn – as when the banker chooses to pass the bank. (An auction is not held.)

Reshuffling The cards are not reshuffled until at least 5/6 of the deck has been used – and usually not until the last few cards are reached.

Player

Player holding	Action	
0,1,2,3,or 4	draw	
5	optional	
6 or 7	stay	
8 or 9	face	

Banker

After giving	Banker stays on	Banker draws on
0 or 1	4,5,6,7	3,2,1, or 0
9	4,5,6,7, (or3)	2,1,0, (or3)
8	3,4,5,6, or 7	2,1, or 0
7 or 6	7	6,5,4,3,2,1, or 0
5 or 4	6 or 7	5,4,3,2,1, or 0
3 or 2	5,6, or 7	4,3,2,1, or 0
Player has stood	6 or 7	5,4,3,2,1, or 0

BACCARAT BANQUE

Also known as *baccarat à deux tables* (double take
baccarat), baccarat banque is the oldest European form of the
game.

The distinctive features of baccarat banque are that:

a the role of the banker rotates more slowly among the
players or may be held permanently by the casino or
concessionaires;

b one bank hand and two non-bank hands are dealt;

c bets can be placed only against the bank.

Except when specifically described here, the rules are the
same as for chemin de fer.

Cards Three standard decks are used.

Banker Sometimes the role of the banker is held
permanently by the casino – or by concessionaires who pay
the casino a percentage of their takings.

Otherwise the procedure is as follows.

a The bank is auctioned to the highest bidder, who pays
2 $^{1}/_{2}$% of his bid to the casino.

Baccarat banque layout

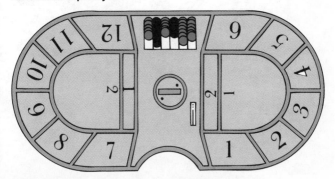

b The banker does not lose the bank if he loses a hand, but holds it until he loses the whole bank or passes.

c The banker cannot withdraw any money from the bank unless he passes – but any part of the bank not bet against on a hand is not at risk.

d When a bank is lost or passed, the bank is again auctioned. As before, the casino takes a 2 ½% cut from the winning bidder.

Betting and play differ from chemin de fer in the following ways.

a The banker deals three hands – one to his right, one to his left, and one to himself.

b Bets against the bank may be placed on either the right or the left hand, or on both hands. Betting on both hands is called betting "*à cheval*" (on horseback).

c Priority for betting on the right table hand begins with the player sitting to the banker's right; for the left table hand, with the player to the banker's left. Calling "Banco" is usually allowed, but not always.

d Each hand is played by a player on the appropriate side of the table. The player playing the right hand always plays first. On the first deal, the hands are played by the players nearest the dealer on his right and left sides.

Thereafter, a player continues playing one of the table hands until he loses a hand After a player has lost a hand, the right to play that side's hand passes to the next player in rotation.

e Table players are bound by the same staying and drawing rules as in chemin de fer. The banker may stay or draw on any hand, and will obviously concentrate on beating the hand on which most money has been bet.

f Players betting *à cheval* lose only if the bank wins both hands, and win only if the bank loses both hands. Otherwise their bets are returned.

BACCARAT-CHEMIN DE FER (LAS VEGAS)

The distinct Las Vegas form of the game may be called baccarat, chemin de fer, or baccarat-chemin de fer.

The distinctive features of the Las Vegas game are that :

a the role of the banker is usually held permanently by the casino, although it may rotate slowly among the players;

b one non-bank hand is dealt;

c bets can be placed either with or against the bank.

Cards Six or eight standard decks are used.

Banker When the role of banker rotates among the players, the rules for the bank are the same as for baccarat banque. More usually the casino keeps the bank, and the procedure is as follows.

a The limit on bets on a hand is not the size of the bank but the house betting limit. (The house betting limit will, however, sometimes be raised when a player requests this.)

b There is no banco bet and no need for rules of precedence in betting.

c A single player can play.

d The casino takes a cut (usually 5%) from winning bets that have bet the bank to win.

Baccarat-Chemin de fer layout

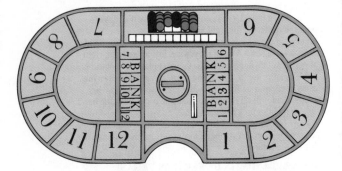

Betting Players may bet with or against the bank.

A player betting the bank to win places his bet on the appropriate numbered section at the table center.

A player betting the bank to lose places his bet on the numbered section in front of him.

A player may also back the bank to have a natural eight or nine, and if successful, he is paid the odds of nine to one.

Play is as in chemin de fer, except that all players' and banker's options are removed to become draw plays. Thus:

a a player must draw if holding a hand totalling five;

b the banker must draw if holding a three hand when he has given a nine, or a five hand after giving a four.

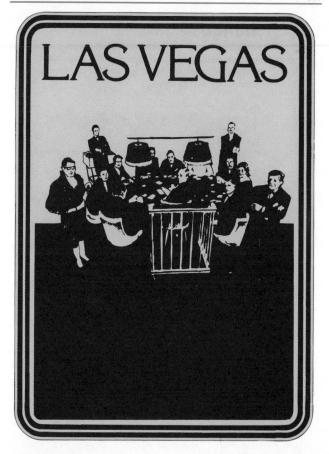

LAS VEGAS

3-10   **Bango**

In this card variant of the bingo played in bingo halls,
players turn over playing cards instead of covering rows of
numbers on a score card.

Equipment
1 two standard 52-card decks, with different backs;
2 betting chips.
Players The game is for three to ten players.
Objective Each player aims to be the first player to turn all
his face up cards face down.
Choice of first dealer is by deal: first ace to appear
(See p 13).
Shuffle and cut The dealer and the player to his left each
shuffle one deck of cards. Each deck is then offered
separately to the player to the dealer's right to be cut as usual
(See p 14).
Ante Before each deal, each player including the dealer puts
an equal agreed amount into the pool.
Deal From one deck, the dealer deals five cards to each
player including himself, dealing them face up and one at a
time. The rest of this deck is then put to one side out of play.
Play The players arrange their cards face up in front of them.
The dealer then takes the second deck of cards and deals the
top card face up onto the table, stating its rank and suit as he
does so.
If any player including the dealer has the identical card from
the first deck face up in front of him, he now turns that card
face down.
The dealer then takes the next card from the top of the
second deck and deals it face up onto the table, stating its
rank and suit as he does so.
Play continues in this way until one player has turned all his
cards face down. He announces this by calling "Bango."

Deal

End of play

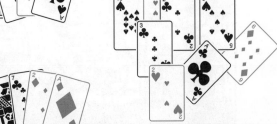

Checking The dealer checks the hand of the player who called against the cards that have been dealt from the second deck, and if no mistake has been made that player wins the pool.

Change of dealer The deal passes one player to the left after each hand.

BANGO VARIANT

In this game players take into account only the rank of the cards turned up by the dealer. The dealer calls the rank and players turn face down all cards of that rank in their hands.

Banker and broker   2+

This simple game has very fast betting action. Also known
as Dutch bank and blind hooker, it is played in a number of
slightly different ways.

Equipment:
1 one standard deck of 52 cards;
2 betting chips (or cash).
Players two or more.
Rank of cards is normal (ace high). Suits are not ranked.
Objective Players try to bet on a card of higher
denomination than that bet on by the banker.
Choice of first banker is by high cut (see p 13).
Shuffle and cut are normal (see p 14).
Betting limits are as agreed.
Basic form of play
1 The banker cuts a number of sections from the deck: one
for himself and one for each of the other players.
2 The other players lay bets on their sections by placing
chips (or cash) beside them.
3 The banker turns all the sections face up to show the
bottom cards.
4 The banker collects the bets on sections showing a lower
denomination card than his own. He pays 1 to 1 on sections
showing a card of higher denomination.
Points of variation
1 Discarding the bottom card: either the banker removes and
discards the bottom card from the deck before cutting; or he
leaves an unused bottom section after cutting.
2 Timing of bets: bets are placed either before or after the
sections are cut.
3 Number of sections cut:
either the banker cuts one section for each player and one for

Deal

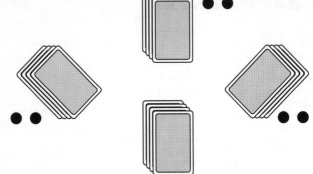

Play

himself (up to a limit of seven), and each player may only bet on the section cut for him; or

the banker cuts three sections, two for the players and one for himself, and each player bets at will on either or both of the players' sections; or

the banker cuts as many sections as he likes, varying the number from deal to deal if he wishes, and the players bet as they please but leave one section for the banker.

4 When the banker's denomination is the same as that bet on by a player: either the bank wins, or the player's bet is returned.

5 Change of banker:

either the bank passes one player to the left after each deal or set number of deals; or

players cut for the bank after each deal or after a set number of deals; or

the bank is passed when a player bets on an ace – if two players (or player and banker) both have an ace, or if two players have bet on the same ace, the deck is cut and the bank goes to the player with the higher card.

2-14   Blackjack

Blackjack is the world's most widespread banking card game. It is also known as BJ, twenty-one, vingt-et-un, pontoon, and vanjohn. There are two main forms: that with a "changing bank" – the usual private game; and that with a "permanent bank"– the casino game. The two forms of the game have many features in common.

Players Games are played by a banker/dealer and from one to six or seven other players (private games can have as many as 14 other players).

Value of cards Standard playing cards are used.

a An ace counts as 1 or 11, at the option of the holder.

b A "face" card counts as 10.

c All other cards count their numerical face value.

Card values A joker, if used, is only an indicator card and does not enter play.

11   10   10   10   10   9   8   7   6   5   4   3   2   1

Objective Each player tries to get a higher point count in his hand than the dealer – but the value of his hand must not exceed 21. A hand whose point count exceeds 21 is immediately lost.

A two-card hand with a value of exactly 21 (a face card, or 10, and an ace) is called a "natural" or a "blackjack."

Betting With the exception of the dealer, each player bets at the beginning of each hand. Only bets against the dealer are allowed.

At the end of each hand, the dealer pays those with point counts higher than his own.

Onlookers may be allowed to bet on any player's hand, but not on the dealer's hand.

Basic sequence of play

1 Betting, and deal of two cards to each player.

Examples of 21-point hands

2 Receipt of further cards on request by each player in turn – with the dealer last.

3 Settlement of bets.

BLACKJACK WITH A CHANGING BANK

Cards A standard deck of 52 cards (or sometimes two decks shuffled together), plus a joker that does not enter play.

Choice of first banker/dealer is by deal: usually the first ace, but in some versions the first black jack, decides (see p 13 for procedure).

Change of banker/dealer There are two alternative systems.

1 Each player has five deals as banker/dealer, after which the role passes to the next player to the left.

2 The deal passes whenever there is a hand in which a "natural" is dealt – ie when a player's first two cards total 21. The player with the natural has the option of becoming the new banker/dealer on the completion of that hand.

When two or more players hold naturals, the player nearest the dealer's left has the first option.

If all players with naturals refuse the option, the present banker/dealer continues – unless he also refuses, in which case the role is offered around the table clockwise, beginning with the player to the immediate left of the present banker/dealer. If all refuse, a new banker/dealer is chosen in the same way as the original one.

Auctioning the bank Private games are occasionally run so that the banker/dealer is always decided by auction.

In all private games, however, a player who no longer wants to be banker/dealer may, between hands, put the bank and deal up for auction.

However, if there are no bids he loses the bank and deal to the first player to his left (or, if that player refuses, the bank and deal are offered clockwise around the table until accepted or until a new dealer has to be chosen in the original way).

Shuffle and cut

1 The dealer shuffles the cards. (Any player has the right to shuffle at any time but the dealer has the right to shuffle last).

2 Any other player cuts the cards. If several players want to cut, each of them must be allowed to do so.

3 The deck is placed, face down, on an upturned joker, which acts as an indicator card. (If no joker is available, the dealer "burns" a card – ie he takes the top card from the deck, shows it to all players and places it face up at the bottom of the deck.

An ace may not be burned, and if an ace is turned up the deck must be reshuffled and cut again).

Betting limits The dealer decides the minimum and maximum allowable bets, and can alter them at will between hands.

Bet and deal for the two forms of the private game
The betting and dealing stage of the private game takes two main forms.

a As in the casino blackjack game, the players place their bets before they have seen any of their own cards.

b As in the pontoon game of the British Commonwealth, the players bet after looking at their own first card.

There is no standard way of distinguishing between these: American rules for private blackjack games may quote the pontoon form, while a few Americans use "pontoon" to mean standard blackjack. We have used the name "blackjack" for form (**a**), and "pontoon" for form (**b**).

Bet and deal: "blackjack"
1 Before any cards are dealt, each player but the dealer puts his bet in front of him in full view.

2 The dealer deals one card to each player but himself, face down, beginning with the player to his immediate left and going clockwise. He then deals one card to himself, face up.

3 A second card is then dealt to each player, including the dealer, face down.

4 If the dealer's face up card is an ace or a card worth 10 points, the dealer looks at his face down ("hole") card to see if he has a natural.

If he has, he immediately announces this and turns his cards face up. The other players then show their own cards. The dealer collects the bets of all players not having naturals; players with naturals usually have their bets returned, but in

Dealer   **Player 1**

some versions of the game they also pay the dealer.

5 If the dealer's face up card is not an ace or a 10 point, or if he finds that he does not have a natural, then the player to the dealer's left commences play.

Bet and deal: "pontoon"

1 The dealer deals one card face down to each player, including himself, beginning with the player to his immediate left and going clockwise.

Each player, including the dealer, looks at his own card.

2 Each player, except the dealer, puts his bet in front of him in full view.

The dealer may call for all bets to be doubled. Any player refusing to double drops out of the hand and loses his original bet.

If the dealer has doubled, any other player may then redouble his own individual bet.

3 The dealer deals a second card, face up, to each player including himself.

4 The dealer then considers if he has a natural, as in the "blackjack" game. If he has a natural, he collects from each player twice the amount of that player's current bet – except that from any other player with a natural he collects only that player's bet.

5 If the dealer's face up card is not an ace or a 10 point, or if he finds that he does not have a natural, then the player to the dealer's left commences play.

First player's hand The player to the dealer's left looks at his hand and commences play.

a If he has 21 points, he shows his cards, claims a natural, and is paid by the dealer unless the dealer also has a natural.

b If his card total is less than 21 points, he has the option of taking further cards.

If he feels that the points count he already holds is closer to 21 than the dealer is likely to achieve, then he can say "I stand," and he receives no further cards.

If he decides to attempt a total closer to 21, he can say "I draw" or "Hit me," and receives another card face up.

He can repeat this until he is satisfied with his hand, when he says "I stay." However, if his points count goes over 21 he must announce this immediately by saying "I bust."

If a player goes "bust," he turns his cards face up, the dealer collects his bet, and the player's cards are placed face up at the bottom of the deck. He is then out of the game until the next hand.

Subsequent player's hands Once a player has said "I stand," "I stay," or "I bust," play passes to the player to his left. This continues until all players have had the chance of drawing further cards.

Dealer's hand The dealer plays last.

If all players have bust, he simply discards his cards and begins the next hand.

Otherwise he turns his hidden card face up, and decides to stay or to "draw" (giving himself further cards, face up) until he is satisfied or he exceeds 21 (busts).

Once the dealer's hand is completed, all hands still in the game are shown.

Doubling down is a procedure allowed in the "permanent bank" game and often incorporated in the "blackjack" form of the "changing bank" game.

In his turn a player may, after looking at his first two cards, decide to "double down" – ie with his original two cards face up, he doubles his original bet and receives one further card only, face down. He may not look at this card until the dealer turns it up after all other players and the dealer have completed their turns of play.

(Sometimes doubling down is allowed only when the first two cards total 10 or 11).

Buying is a procedure sometimes played in the "pontoon" form of the "changing bank" game.

At his turn, a player may "buy" a card: instead of receiving a further card face up, he adds to his original bet and receives a further card face down. The amount of the additional bet must be at least the minimum, but no greater than the original bet.

Buying can be repeated for further cards if the player wishes; or he may "twist" – ie draw further cards face up in the normal way. However, once a player has twisted he is not allowed to buy.

Splitting pairs is a procedure allowed in the "permanent bank" game, and often incorporated in both the "blackjack" and "pontoon" forms of the "changing bank" game.

If a player's first two cards are a pair (eg two 6's or two kings), they may be "split" if the player wishes – ie they may be treated as the basis of two separate hands.

In his turn of play, the player with the pair turns it face up – one card to his right and one to his left. He places his original bet by one of the cards and an equal amount by the other. The dealer then deals one card, face up, to the card to the player's right – after which the player plays this hand off in the normal way. When he has finished (stood, stayed, or bust), he receives another face up card, dealt to the card to his left, and then plays off this hand.

If , on splitting and receiving a new card other than an ace, a player forms a further pair, he may split the pair again if he again puts out an amount equal to his original bet. Any further pairs may also be split.

If aces are split, one card may be drawn to each split ace.

A 21 point count made in two cards after splitting does not count as a natural – it is paid off at even money and the bank does not change hands.

Irregularities

a If a player is missed on the first round of dealing, he must ask for a card from the top of the deck before the second round of dealing begins, or must stay out for that deal.

b If a player receives two cards on the first round of dealing, he has the choice of: discarding either one, or playing both hands with his original bet on each.

c If a player in the "pontoon" game receives his first card face up, he can either: bet, and receive the next card face down, or drop out of that hand.

d If a player receives two cards on the second round of the dealing, he discards either one.

e If a card appears face up in the deck, a player has the choice of accepting or refusing it.

f If a player receives a card that he did not ask for, he may either keep or discard it.

g If a player has stood on a total of over 21, he pays the dealer twice his original bet even if the dealer has bust. (All discards are placed face up at the bottom of the deck. They may not be claimed by the next player in turn.)

Settlement If the dealer goes bust, he pays all players who have not bust.

If he does not bust, he collects the bets of all players with a lower total, and pays out to players with a higher total who have not bust.

Where a player and the dealer have the same total, rules vary. Sometimes the player's bet is returned, but often (more commonly in the "pontoon" game) the dealer collects.

All winning bets are paid off by the dealer at even money, except that a player who has beaten the bank with a natural is paid off at two to one.

Continuing play As each bet is settled, the player's cards are given to the dealer and placed face up at the bottom of the deck.

Play of further hands then continues from the same deck, without a shuffle, until the face up cards are reached. All face up cards are then shuffled by the dealer, cut by another player, and a joker or burnt card is used as an indicator as before.

Bonus payments In the "pontoon" game, a player other than the dealer can win his bet with certain special hands. These hands are declared and paid off as soon as they have been achieved.

a A hand with five or more cards totalling 21 or under:
for a five-card hand, a player receives double his bet;
for a six-card hand, a player receives four times his bet;
for a seven-card hand, eight times his bet; and so on.
The win stands even if the dealer achieves a total nearer to 21.

b Triple 7s: for a 21 made with three 7s, a player receives three times his bet.

c 8,7,6: for a 21 made with an 8,7, and 6, a player receives double his bet.

None of these is a special hand if held by the dealer. They are then judged only according to their points count: a banker's five-card hand is beaten by a player's hand with a higher point count, and a player's win on a natural stands against a banker's triple 7s or 8,7,6. (See sample play overleaf.)

**Bonus
payments**

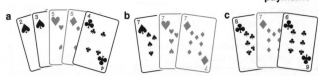

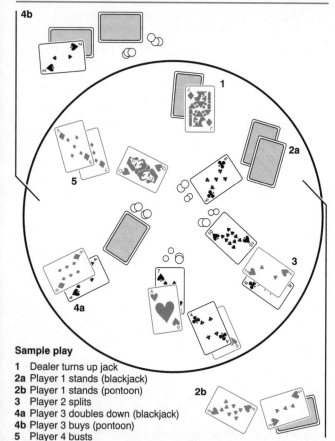

Sample play

1   Dealer turns up jack
2a Player 1 stands (blackjack)
2b Player 1 stands (pontoon)
3   Player 2 splits
4a Player 3 doubles down (blackjack)
4b Player 3 buys (pontoon)
5   Player 4 busts

BLACKJACK WITH A PERMANENT BANK
Equipment:

1 a regulation blackjack table, with six or seven betting spaces on the layout;

2 a rack containing betting chips;

3 a card-dealing box ("shoe");

4 a discard receiver;

5 one, two, or four standard 52-card decks, shuffled together;

6 two blank or advertising cards to be used as indicator cards – one to cut the deck and one to mark the end of the shuffled cards.

Participants:

1 a permanent house dealer/banker;

2 one to six or seven active players.

There is also a casino observer/supervisor, who controls play and whose decision is final.

Shuffle and cut

1 Only the dealer shuffles. He may reshuffle at any time.

2 After he has shuffled, he offers the deck to a player to cut. (Casino regulations may require an "indicator card" cut, in which the dealer holds the deck and the player inserts a blank or advertising card to indicate the point where he wants the deck cut. The dealer then cuts the deck, with the indicator card going to the bottom.)

3 In many casinos, the dealer then inserts a second indicator card about 40 cards from the bottom of the deck to prevent the last cards of any shuffle coming into play.

4 If a shoe is being used, the dealer places the deck in it, face down.

5 The dealer then deals a few (usually three) cards from the top of the deck and places them to one side, out of play.

Betting limits The casino sets the minimum and maximum bet limits. (A casino will often agree to raise the maximum at a player's request.)

Bet and deal

1 Before any cards are dealt, each player except the dealer puts his bet on the layout in the betting space directly in front of him. If empty betting spaces are available, players are allowed in most casinos to bet on and receive more than one hand.

2 The dealer deals one card to each player, beginning with the player to his immediate left and going clockwise, and then deals one card to himself.

Then in the same way he deals a second card to each player and to himself. Whether cards are dealt face up or face down varies from casino to casino (see the section below on dealing possibilities, p 15).

3 If the dealer's face up card is a 10 point or an ace, he looks at his face down card to see if he has a natural, exactly as in the "changing bank" game. If he has a natural, he immediately collects the bets of all players who do not have naturals; players with naturals always have their bets returned.

(In some casinos, to prevent cheating by the collaboration of a player and a crooked dealer, the dealer is not allowed to look at, or sometimes even to deal, his own face down card until all other player's hands are completed).

4 If the dealer's face up card is not a 10 point or an ace; or if he finds that he does not have a natural; or if he may not look at his face down card: then the player to the dealer's left commences play.

Dealing possibilities The usual arrangements are listed here, and shown in the diagrams.

a Dealer and all players: first card received face down, second face up.

b Dealer's first card face up, second face down; players' first and second cards face down.

c Dealer's first card face up, second face down; players' first and second cards face up.

d Dealer's first card face down, second face up; players' first and second cards face up.

e Dealer's first card face up, second face down; players' first card face down, second face up.

Dealing possibilities

Insurance bet If the dealer's face up card is an ace, players are in many casinos allowed to place an insurance bet against being beaten by a dealer's natural.

Before the dealer looks at his face down card, a player wishing for insurance puts out an amount equal to half his present bet. If the dealer has a natural, the player gets two to one on his insurance bet; otherwise the insurance bet is lost.

Play If a player is playing more than one hand, he must play out the hand farthest to his right before looking at his next hand or hands.

Play is as for the private game, with splitting and doubling down but no buying allowed.

Dealer's play In the "permanent bank" game, the dealer has no decisions to make:

a if his count is, or reaches, 17 or more – he must stay;

b if the count is 16 or less he must draw;

c when he holds an ace he must accept a count of the ace as 11 and not draw if this gives him 17 or more without busting. (As the dealer has no option in his play, it does not matter if he sees the players' hands. For this reason players' hands are dealt face up in some casinos.)

Settlement is as for the "changing bank" game, except that:

a when a player and the dealer have the same total, the player's bet is always returned;

b naturals are paid at odds of three to two, not two to one;

c there are no bonus payments.

Irregularities are treated in the same way as in the "changing bank" game.

VARIANTS OF BLACKJACK

There are a number of games whose basic differences from blackjack are the card values and the points count that the players are attempting to reach.

SEVEN AND A HALF

This is an Italian-American variant of blackjack. The rules are as for blackjack with the following exceptions.

Cards The 8s, 9s, and 10s are removed from a standard deck to give a deck of 40 cards. No indicator card is used.

Objective Players aim to get a total points count of 7 $\frac{1}{2}$: non-face cards count their face value, with aces 1 point; the king of diamonds can be given the value of any card the holder chooses;

other face cards each count $\frac{1}{2}$ point.

Play The player receiving the king of diamonds in a preliminary deal becomes the dealer for the first hand. The dealer decides and alters betting limits at will. A player not wishing to bet on a round can say "Deal me out."

The deal is one card face down, after which a player stands or draws one or more cards face up.

7½ in two cards is announced and settled immediately. Unless the dealer also has 7 ½ in two cards, it is paid double and wins the bank. (If two or more players have 7 ½ in two cards, the bank goes to the player nearest the banker's left.)

Bust – 8 or more with any number of cards – is also settled immediately.

The dealer then plays, and pays surviving players with a higher total. He returns the bet of any player with the same total as himself.

The dealer shuffles the deck after every round.

Seven and a half: values

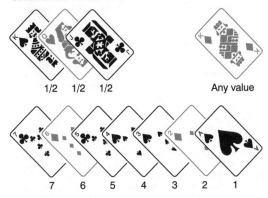

1/2   1/2   1/2   Any value

7   6   5   4   3   2   1

TEN AND A HALF

Ten and a half or "*saton pong*" is the Dutch equivalent of
seven and a half. The rules are as for seven and a half, with
the following exceptions.

It is played with a standard 52-card deck.

Players aim for total points count of 10 1/2. A count of 10 1/2
is announced immediately. 10 1/2 in two cards is paid double.
The dealer places discards at the bottom of the deck, face up.
The deal changes by passing to the left when the whole deck
has been used – though the current dealer is allowed to
reshuffle used cards to complete a half finished hand.

Ten and a half: values

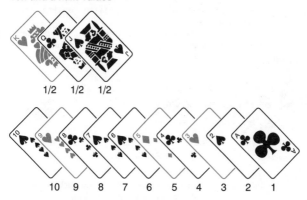

1/2   1/2   1/2

10   9   8   7   6   5   4   3   2   1

MACAO

Macao or "three naturals" is a variant of blackjack that was popular in the 1920s and 1930s.

It is played with a standard 52-card deck.

Players aim for a total points count of 9 in one or more cards. Card values are:

zero for face cards and 10s;

the face value of all other cards (with aces counting 1).

The deal is one card, face down.

A player with a 9,8, or 7 in one card announces it immediately. The dealer then shows his own card, and pays if the player's card is higher.

For a 9 in one card a winning player is paid three times his bet, for an 8 twice, and for a 7 one for one.

Players and dealer without a 7,8, or 9 in one card then draw one or more cards toward a total of 9.

The dealer then collects and then pays out on remaining bets.

A player who ties with the dealer has his bet returned.

Macao: values

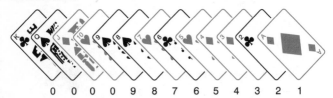

0   0   0   0   9   8   7   6   5   4   3   2   1

FIFTEEN

Fifteen, also called quince, cans, or ace low, is a blackjack variant for two players with one acting as dealer.

Players aim for a points count of 15. Face cards count as 10; other cards their numerical face value (with ace as 1).

Dealer and nondealer place equal amounts in a pool before the deal.

The deal is one card face down. The nondealer stands, or draws one or more cards face up. He does not announce if he

Fifteen: values

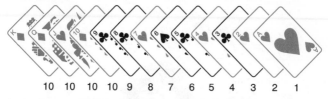

busts – he says only "I stay." The dealer then stands or draws. Both players then show their face down cards. The player nearer 15 without busting wins. If both players tie or bust, bets are left in the pool for the next deal.

The loser of one hand deals for the next.

FARMER

This is an interesting variant of blackjack for two to eight players.

One player, the "farmer," is the equivalent of the banker/dealer in other games of the blackjack family, but in this game players also make an ante bet into a central pool or "farm." The money in the farm is won only when a player has a points count of exactly 16; other settlements are made between player and farmer after each round.

Cards 45 cards are used, a standard 52-card deck with all the 8s and three of the 6s removed (the 6 of hearts is retained in the deck).

Farmer: values

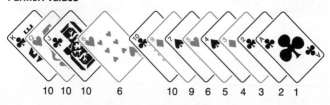

Objective Players aim for a total points count of 16: face cards count 10 points; other cards their face value (with ace as 1).

Choice of first farmer is as for the banker/dealer in blackjack, except that the deciding card is the 6 of hearts.

Ante bet Each player puts one unit into the farm.

Shuffle The farmer shuffles. Any other player has the right to shuffle, but the farmer has the right to shuffle last.

Cut The player to the farmer's right is offered the cut. If he does not wish to cut, any other player may do so. If no other player wishes to cut, the farmer must cut.

Deal The farmer deals one card face down to each player, including himself, beginning with the player to his left and going clockwise.

**Farmer:
sample settlement**

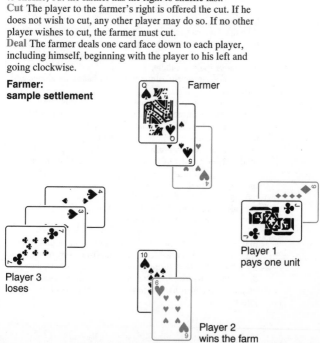

Farmer

Player 1
pays one unit

Player 3
loses

Player 2
wins the farm

Play The player to the farmer's left begins. He looks at his card and then receives one further card from the farmer. If his total now exceeds 16, he does not announce this but says "I stay" and receives no further cards. He does not show his hand.

If his card total is less than 16, he can either stay or receive further cards as he wishes.

When he is satisfied with his hand or when his total exceeds 16, he says "I stay," receives no further cards, and keeps his hand concealed.

Play then passes to the player to the first player's left, and play continues as described until all other players, including the farmer, have received at least one further card and had the chance to draw others.

Settlement At the end of the round, all hands are shown and settlement is as follows.

a Each player who has a count of over 16 points must pay one unit to the farmer who dealt the hand. (The farmer does not have to pay anyone if his hand exceeds 16 points).

b A player holding 16 points wins the farm (the central pool) and becomes the next farmer. If more than one player holds a total of 16, the order of precedence when deciding the new farmer is:

the player with the 6 of hearts;

the player with the fewest cards;

the current farmer if he has 16 points;

the player nearest the farmer's left.

c If no one holds a total of 16, the farm is not won. The player with the total nearest 16 then receives one unit from each player with a lower total (but not from players who have bust). If two or more players have equal totals, they divide the units won from the other players. The same farmer then deals the next hand, and all players put a further ante into the farm.

Blücher

3+

This private banking game is named after a Prussian general who fought against Napoleon. Modified rules are given here.

Equipment:
1 one standard deck of 52 cards;
2 betting chips;
3 a betting layout with areas representing each denomination of card (it can be made up of cards from another deck, or may be drawn on paper).

Players three or more.

Objective Players aim to bet on a denomination on the layout that is not matched during the hand.
A denomination is matched when the player, having called that denomination, turns up a card of that rank.

Choice of first bank is by high cut (see p 13).

Shuffle and cut are normal (see p 14).

Betting limits are agreed beforehand.

Betting Each player but the banker places as many bets on the layout as he wishes. Each bet must be placed on only one denomination.

Play The banker turns up cards one at a time from the top of the deck to form a face up pile on the table. As he turns the first card up he says "Ace." He says "Deuce" for the second, "Three" for the third, and so on. For the eleventh, he says "Jack" for the twelfth "Queen" and for the thirteenth, "King."
For each card, if the denomination of the exposed card matches the rank called, the bank collects any bets placed on that denomination on the layout.
For example, if the eighth card is an 8, the banker wins the bets on section 8; if the twelfth card is a queen, he wins the bets on the queen's section.
Each time the banker wins a bet on the layout, he is paid an additional equal amount by the player who made the bet.

When the banker has counted to king he begins again from ace, still turning up a card from the deck for each rank he calls.

The players may not add to, remove, or change their bets. The banker collects bets as before, if rank and card match. Play continues in this way until the banker has counted from ace to king four times. All the deck has then been dealt.

Doubling This occurs if at any time the banker counts from ace to king without any of the 13 cards matching the rank called.

The banker must then, with his own chips, double all players' bets that are then on the layout.

However, the bets stay on the layout and are still at risk.
This doubling only takes place once in a single deal. If the
banker counts from ace to king again without any cards
matching, he does not add again to the players' bets.

If the banker wins a player's bet that has been doubled, he
wins all the doubled bet plus an equal amount from the
player.

Final settlement Any bets still on the layout at the end of
the game are returned to the players who placed them.

Continuing play Bank and deal pass one player to the left.
All the cards are collected for the next deal, and new bets are
placed.

3-12 **Brag**

Brag was one of the ancestors of poker and still remains very popular in Britain. There are many forms and variants but basically the game is a form of three-card poker with no "draw."

Equipment:
1 one standard deck of 52 cards;
2 betting chips or cash.
Rank of hands A "hand" at brag contains only three cards. Originally only threes and pairs scored but today, through poker influences, all the following are generally recognized (with the highest listed first).
a "Pryle": three cards of the same denomination.
b "On a bike" run: three cards in sequence from the same suit.
c Run: three cards in sequence.
d Flush: three cards of the same suit.
e Pair: two cards of the same denomination and one unmatched card.
f "High card": three unmatched cards.

Hands

a   **b**

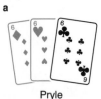

Pryle   On a bike run

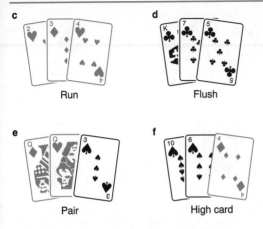

c
Run

d
Flush

e
Pair

f
High card

Rank of cards The cards rank in normal order, with ace high, except:

a ace can rank low to make a 3, 2, ace run or on a bike run – which then counts as the highest hand of that rank, beating ace, king, queen.

b for pryles only, a specified denomination varying with the game played (eg three 3s) is ranked above three aces.

Wild cards Today brag is usually played with no wild cards, or sometimes with 2s (deuces) wild. (See diagram overleaf.) However, the traditional wild cards for the game, listed in order of rank, are: ace of diamonds; jack of clubs; 9 of diamonds.

Wild cards

Hands of the same rank are valued according to the denomination of cards used – as in poker. For two special cases, see "rank of cards." Otherwise:

1 for pryles, on a bike runs, flushes, and high cards, the hand with the highest denomination card wins;

2 for pairs, the hand with the highest denomination pair wins or, if these match, the hand with the highest ranking odd card wins.

Rank of hands with wild cards A hand using wild cards is valued in the usual way (with the wild card valued according to the card it represents). However, a hand using wild cards loses to a hand that has none.

Note that a pair using a wild card loses to the same pair in natural cards even if the wild card hand has the higher odd card.

Arrangements

1 choice of first dealer is by low cut (see p 13).

2 shuffle and cut are normal (see p 14).

THREE-CARD BRAG

This is the basic form of the game.

Players From three to 12.

The objective on each deal is to win the pool by holding the best ranking hand on a showdown or by having all the other players drop out of the betting.

Betting limits are agreed beforehand. Typical limits would be:

1 maximum one unit bet or raise;

2 one to five or one to ten units bet or raise.

Ante Sometimes rules specify that, before each deal, each player must contribute one unit to the pool.

Deal The dealer deals one card face down to each player, including himself, beginning with the player to his left going clockwise, and continuing until each player has three cards.

Play Players look at their hands and bet accordingly, beginning with the player to the dealer's left and going clockwise. Bets are placed in a central pool. Players may bet on any hand – bluffing is unrestricted.

There is only one betting interval. A player cannot "pass" and stay in the game – he must bet or drop out. If all the players but one drop out the remaining player wins the pool. Otherwise betting continues until there is a showdown, when the player with the best hand wins. A showdown is not allowed until all players but two have dropped out.

Dealt cards are replaced at the bottom of the deck, face down. The cards are reshuffled for the next hand only if a pryle has just appeared on showdown.

Betting principles There are several alternatives:

a "round the table";

b "bet or raise";

c poker betting.

Round the table betting Each time it is his turn to bet a player must bet one unit or drop out.

This continues even when there are only two players left, but then either player may in any of his turns pay a double amount to "see." Both players then show their cards without further betting.

Bet or raise In this system limits are agreed beforehand and affect only the opening bets and raises.

In the betting interval betting is as for the round the table system, but in any turn a player may choose to bet more than one unit.

All active players must then bet exactly the same amount each time their turn comes around – or must drop out or raise again.

Raises are therefore not like the raises in poker. Instead of players just having to "call," they set a new minimum contribution to the pool per turn.

Each player must contribute at least that full amount in subsequent turns – regardless of his previous contributions to the pool – or must drop out.

Each time the bet is raised only the increase is limited. The total bet of a player in a turn can therefore exceed the "limits."

As in the round the table system this can continue when only two players remain in– until one of them pays double the amount at that time to see.

Poker betting is sometimes used (see poker, p 285). In this system the interval ends when bets are equalized.

However, unless modified, poker rules can leave more than two active players at showdown. This can be accepted, or the following rules may be observed:

a when there are three or more active players, a player may not call if this equalizes all players' bets (he must raise or drop out);

b if a player drops out and so equalizes the bets between the remaining three or more active players, the last player to raise must raise again.

"Blind" betting It is sometimes ruled that a player may bet without looking at his cards.

In this case, any player who has looked at his cards must in each turn pay double to the blind bettor if he is to stay in. When only two active players are left an "open" bettor cannot double his stakes to see a blind bettor. To remain in the game he must continue to bet until the blind bettor doubles his bet to see him.

When the last two active players are both blind bettors either of them can pay double to see the other.

Covering the kitty If a player runs out of money during the betting interval he places his hand face down on the pool. Subsequent bets by other players are then placed in a side pool.

Showdown is then between three players: between the last two active players for the side pool and between these two and the player who covered the kitty for the main pool.

SEVEN-CARD BRAG

This version is for two to seven players.

Before each deal, players contribute equal amounts to a pool. Each player then receives seven cards, looks at them, discards one face down, and visibly splits the remainder into two unexposed three card brag hands.

When all are ready, each player in turn exposes one hand, beginning with the player to the dealer's left.

Then each player in turn exposes his other hand, beginning with the player whose first hand was highest.

Seven-card brag: pryles

7s beat aces

A player has complete discretion on how he splits his cards between the two hands, but he must expose the best hand first. The rank of cards is as in three-card brag, except that the highest pryle is three 7s, followed by three aces. (Three 3s rank normally – below three 4s and above three 2s.)

If the same player has the highest hand both times, he wins the pool.

Alternatively, a player whose original seven cards contained four cards of the same denomination wins the pool if he declares this at once without discarding.

Otherwise the pool is not won, but players still contribute again before the next deal.

A deal is usually one card at a time, face down. It may however, be three cards to each player, followed by another three, and then by a single card.

In the latter case, dealt cards are usually not shuffled between hands but replaced face down at the bottom of the deck with no shuffle or cut.

NINE-CARD BRAG

This is similar to seven-card brag. A maximum of five can play, as nine cards are dealt to each player. The deal is usually in ones, but sometimes in threes.

Players divide their cards into three brag hands, exposing the highest hand first. Any player with the highest hand in all

Nine-card brag: pryles

9s beat aces

three exposures wins the pool (or, under some rules, the pool is won by a player with two out of three highest hands). Alternatively, as in seven-card brag, the pool is won immediately by a player with four cards of a kind.

The rank of hands is as in three-card brag, except that the highest pryle is three 9s, followed by three aces. (Three 3s rank normally – below three 4s and above three 2s).

If no one wins the pool, players still contribute again before the next deal.

Sometimes a pool may not be won for many hours – by which time it can be very large.

STOP THE BUS

This British students' game is a variant of three-card brag. All players start with an equal number of betting chips. An additional three-card hand – the dummy – is dealt face up onto the table. In play, each player in turn may exchange one card in his hand for one from the dummy. The discarded cards go into the dummy face up.

This continues until one player does not wish to alter his hand. All players then show their cards, and the lowest hand pays a previously agreed amount into the pool (eg five units).

Further hands are played until only one player has any chips remaining. He then wins the whole pool.

2+   Card craps

This game was created to bypass laws banning dice craps.
The "shooter" deals cards instead of throwing dice.

Equipment:
1 a special deck of 48 cards. It is made up of six
denominations only - ace, 2,3,4,5, and 6. In each
denomination there are eight cards, two in each suit. For
example there are eight 6s made up of two hearts, two
spades, two diamonds, and two clubs;
2 betting chips or cash.

Cards used

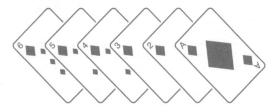

Players Any number can play from two upward. One person
is dealer and is known as the "shooter."
Choice of first shooter is by any agreed method.
Shuffle See p 14.
Cut Any player may cut; but the player to the dealer's left
has the right to cut last. If he does not wish to do so, the right
to cut last passes clockwise.
Basic play The shooter deals two cards from the top of the
deck face up onto the table. This constitutes a "throw." The
value of the two cards added together gives the score for the
throw in just the same way as the two dice in dice craps. The

first throw in a shooter's turn is called a "come-out" throw,
as is the first throw after each time the cards win or lose.
On a come-out throw:

a if the shooter throws a 7 or 11, he has thrown a "natural":
the cards "pass" (ie win) immediately.

b If the shooter throws a 2,3, or 12, he has thrown "craps":
the cards "miss out" or "crap out" (ie lose) immediately.

c If the shooter throws a 4,5,6,8,9, or 10, he has thrown a
"point": for the cards to win he must "make the point," ie
throw the same number again before he throws a 7 – no other
numbers matter.

If the shooter throws the same number again before he
throws a 7, the cards pass (win).

If he throws a 7 before he throws the number again, the cards
miss out or "seven out" (lose).

After a come-out throw the shooter shuffles the two cards
back into the deck and he cuts the deck.

If the shooter then still has to make a point, he deals further
throws but does not shuffle these back into the deck. This
continues until he makes the point (wins) or sevens out
(loses) – ie until a "decision" is reached. The entire deck is
then shuffled together and cut.

If, on a point, the whole deck is used without a decision, the
shooter reshuffles and cuts the deck; he then continues,
trying for the same point.

Change of shooter If the shooter sevens out he must give up the cards. He may also give up the cards if:

a he has not made any throw in his turn; or

b he has just thrown a decision.

The cards pass to the next player to the left.

Change of deck When two decks are available, any player may request a change of deck at any time. The change is made immediately before the next come-out throw.

Betting and odds Players arrange bets among themselves.

Center bet On each come-out throw, the shooter places the amount he wishes to bet in the center of the playing area. He announces the amount, saying "I'll shoot...."

Any of the other players then "fade" (accept) whatever part of the total they wish, by placing that amount in the center alongside the shooter's bet.

Unless agreed at the beginning of the game, there is no set order or amount by which players fade center bets. Players simply place money in the center until all the shooter's bet has been faded, or until no one wishes to place any further amount. (However, it is sometimes agreed that any player who faced the entire center bet on the preceding come-out, and lost, can claim the right to fade the entire present bet). If the center bet is not entirely faded by the players, the shooter may either:

a withdraw the part not faded; or

b call off all bets, by saying " No bet."

Players may not fade more than the shooter's center bet; but if the players show eagerness to bet more, the shooter can decide to increase the amount of his bet.

Settlement of center bet If the cards miss out (lose), the players who faded the center bet each receive back their money together with the equivalent amount of the center bet. If the cards pass (win), all the money in the center is collected by the shooter.

The center bet is therefore an even money (1 to 1) bet. Since the probability of the cards passing is in fact 970 occasions in 1,980, the shooter has a 1.414% disadvantage on the center bet.

Other bets are known as side bets. Like the center bet, they must be arranged before the cards are dealt.

Note that the shooter himself may make any of the side bets he wishes, in addition to the center bet.

Hardway bet (or gag bet) This is a bet on whether the shooter will throw a certain number "the hard way" – ie as the sum of a double. Hardway bets can be placed on 4 (2+2), 6 (3+3), 8 (4+4), or 10 (5+5).

The right bettor loses if a 7 is thrown, or if the number bet on is thrown any other way before being thrown as a double.

Double hardway This is not a bet but a double payment made when the shooter throws a point number (4,6,8 or 10) with two cards that are pairs of the same suit, eg 8 with two 4s of hearts.

The payment is made by wrong bettors to those who have taken a normal "right bet" on the shooter making the point. This serves to equalize the right and wrong bettors' chances on even number points.

Off-number bet Two players agree to bet on any number they choose. The right bettor wins if the shooter throws the number before he throws a 7. Bettors may call off the bet before a "decision" is reached.

Proposition This refers to any other kind of side bet agreed upon – limited only by players' imaginations!

Such bets are always offered at odds designed to give the proposing player an advantage. There are two main categories:

1 bets on whether the specified number(s) will appear within a certain number of throws after the bet: "one-throw bets," "two-throw bets," three-throw bets;" or

2 bets on whether the specified number(s) will appear before other specified numbers or before a 7.

In each case, the specified number(s) bet on may be:

a a certain number to be thrown in any way;

b a certain number to be thrown in a specified way;

c any one of a group of numbers (eg a group of specified numbers, odd numbers, (numbers) before 7, etc).

Right and wrong bets All these bets require agreement between two players.

One is the "wrong" bettor: he "lays" odds that the cards will not pass or will not make the number(s) bet on.

The other is the "right" bettor: he "takes" odds that the cards will pass or will make the number(s) bet on.

The bet and odds may be proposed by either the right or the wrong bettor; in practice, however, more experienced players tend to be "wrong" bettors and propose odds that the less experienced player will "take."

Flat bet This is a normal bet on whether a shooter's come-out throw will pass, and is made as a side bet between two players (of which one may be the shooter). Flat bets occur especially if one player has faded the entire bet.

Point bet If the shooter throws a point on his come-out throw, players may bet on whether he will "make the point." (The center and flat bets still remain to be settled in the same way).

Come bet This is a bet on whether the cards will pass – but treating the next throw after the bet as the bet's come out throw (when in fact the shooter is throwing for a point). If on this throw the shooter throws a 7, he sevens out on his point – but for the come bet the cards "come," because a 7 on a come-out throw is a natural.

Similarly, 11 is a natural for the come bet, but 2,3, or 12 is craps – the cards "don't come." (But all of these leave the center bet undecided, because they are neither the point number nor a 7).

If the shooter throws a point number on the come-out throw for the come bet, this number becomes the point for the come bet. The outcome then depends, in the usual way, on whether the point or a 7 appears first.

If the shooter makes the point on his center bet without making the come bet point, the players making the come bet can agree to withdraw the bet or to continue the number sequence into the shooter's next turn.

True odds Table 1 overleaf gives the true odds for various bets on or between single numbers, and provides the information from which the true odds for any bet between groups of numbers can be calculated. (A player should particularly avoid accepting 1 to 1 odds on 6 to 5 bets).

Table 2 overleaf gives the true odds for hardway bets.

Table 1: True odds for bets on or between single numbers

Number	A Single throw	B Before a 7	C Comparative odds
12	35-1	6-1	**12**
11	17-1	3-1	2-1 **11**
10	11-1	2-1	3-1 3-2 **10**
9	8-1	3-2	4-1 2-1 4-3 **9**
8	31-5	6-5	5-1 5-2 5-3 5-4 **8**
7	5-1	—	6-1 3-1 2-1 3-2 6-5 **7**
6	31-5	6-5	5-1 5-2 5-3 5-4 1-1 5-6 **6**
5	8-1	3-2	4-1 2-1 4-3 1-1 4-5 2-3 4-5 **5**
4	11-1	2-1	3-1 3-2 1-1 3-4 3-5 1-2 3-5 3-4 **4**
3	17-1	3-1	2-1 1-1 2-3 1-2 2-5 1-3 2-5 1-2 2-3 **3**
2	35-1	6-1	1-1 1-2 1-3 1-4 1-5 1-6 1-5 1-4 1-3 1-2 **2**

Table 2: Hardway bets

Bet	Odds against hardway	Payment on double hardway
10	8.1	4.1
8	10.1	12.5
6	10.1	12.5
4	8.1	4.1

Notes on table 1

A Odds against making a number on a single throw.

B Odds against throwing the number before throwing a 7: for point and off-number bets.

C Odds against making the higher number before the lower number (eg 12 before 4: 3-1). Reverse the odds to give odds against making the lower number before the higher (eg 4 before 12: 1-3).

To calculate the odds between any groups of numbers: add all ways of making the numbers in one group, and compare with the total of all ways of making the numbers in the other group.

True odds for other one-throw bets:

a against any specified pair (eg 3+3): 35-1;

b against any specified combination of two different numbers (eg 6+5): 17-1;

c against any craps (2,3, or 12): 8-1.

2-8   Card put-and-take

Taking its name from the game of put-and-take played with a specially marked teetotum, this private banking card game has some features in common with red dog.

Equipment:
1 one standard deck of 52 cards;
2 betting chips.
Players From two to eight.
Objective On the "take" deal each player aims to hold, and on the "put" deal not to hold, cards of the same rank as those turned up by the banker.
Choice of first banker/dealer is by high cut (see p 13).
Shuffle and cut are standard (see p 14).
Deal The banker deals five face-up cards to each player except himself, dealing them one at a time in a clockwise direction.
Betting limits Payments are one to 16 chips. One chip's value is agreed beforehand.
Play
1 Players look at their cards.
2 The put deal is made. The banker deals five face-up cards one at a time onto the table.
After each card is dealt, any player holding a card of the same rank must pay chips into a pool. The payment doubles with each card: one chip for the first card turned up; two for the second; four for the third; eight for the fourth; and 16 for the fifth. A player with two or more cards of the same rank as the banker's card must pay for each one.
The banker makes no payments.
3 The banker takes the five cards from the table and places them face up at the bottom of the deck.
4 The take deal is made, for which the banker deals five more cards as before. This time each player takes chips from

Sample play

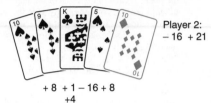

Player 2:
− 16 + 21

+ 8 + 1 − 16 + 8
+ 4

Player 1:
− 14 + 0

− 2 − 4
− 8

Player 3:
− 1 + 23

+ 1 − 1
+ 4 + 2
+ 16

Put deal

| 1 | 2 | 4 | 8 | 16 |

Take deal

the pool for each of his cards of the same rank. The number
of chips taken increases exactly as in the put deal.

5 Any chips left in the pool after the five cards have been
played go to the banker. Any chips still owing are paid by
the banker from his own chips.

Change of banker/dealer After each hand the bank and deal
pass to the player to the banker's left.

VARIANTS

Ante payment Sometimes each player but the banker puts
one chip into the pool before each hand.

Easy go has an additional payment and claim. Players pay –
and take – one additional chip to each card that, besides
being of the same rank as the card played by the banker, is
also of the same color.

Red and black has an additional payment and claim for any
player with three or more cards of the same suit as the card
played by the banker.

Players pay – and take – one chip for the first card the banker
turns up, two for the second, three for the third, four for the
fourth, and five for the fifth, in addition to regular payments.

Up and down the river has a different payment and claim
system. Each player pays – and takes – according to the rank
of the matching cards, not according to whether it is the first,
second, third, fourth, or fifth card turned up.

Payment for an ace is one chip; for a jack, 11 chips; for a
queen, 12 chips; and for a king, 13. Payments on the other
cards match their face value.

Chinese fan-tan

2+

This simple game works on the same principle as the Chinese bean game of fan-tan. It was once an American gambling house game but disappeared because it gives no advantage to the banker.

Equipment:
1 one standard deck of 52 cards;
2 one joker to be used for the betting layout;
3 betting chips – preferably a different color for each player.
Players The game is for two or more players.
Objective Players aim to guess how nearly the number of cards in a section cut from the deck will be divisible by four.
Choice of first banker is by high cut (see p 13).
Betting limits Are agreed beforehand.
Bank Because each player may make more than one bet, the betting limits do not limit a bank's losses. A banker therefore places to one side, before his first hand as banker, any of his fund of chips he is not prepared to put at risk. The remainder constitutes the bank. Any winnings gained during a player's turn as banker must remain at risk in the bank until the role of banker passes to the next player.
The betting layout consists of the joker, turned face up in the center of the table. The card is placed so that one of its short sides is facing the banker.
Each of the joker's corners is allocated a number. As the banker looks at the card, the bottom left hand corner is 1, the top left hand corner 2, the top right hand corner 3, and the bottom right hand corner 4.
Bets at the corners of the joker are on one number only. Bets along the side of the joker are on the numbers of the two adjacent corners. In the example illustrated overleaf, bet (**a**) is on 3, bet (**b**) on 3 and 4, and bet (**c**) on 4 and 1.
A player may place as many bets as he likes, provided each

bet is within the betting limits. For each bet, he puts down the number of chips he wishes to put at risk.

More than one player may make the same bet. The banker does not bet.

Betting   **Play**

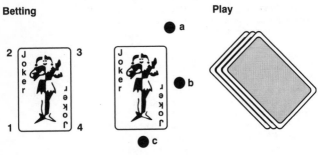

Layout

a bets on 3
b bets on 3 and 4
c bets on 4 and 1

Shuffle The player to the banker's left shuffles the deck thoroughly and gives it to the banker.

Play The banker cuts a section of at least one third of the cards from the deck, and then counts them out face down onto the table in groups of four.

If the section divides exactly into groups of four, 4 is the winning number.

If a number of cards is left over after counting out in fours, the number left over is the winning number.

In the example illustrated, the section comprised 15 cards – three groups of cards and three over.

Settlements of bets The banker first collects losing bets and then pays winning ones.

Bets on single numbers are paid as 3 to 1 – bet (**a**) in the example illustrated opposite. Bets on two numbers are paid at evens – bet (**b**) in the example; bet (**c**) loses.

The banker first pays any winnings due to the player to his left and then those due to the other players in turn.
If the bank is emptied before all winnings have been paid, the winning bets that remain unpaid are simply returned to the bettors.

Settlement

a is paid at 3:1
b is paid at evens
c loses

Three cards over

Change of banker Unless the bank has been emptied, bank and deal remain with one player for a set number of hands agreed beforehand. After this the banker receives all the chips then in the bank, and bank and deal pass one player to the left. The bank and deal pass immediately if a bank is emptied.

2-10   Faro

Faro or farobank is a very old banking game. It was known as pharaon in the French court of Louis X1V. In the 1700s it was the most popular gambling house game in England. The following century it became equally popular in the United States, where it was often called "bucking the tiger."

Equipment

1 A table covered with green baize, bearing the faro layout. The complete spades suit is usually used for the layout.
2 A dealing box from which one card can be slid at a time.
3 A casekeeper. This is a frame like an abacus used to show which cards in the deck have been played.
4 A standard deck of cards.
5 Betting chips.
6 Faro "coppers" – round or hexagonal chips of either red or black – used for betting a denomination to lose.
7 Bet markers – small flat oblongs of ivory or plastic – used to make bets over the limit of a bettor's funds.

Players Up to ten can play. House officials are a dealer, a lookout who supervises betting, and a casekeeper official. The house always banks.

Objective Players try to predict whether the next card to appear, of the denomination bet on, will be a winning or a losing card.

Cards appear in play two at a time. The first in each pair is always the losing card, the second the winning card.

Shuffle, cut and bet The dealer shuffles the cards, cuts them, and puts them in the dealing box face up. The exposed top card is called the "soda." It is ignored for betting. Bets are now placed (see p 247).

First turn The dealer puts the soda card face up to one side to start the discard pile or "soda stack."

He then takes the next exposed card from the box and places

it face up to the right of the box. This card is the losing card.
The card now exposed in the box is the winning card.

Between turns Any bets on the two exposed denominations
are settled. Other bets may be changed and new bets made.
The casekeeper is altered to show the cards that have already
appeared.

Continuing play Play continues through the deck. In each
turn:

1 the dealer removes the last winning card from the box and
places it face up on the discard pile;

2 a new losing card is taken from the box as in the first turn;

3 the new winning card is exposed at the top of the box.

The casekeeper has pictures of the 13 denominations, with
four large wood buttons on a spindle opposite each picture.
At the beginning of the deal all the buttons are positioned at
the inner ends of the spindles.

As a card is taken from the box, one of the buttons on the
relevant spindle is moved along toward the outer end of the
frame.

Casekeeper

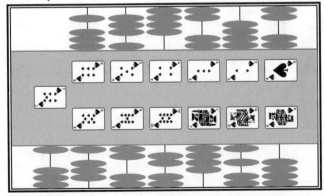

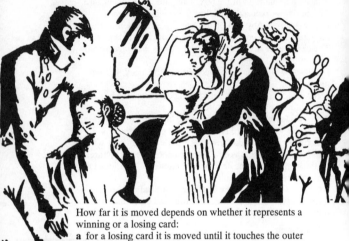

How far it is moved depends on whether it represents a
winning or a losing card:

a for a losing card it is moved until it touches the outer
frame or an earlier button on the same spindle;

b for a winning card a gap of about $1/2$ in is left between the
button and the frame or between this and an earlier button.
When the fourth card of a denomination appears, whether it
is a winning or a losing card, all four buttons are pushed
together against the outer frame to show that betting on this
denomination is at an end.

The last turn Three cards are left in the box for the last turn.
The casekeeper shows which cards they are. The last card in
the box is called the "hoc" or "hock" card.

For the last turn players may normally:

a bet on any one of the cards to win or lose as usual;

b "call the turn" – ie try to predict the precise order of all
three cards (eg, queen first to lose, 6 second to win, ace last).
The turn is played in the usual way, except that when the
winning card has been removed from the box the losing card

is half slid out to confirm the denomination of the hoc card.
A player's bet is returned if the card that he bet to win or
lose appears as the hoc card.

Continuing the game After the last turn all cards are
gathered and shuffled for the next deal.

Betting There are three kinds of bet apart from bets on the
last turn:

bets on a single denomination;

bets on a set of denominations;

bets that take action in every turn.

Bets on a single denomination are settled when a card of
that denomination appears. To make the same bet again a
player places a new stake on the layout.

Bets on a set of denominations are bets on groups of
different numbers that appear close together on the layout
(see placing of bets diagram and explanation). They are
settled as soon as any one of the denominations bet on
appears.

To make the same bet again, a player places a new stake on the layout.

Bets that take action in every turn remain on the layout until removed by the player. There are two such bets: a "high card" bet an an "even or odd card" bet.

In a high card bet the player bets that the higher denomination card of each pair will win in each turn, or, if he has "coppered" the bet, that the higher card will lose. (For this bet ace ranks low.)

In an even or odd card bet the player bets that either the even card or the odd card will win in each turn. (For this bet ace, jack, and king count as odd, and queen is even.)

With these two bets the player wins or loses on every turn. Each time he loses he gives the dealer a number of chips equal to his stake. Each time he wins he receives an equal number. The actual stake remains on the table until the player stops making the bet.

Explanation of placing of bets diagram:

a bets a single denomination (5);

b bets two denominations horizontally adjacent (2+3);

c bets two denominations diagonally adjacent (6+9);

d bets two denominations vertically adjacent (2+q);

e bets 6+7;

f bets 7+8;

g bets two denominations horizontally adjacent and separated by one other denomination (j+k);

h bets three denominations horizontally adjacent (8,9,10);

i bets three denominations in a right angle (3,10,j);

j bets 6,7,8;

k bets adjacent denominations in a square (4,5,9,10);

l bets the even denomination card in each turn (the chip position is between the 2 and the table edge);

m bets the odd denomination card in each turn (the chip position is between the 5 and the table edge);

n bets the higher denomination card in each turn.

Placing of bets

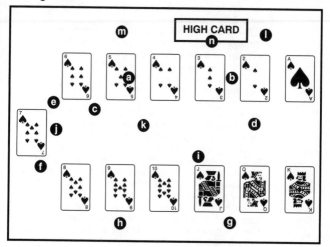

Bets to win using one or several chips All bets may be
made with one chip or several chips.

If several chips are used, they are stacked vertically except
for bet (**c**). For that bet they are tilted or "heeled," by
moving the bottom chip in to rest on the corner of one card
and tilting the remainder toward the other card.

Bets to lose using one or several chips In general these bets
are placed as for bets to win but are "coppered" – ie a faro
copper is placed on top of the betting chip(s).

The only exception is where bet (**c**) is made with a single
chip. In this case the copper is placed in the usual position
not far from the tip of one of the cards, with the chip on top
of it tilting toward the other card.

Betting one card to win and one to lose This bet can be
placed on any two adjacent denominations or on bet (**g**).

If the bet is made with a single chip, a copper is placed on the edge or corner of the lose card and the chip is tilted toward the win card.

If the bet is made with several chips, one chip is placed on the edge or corner of the lose card and the remaining chips are tilted on it in the direction of the win card.

This bet is settled as soon as one of the denominations appears as a winning or losing card.

Last turn bet: "calling the turn" The stake is placed on the card bet to lose and angled toward the card bet to win.

a When made with a single chip, a copper is placed on the card bet to lose on the edge nearest the card bet to win. The single chip is placed on it, tilted toward the card bet to win. Another copper is placed on top of the single chip.

b When made with several chips, one chip is placed on the card bet to lose on the edge nearest the card bet to win. The remaining chips are tilted on the bottom chip so that they point toward the card bet to win.

When the third card lies between the winning and losing cards, the bet is tilted toward the outside of the layout. This shows that it avoids the middle card, ie the middle card is bet to be the hoc card.

Last turn bet: "cat hop" The stake is placed as for calling the turn.

Bet markers are used when a player wants to place on the layout at one time more bets than he has funds for. For each marker placed on the layout the player must have staked an equal value in chips elsewhere on the layout. If one of the player's bets loses, the dealer takes payment in chips. The player must then withdraw his marker bet unless the value of his chips on the layout still exceeds the value of the markers he has used.

If one of the player's bets wins, the player wins an equivalent amount in chips.

A "split" occurs in a turn when a single bet has covered both winning and losing cards.

a A split on a single denomination occurs when two cards of the same denomination appear in a turn. The house takes half of any bet on that denomination; the other half is returned to the bettor.

b A split on a set of denominations occurs when two cards of a group bet on by a player appear in a single turn. The bet is returned to the bettor.

c A split on bets that take action in every turn occurs when both cards in a turn are of the same denomination or are both odd or both even. The bet remains on the table and the bettor neither makes nor receives any payment.

Betting on "cases" When only one card of a denomination is left in the box, this is called "cases" – eg "cases on the queen."

Most houses forbid a player to bet on cases until after he has bet on a denomination that could be split.

"Cat hop" bet On the last turn the casekeeper may show that the three cards left are not all of different denominations. "Calling the turn" is then replaced by the "cat hop" bet. It may be made on denominations or colors.

a If two of the three cards are of the same denomination, a player may make a cat hop on denominations, predicting the order of denominations as usual – eg, 10,6,10. (A player may still bet one denomination to win or lose as usual).

b If all three cards are of the same denomination, a player may make a cat hop on color, predicting the order of suit colors – eg, red, black, red.

Cat hop bets are placed in front of the dealer according to whatever temporary regulations he states.

Settlement A player who calls the turn successfully is paid at 4 to 1. A player who makes a successful cat hop bet is paid at 2 to 1. All other bets are paid at even money (1 to 1).

2+ **Hoggenheimer**

A game of pure chance in which the settlement of bets depends on how soon the banker turns up a joker.

Equipment:
1 one standard deck of 52 cards from which the 2s,3s,4s,5s, and 6s have been removed.
2 one joker (or any discarded card if a joker is not used);
3 betting chips.
Players The game is for two or more players.
Objective Players try to bet on a card (or cards) exposed before the joker is exposed.
Choice of first banker is by high cut (see p 13).
Shuffle and cut are normal (see p 14).
Dealing the layout The banker deals four rows of eight cards face down, and the 33rd card face down to one side. He takes care that no card's face is seen during the deal.
Betting limits are agreed beforehand.
Betting Each player except the banker places as many bets as he likes. The card bet on is shown by the bet's position on the layout. The top row represents spades, the next hearts, the next diamonds, and the bottom row clubs. The column farthest to the right represents 7s, the next 8s, and so on; the column farthest to the left represents aces.
Examples of betting are shown in the illustration opposite:
a is a bet on the jack of hearts;
b is on the king of diamonds;
c is on two adjacent cards – the 7s of spades and hearts;
d is on two adjacent cards – the 9 and 10 of spades;
e is on four cards in a square – the 8s and 9s of hearts and diamonds;
f is on a column of cards of a single denomination – all the 10s;
g is on a row of cards of the same suit – all the diamonds.

Betting

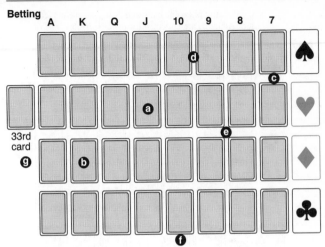

Play The banker turns the 33rd card face up.

If it is a joker the deal ends and the banker collects all bets.

If it is any other card the banker places it face up in its correct position on the layout.

Any bet on that position is replaced on top of the card.

The face-down card that was in that position is removed, turned face up, and placed in its correct position in the layout. Play continues in this way until the joker appears. (See diagram overleaf)

Settlement A player's bet wins if all the cards bet on are turned up before the joker. The banker collects all other bets. In the example illustrated: bets (**a**),(**c**), and (**d**) win; bets (**b**), (**e**), (**f**), and (**g**) lose.

Bets on single cards are paid 1 to 1. Bets on two cards are paid 2 to 1. Bets on four cards in a square or column are paid 4 to 1. Bets on eight cards in a row are paid 8 to 1.

Continuing play The bank and deal pass one player to the left. All cards are collected for the next hand.

Play

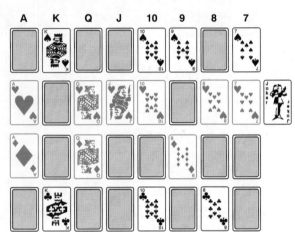

Horse race

3+

An exciting game emulating the thrills of the racetrack. Bets are laid on cards that are moved like horses toward the finishing line.

Equipment:
1 one standard deck of 52 cards;
2 betting chips.
Players The game is for three or more players.
Objective Player try to "win the race" by betting on the first suit to appear eight times in a deal.
Choice of first banker is by high cut (see p 13).
The "horses" The banker takes the four aces from the deck and lines them up in any order.
Shuffle and cut are standard (see p 14).
The "course" After the shuffle and cut, the banker deals seven face-up cards in a line at right angles to the horses. (See diagram overleaf.) If five or more of the cards dealt are of the same suit, the banker takes them all up, reshuffles, and deals the course again.
Betting limits are decided by the banker for each race.
Betting The banker declares the odds on each horse (suit), taking into account the cards that were dealt to form the course. If one suit has appeared predominantly in the course, there will be fewer cards of that suit to appear in the race. The table gives an example of the odds that a banker might offer. He will choose odds that give him some degree of advantage; it is up to each player whether or not to place a bet at those odds.
The players then state their bets, placing their stakes in front of them. The banker makes a note of how much each player bets on each horse and what the odds are.
The "race" The banker deals the top card from the deck face up onto the table. The horse (ace) of the same suit as the

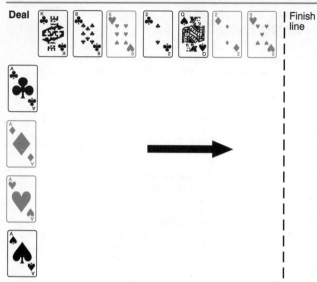

dealt card is then moved up the course one space. The banker then deals another card face up on top of the first, and again moves the horse of the corresponding suit one space. This continues until one horse has passed the end of the course. This horse is the winner. (See diagram opposite.)

Settlement of bets The banker collects all bets placed on the losing horses. He pays at the quoted odds each bet on the winning horse.

Change of banker After each hand, the bank and deal pass one player to the left.

Play

Finish
line

Betting odds

Number of cards of suit in course	Odds offered on suit
0	Evens
1	2-1
2	3-1
3	5-1
4	10-1
5 or more	Layout redealt

2-15 **Injun**

This fast, amusing game is very simple to play. But it can see a lot of money change hands very rapidly, and offers opportunities for skilful judgment to anyone familiar with mathematical odds. Bets are placed in a central pool; there is no banker.

Equipment:
1 one standard deck of 52 cards;
2 betting chips or cash.
Players from two to about 15.
Rank of cards The cards rank in normal order, with ace high. The suits are not ranked.
The objective is to bet on holding a higher ranking card than any other player.
Choice of first dealer is by deal: first ace to appear (see p 13).
Shuffle and cut are normal (see p 14).
Ante Before each deal, each player, including the dealer, puts an equal amount into the center of the table to form a pool.
Deal The dealer deals one card face down to each player including himself, beginning with the player to his left and going clockwise.
Play Players are not allowed to look at their own cards. Each picks up his own card and puts it against his forehead.
He holds it there, face outward, so that all the other players in the game can see the card.
Players should watch carefully at this stage of play to check that no player glimpses his own card.
Betting begins with the player to the dealer's left, and goes clockwise.
Each player bets according to his judgment of whether his own card, which he cannot see, is likely to be higher in rank

than all the others players' cards – which he can see.
A player must bet to stay in the game. If he drops out at any time, he places his card face down on the table in front of him.
All bets are placed in the pool.
Betting principles There are two alternatives:
a poker betting;
b brag betting.
Poker betting In this alternative each player in turn bets, calls, raises, or drops out until the bets are equalized. When this happens, betting ends and there is a showdown between all active players.
Brag betting In this alternative, betting is as in the "round the table" system in brag. Each player in each of his turns contributes one unit to the pool, or drops out.
No one can raise and betting continues until all but two players have dropped out. These last two active players then continue to put bets of one unit each into the pool, until:
a one of them drops out leaving the other player the winner; or
b one of them pays two units to "see the other" and there is a showdown between these two players.
Showdown On showdown all active players look at their own cards. The player with the highest card wins the play and takes the pool. Ties for highest card divide the pool.

"Covering the kitty" If a player runs out of money during betting he places his card face down on the pool – allowing all players to remind themselves of its rank before he does so. Subsequent bets of other players are then placed in a side pool. Showdown is then between three players: between the last two active players for the side pool, and between these two and the player who covered the kitty for the main pool.

Continuing play After the pool has been won the deal passes one player to the left and all players ante for the next play.

Kentucky derby

3+

Also called pasteboard derby, this pool betting game has a
varied race and simple betting.

Equipment:
1 one standard deck of 52 cards;
2 betting chips or cash.
Players three or more.
Objective Players try to bet on the winning "horse."
Choice of first dealer is by high cut (see p 13).
Shuffle and cut The four aces are removed from the deck.
The rest of the deck is shuffled and cut as usual (see p 14).
The "course" After the shuffle and cut, the dealer forms the
course by dealing seven face down cards in line.
The "horses" The four aces are the horses – they can be
given the names of favorites. These cards are lined up just
below the first course card, in the order: hearts, diamonds,
spades, clubs.
To make judging easier, the two red aces are put to one side
of the course and the two black aces to the other.
The player to the dealer's left lines up the aces and moves
them during the race.
Ante Before the game, each player including the dealer puts
an equal agreed amount into the pool.
Betting Each player decides which horse he will back. A
player may bet only on one horse; more than one player may
bet on the same horse.
A horse still runs even if no one bets on it.
It is best to write down the selections if there are several
players. This is done by the player to the dealer's right. He
also has charge of the pool and pays out the winnings at the
end.
Starting the race The dealer deals the top card from the
deck face up onto the table just behind the ace of hearts.

The player to the dealer's left moves the ace of hearts the appropiate number of spaces up the course, if any (see moves table, p 264).

The dealer then deals a card behind the ace of diamonds, and so on.

Running the race How far a horse moves depends on the card dealt. The dealer deals one card to each ace in turn, in the order: hearts, diamonds, spades, clubs, and then starts again. Further cards dealt to each ace are placed face up on top of the cards first dealt, forming four discard piles.

Finishing the race A horse finishes when it passes the last course card.

But the winner is only decided when all horses have had an equal number of turns. The winner is then the ace that has gone farthest over the finishing line.

If the second place horse is to be decided too, and only the winning horse has crossed the finishing line, then the winner's discard pile is turned face down, and play continues with the remaining aces.

Splitting "dead heats" Sometimes two aces have gone an equal distance over the finishing line on the same turn. Each is then dealt a further card from the deck. This continues until, with an equal number of cards dealt, one horse has gone farther past the post than the other.

Settlement: winning horse only With fewer than six players, races are run for first place only. The pool is won by the player or players betting on the winning horse. If there are two or more sucessful bettors, the pool is split equally between them. If the pool does not divide equally, any chips over stay in the pool for the next race.

Settlement: winner and second place With six or more players, races may be run for first and second places. Bettors on the second place horse receive back their ante from the pool. The remainder of the pool is won (and divided if necessary) by the player(s) who bet on the winning horse.

Preparing for the next race The deal passes to the player to the dealer's left. He collects all the cards (except the aces) and reshuffles them.

The player to the new dealer's left controls the horses, and the player to his right the bets.

The moves

	Card played	*Distance moved*
Ace moves forward	king	2 lengths
	queen	1¹/₂ lengths
	jack	1 length
	7,8,9,or 10 same color as ace	1 length
	3,4,5, or 6 same color as ace	¹/₂ length
	Any card dealt of the same suit as ace adds ¹/₂ length	
Ace moves back	2 same color as ace	¹/₂ length back
	2 not same color as ace	1 length back
No move	2 dealt while ace still on starting line	

Sample play

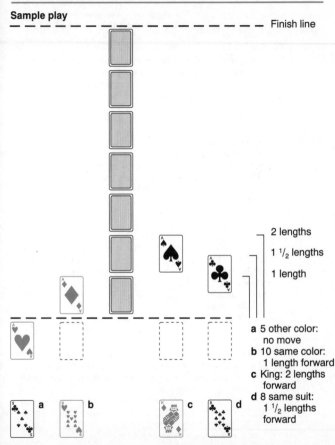

Finish line

2 lengths

1 ¹/₂ lengths

1 length

a 5 other color:
no move
b 10 same color:
1 length forward
c King: 2 lengths
forward
d 8 same suit:
1 ¹/₂ lengths
forward

2+   Lansquenet

This private banking game is said to have been popular with
German mercenaries in the 1600s. Its name derives from
Landsknecht, the German word for mercenary. It is closely
related to ziginette and skinball.

Equipment:
1 one standard deck of 52 cards;
2 betting chips.
Players two or more.
Objective Players aim to bet on a card that has not been
"matched" by the time the banker's card is matched.
A card is matched when a card of the same denomination is
dealt from the deck.
Choice of first banker is by deal: first ace to appear
(see p 13).
Shuffle and cut are normal (see p 14).
Dealing the layout Provided that none of the cards dealt for
the layout matches, the procedure is as follows. The banker
deals the top two cards from the deck (the "hand" cards) face
up onto the table. He then deals one card face up to himself
(the "banker's card"), followed by another one face up (the
"players' card").
Matching cards in the layout The following procedure
must be observed if matching cards are turned up for the
layout.
1 If the card dealt for the second hand card matches the first,
it is placed on top of it. A further card is then dealt as the
second hand card. If necessary this process is repeated until
the hand cards do not match.
2 If the card dealt as the banker's card matches one of the hand
cards, it is placed on top of that card and a new banker's card
dealt. This process is repeated if necessary until the banker's
card is of a different denomination than the hand cards.

3 If the card dealt as the players' card matches one of the hand cards, the procedure is as for the banker's card. If the players' card is the same denomination as the banker's card, the deal is void and a new deal made.

Betting limits are decided by the banker for his hand's duration.

Betting Each player places his bet alongside the players' card. If all chips are of the same color, the bets may be placed at different corners of the card to distinguish them.

First turn The banker deals one card from the top of the deck face up onto the table.

If the dealt card does not match any card on the layout, it is placed face up next to the players' card. It is now a further players' card, on which players may place bets.

If the dealt card matches one of the hand cards, it is placed on top of the matched card. This denomination is now out of play.

The hand cards have no effect, except to remove two denominations from the betting.

If the dealt card matches the players' card, the banker wins the players' bets. There is then no further betting on the matched denominations for the rest of the deal.

The matched and matching cards are dead, but are left on the layout, on top of each other, as a reminder that this denomination is out of play. Any further cards of that denomination are placed on top of the matched cards.

If the dealt card matches the banker's card, the banker pays all bets at even money, ie each winning player receives his stake plus an equal amount from the bank. Play on this deal then ceases and the bank and deal pass one player to the left.

Continuing play If the banker's card is not matched immediately, play continues in the same way until it has been matched – when the banker pays all outstanding bets. A card is dealt in each turn – and either matches a card on the layout or becomes a new players' card.

Each time one of the players' cards is matched, the banker collects the bets on that card.

Between turns, players may place new bets on the players' cards. But a bet that has once been placed may not be removed or transferred to another card.

Explanation of play diagram

a The 8 was dealt first, and became a players' card.

b The king was dealt, matching a hand card and having no effect on play.

c The 6 was dealt. It matches the banker's card – so players win all bets and the deal ends.

Betting   **Play**

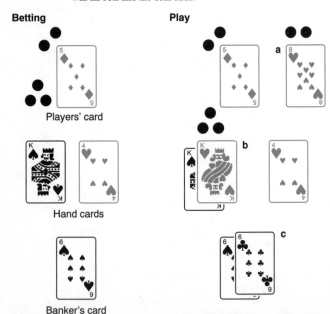

Players' card

Hand cards

Banker's card

Monte bank   *2+*

Monte bank is the major banking card game of illegal
gambling clubs. It is also called monte or Spanish monte.

CASINO VERSION
Cards: a standard deck with the 10s, 9s, and 8s removed.

Cards used

Players From two to as many as can get around the gaming
table. One of the players is banker.
There is also a non-playing house official called a "cutter."
He assists the banker and collects a 25% cut from certain
bets.
When the bank passes, the amount collected by the cutter is
divided equally between the house and the retiring banker.
The objective for a player is to bet on the layout card or
cards that will first be matched in play.
Normally a card is "matched" when another card of the same
denomination appears at the top of the deck.
Choice of first banker/dealer is by low cut.
Bank The banker places in front of him, in cash, the total
amount he wishes to put at risk. The banker does not have to
pay out an amount greater than this on any one hand. If the
result of a hand presents a banker with losses exceeding the
bank total, he pays off the highest bet first, then the next
highest, until the bank is exhausted. Other bets are then void
and are returned to the players.

Betting limits The minimun bet is governed by house rules. The maximum bet is the amount of the bank. A player betting the maximum on a hand does not prevent other players betting because his bet may lose.

Shuffle and cut The dealer shuffles. Any other player may claim the right to shuffle before the cut but the dealer shuffles last. The dealer then places the cards in front of the player to his right. Any other player may claim the right to cut, but the player to the dealer's right must cut last.

Dealing the layout Holding the deck face down, the banker deals two cards from the bottom. He places them face up on the table, slightly apart. These form the "top layout". He then deals two cards from the top of the deck and places them face up on the table just below the first two cards and slightly apart. These form the "bottom layout."

Pairs and triples If the two cards of the bottom layout are of the same denomination, the deal is void. The cards are collected and reshuffled.

The same applies if two cards, one in each layout, are of the same denomination.

If the two cards of the top layout are of the same denomination, the dealer places them on top of the other and deals another card alongside.

If this card is also of the same denomination, it is placed with the others and a further card is dealt.

If this card is the fourth of the same denomination, the deal is void.

The cards are collected and reshuffled.

Betting involves predicting which of two cards or two groups of cards on the layout will be matched earliest. Players back a certain card or cards to be matched before another specified card or cards. Normally a card is "matched" when another card of the same denomination appears at the top of the undealt portion of the deck.

Bets are placed in cash on the layout. The position of a bet shows the card(s) bet and the card(s) bet against. There are four types of bet:

Sample layouts

Top layout

Bottom layout

Pair in Top layout

Top layout

Bottom layout

Triple in Top layout

Top layout

Bottom layout

1 circle bet;
2 crisscross bet;
3 doubler bet;
4 Monte Carlo bet.

Circle bet The player bets that a specified card will be matched before any of the other three cards on the layout (**a**). A successful circle bet is paid at 3 to 1.

Crisscross bet The player bets that a specified card will be matched before another one specified card on the layout (**b**). A successful crisscross bet is paid at evens (1 to 1).

Doubler bet The player bets that one of the cards (unspecified) in the top layout will be matched before either one of the cards in the bottom layout (**c**), or vice versa. Alternatively, he bets that one of the cards (unspecified) to the dealer's right will be matched before either one of the cards to the dealer's left (**d**), or vice versa. A successful doubler bet is paid at evens (1 to 1).

Monte Carlo bet This is a combination of the other three types of bet.

Types of bet

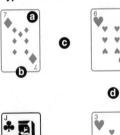

a Circle
b Crisscross
c Doubler (top before bottom)
d Doubler (right before left)

Matching with pairs and triples in the layout When cards of the same denomination have been dealt to the top layout, they are placed together (see sections on pairs and triples). A pair or triple is matched as usual when a further card of the same denomination appears from the undealt part of the deck.

But other cards on the layout are not necessarily matched when a card of their own denomination appears. To give all cards an equal chance, the color of the cards appearing at the top of the deck is taken into consideration.

Matching with pairs in the layout When a denomination in the top layout has been paired, then another card on the layout is matched only by a card which is of its own denomination and of a different color.

Matching with triples in the layout When a denomination on the layout has been tripled, another card on the layout is matched only by a card which is of its own denomination and of the same color.

Matching with pairs

Same color: no match

Other color: match

Matching with triples

Other color: Same color:
no match   match

Crisscross bets An unmatched pair or triple will be involved
in some way in all bets on a layout, with the exception of
those crisscross bets in which neither of the two cards bet is
the pair (or triple).

Such crisscross bets are settled as soon as one of the two
cards involved is matched in the normal way, ie by the
appearance of any card of its denomination.

For other purposes the card is not considered matched.

Play After bets have been placed the cutter says "That's all."
The dealer then turns the deck face up, showing the bottom
card only.

If the card matches any of the cards on the layout, all bets
involved are settled and the matched card is removed from
the layout.

If the card does not match any card on the layout, or if there
are still other bets unsettled, the dealer removes the bottom
card and places it to one side, exposing the next face-up
card. This continues until all bets have been won or lost,
each exposed card being added to the discard pile.

The deal is complete as soon as the last bet on the layout has been settled. (This will happen before all cards on the layout have been matched.) The dealer then gathers all cards and shuffles them for the next deal.

House cut and banker's cut When a player wins because the card he has backed is matched by the very first card exposed, the house takes a 25% cut from the player's winnings.

When the bank passes, the total collected is divided equally between the house and the retiring banker.

House cuts are collected by the cutter.

Change of banker A banker may hold the bank for as long as he wishes or he may be limited to a set number of deals agreed by players beforehand. However, a banker may pass the bank at any time when there are no unsettled bets on the table. He indicates that he is passing the bank by saying "Aces."

If the bank becomes exhausted, the role of the banker passes immediately.

The role of the banker always passes to the next player to the left.

Variant Sometimes the dealer adds unmatched cards from the deck to the layout. Players may place further bets on them as in ziginette.

Sample betting (see diagram overleaf)

a bets 7 of spades;
b bets ace of diamonds;
c bets 7 of spades against 3 of clubs;
d bets king of hearts against ace of diamonds;
e bets 3 of clubs against king of hearts;
f bets ace of diamonds against 7 of spades;
g bets left layout;
h bets bottom layout.

Sample play with pairs Cards turned up:
1 jack of clubs, no action;
2 ace of hearts, bet (**d**) loses (crisscross bet not involving pair); all other bets undecided;

3 7 of hearts, bet (**a**) wins, paid 3-1; bets (**c**) and(**g**) win, paid evens; bets (**b**), (**f**) and (**h**) lose; bet (**e**) undecided;
4 6 of clubs, no action;
5 king of diamonds, bet (**e**) loses.

Sample betting and play

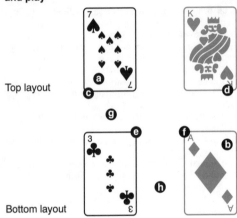

Top layout

Bottom layout

Cards turned up

MONTE BANK: PRIVATE

This is a simple version of the gambling club game.
Cards are matched by suit, not by denomination.

Equipment:

1 one standard deck of 52 cards with all 10s, 9s, and 8s
removed to leave a 40-card deck;

2 betting chips.

Players The game is for two or more players.

Objective Players bet that one of two cards on a "layout"
(pair of cards) will be matched.

A card is matched when the next card exposed from the deck
is of the same suit.

Choice of first banker/dealer is by low cut (see p 13).

Shuffle and cut are normal (see p 14).

Dealing the layouts Holding the deck face down, the banker
deals two cards from the bottom. He places them face up on
the table, slightly apart. These form the "top layout."

He then deals two cards from the top of the deck and places
them face up on the table, slightly below the first two cards.
These form the "bottom layout."

The deal is valid whatever suits appear – even if all four
cards are of the same suit.

Betting Each player except the banker may bet on the top or
the bottom layout or on both. A bet on a particular layout is
shown by placing the chips between that pair of cards.

Betting limits are agreed beforehand.

Play The banker turns the deck face up, exposing the bottom
card. This card is known as the "gate."

If the gate card's suit matches one (or both) of the cards in a
layout, the players win any bets on that layout.

If the gate card matches cards in both layouts, the players
win their bets on both layouts.

If no layout card is matched all bets are lost.

Settlement The banker collects all losing bets.

Winning bets are paid at 1 to 1, even if both cards in a layout
were matched.

Continuing play The banker collects together the layout cards, and places them to one side to form a discard pile. He then turns the deck face down, takes the next gate card from the bottom of the deck and puts it on the discard pile. He then deals the layout cards for the next hand. There is no shuffle or cut.

Change of banker Bank and deal remain with one player for a previously agreed number of hands (up to a maximum of six).

At least 10 cards of the deck should remain unplayed to prevent players calculating which suits remain.

The bank and deal then pass one player to the left. All cards are collected, and the deck shuffled and cut as before. If the bank is emptied at any time, bank and deal pass.

Poker

Poker is played all over the world. It has been called the national card game of the United States, where it developed its present form. Poker ranks with blackjack among card games. Although the betting element is central to both games, they also allow for great skill; it is this that sets them apart from most pure gambling games.

Equipment:
1 One standard deck of 52 cards (see also the section on arrangements p 294).
2 One or two jokers as "wild" cards if desired (see also the section on wild cards p 282).
3 Betting with chips or cash.
Players Two to eight or more. Certain forms of poker can be played by up to 14 people. No alliances are allowed; a player may play only for himself.
Basic terms The usage of some poker terms is not standard. In the following text a "hand" means the cards, or the particular combination of cards, held by a player.
A single game, from one shuffle to the next, is here called a "play" (rather than a "hand").
Objective Each player tries to maximize his winnings.
On each play all bets are put into a common pool (the "pot"). One player wins the pool on a play if:
a he holds a higher-ranking hand than anyone still betting at the end (the "showdown"); or
b all other players drop out of the betting before the showdown in the belief that they cannot win.
Rank of cards Cards rank in the normal order. Ace usually ranks high, except in the 5, 4, 3, 2, ace sequence; in a "high-low" game it may rank either high or low (see p 312). Sometimes low-ranking cards (2s, 3s, and even 4s and 5s) are removed from the deck to speed up the game.

The suits are ranked.

Poker hands In standard poker all hands must, for scoring (showdown) purposes, contain five cards, although fewer or more than this may be held at different stages of the game. The following hands are universally recognized. Each hand loses to the one listed before it, and defeats the one listed after it. This order derives from the mathematical probabilities involved.

1 Straight flush: five cards in sequence of the same suit. (a,k,q,j,10, of the same suit is known as a "royal flush").

2 Four of a kind or "fours": four cards of the same denomination, and one unmatched card.

3 Full house: three cards of one denomination, and two cards of another denomination.

4 Flush: five cards of the same suit, but not in sequence.

5 Straight: five cards in sequence, but not of the same suit.

6 Three of a kind or "threes": three cards of the same denomination, and two unmatched cards.

Rank of hands

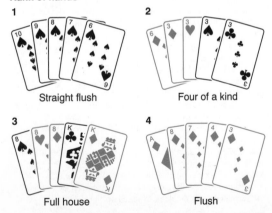

1

Straight flush

2

Four of a kind

3

Full house

4

Flush

7 Two pairs: two cards of one denomination, two cards of another denomination, and one unmatched card.

8 One pair: two cards of the same denomination, and three unmatched cards.

9 High card: five unmatched cards.

Other hands are sometimes accepted locally (eg a "blaze" denotes any five court cards). Their inclusion and their ranking should be agreed before the game begins.

Hands of the same rank When poker hands are of the same rank, the winning hand is decided by the rank of the cards involved.

The following rules apply where no wild cards are used.

1 Straight flush: the highest ranking card in a sequence decides the best hand. Thus a royal flush is the highest when there are no wild cards. Note that the ace in a 5,4,3,2, ace sequence ranks low, so this hand would be beaten by 6,5,4,3,2. The same rule applies to straights.

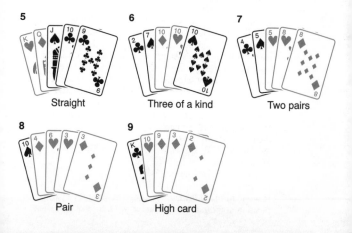

5

Straight

6

Three of a kind

7

Two pairs

8

Pair

9

High card

2 Four of a kind: the hand with the highest ranking matched cards wins.

3 Full house: the hand with the highest ranking "three of a kind" wins.

4 Flush: the hand with the highest ranking card wins. If the highest cards are the same denomination, the next highest are compared. This continues down to the lowest, until a difference is found.

5 Straight: as for straight flush.

6 Three of a kind: as for four of a kind.

7 Two pairs: the hand with the highest ranking pair wins. If the higher pairs in two hands are the same, the lower pairs are compared. If both pairs in two hands are the same, the hand with the best-ranking unmatched card wins.

8 One pair: the hand with the highest ranking pair wins. If the pairs in two hands are the same, the highest unmatched cards are compared. If these are the same, the next highest are compared. This continues down to the lowest, until a difference is found.

9 High card: as for flush.

Hands tie if they contain exactly the same denominations: the suits are irrelevant. Hands that tie as highest in a showdown divide the pool between them. If the pool is not exactly divisible, the amount left over goes to the player who was "called" (ie the player who first made the highest bet).

Wild cards Sometimes players agree at the beginning of a game to designate certain cards "wild." A wild card is one that may represent a card of any denomination.

Any card or group of cards may be agreed on, but the following are popular choices:

the joker (or two jokers);

the "deuce" (2 of spades if no joker is available);

all the deuces;

all the deuces and "treys" (3s);

red 10s.

In some forms of the game, a card that occupies a particular position in the game may count as wild, for example each

Wild cards

player's "hole" (concealed) card in some stud poker games. Two alternative rules govern the use of a wild card. The holder may either:

a use it to represent any card (denomination and suit) he does not hold; or

b use it to represent any card even if he holds that card.

In either case, a wild card ranks the same as the card it represents.

If a joker is used as a wild card, it may be used either like any other wild card, or alternatively as a "bug." The bug may be used to represent only an ace or any card the player needs to complete a straight or a flush. Again, the use of the joker as the bug may or may not be limited to cards not held by the players.

Hands with wild cards Wild cards rank exactly the same as the cards they stand for, so when comparing hands of the same rank, ties are possible between same-denomination fours, full houses, and threes. With fours and threes, the rank of the other cards in the hands decides the winner where possible.

If hands with wild cards are of identical rank, the hand with no or fewer wild cards win. If there are the same number of wild cards, the hands tie.

Where wild cards are used for any card (even one held by the player) two new hands are possible.

1 Five of a kind: five cards of the same denomination. This ranks as highest hand, above a straight flush.

2 Double ace high flush: flush including two aces. This ranks above flush and below full house.

Sometimes, a wild card may be used only to make five of a kind – but not to make double ace high flush. This must be decided before the start of play.

Hands with wild cards

Five of a kind

Double ace high flush

Prohibitions A player may not:

a attempt to make a private agreement with any other player (eg divide the pool without a showdown);

b waive his turn as dealer, unless physically unable to deal;

c look at the discards (either before or after showdown), at undealt cards, at another player's hand, or at a hole card (in stud poker);

d take chips or money from the pool during play, except as correct change for a verbally stated bet;

e leave the table taking his cards with him (he should ask another player, preferably a non-active one, to play his hand for him – if he fails to do so and misses his turn, his hand is dead).

Bluffing is allowed (ie trying to mislead other players by statements, actions, or manner). Bluffing may include: making announcements out of turn about one's hand or plan of play that are not true or are not subsequently kept to; playing so as to make one's hand seem weaker than it is . Sarcasm, heckling, and derision are allowed – help is not!

Betting intervals In a single play there will be at least one betting interval, and normally two or more.

These always follow receipt of cards by players, but the precise number and when they occur depend on the form of poker being played.

In each betting interval, a certain player will have the right to bet or not to bet first. (How he is chosen depends on the form of the game.)

Thereafter players bet or do not bet in clockwise rotation.

Principles of betting All bets on a play are placed together near the center of the table to form a pool. One player bets first ("opens the betting"). Thereafter each player in turn must either "drop out," "stay in," or "raise."

In his turn, a player announces what he is doing before he places any chips in the pool.

For a first bet or a raise, he also announces the amount of the bet or raise.

A bet is not considered made until the bettor has removed his
hand from the chips bet: until then it can be withdrawn.
a Drop out (or "fold"): the player discards his hand and
gives up his chance of winning the pool on this play.
A player may drop out at any time, even if he has previously
bet on this play in an earlier interval or in this interval; but
any chips he has already bet remain in the pool and go to the
pool winner.
A player who has dropped out is no longer "active," and may
not take further action in this play.

b Stay in (or "call" or "see"): the player puts in just enough chips to make the total he has bet so far in this play exactly equal to the total bet by the player with the highest total bet.

c Raise (or "up" or "go better"): the player puts in enough chips to stay in, plus an additional number. The additional amount is that by which he "raises the last bet."

Every other player in the game must then either stay in (by bringing his total bet up to the raised amount), drop out, or raise again ("reraise").

Checking is allowed in many games of poker. A player who checks at the beginning of a betting interval stays in the game for the moment without making a bet. If all active players check, the betting interval ends.

But if one player bets, the interval continues as usual: all other players (including those who have checked) must now stay in, drop out, or raise. To stay in, a player who has checked must equal the highest bet made so far.

If all players check on the first betting interval, the play is void and ends. The next player in turn deals the next round (see the section on the pattern of play, p 297).

A betting interval ends when either:

a all players have checked;

b only one player is still active (and therefore wins), all the others having dropped out; or

c the bets of active players are equalized. This happens when all players still active have put equal amounts in the pool, and the turn has come round again to the last person to raise (or, if no one raised, to the person who opened the betting): he may not then raise again. As long as the bets are unequal any player may raise, but as soon as the bets are equal, no one may raise.

Passing may mean either:

a to drop out; or

b to check (where checking is allowed).

In games where checking is allowed, a player who says "Pass" is assumed to be checking, if checking is available to

Example of a betting interval

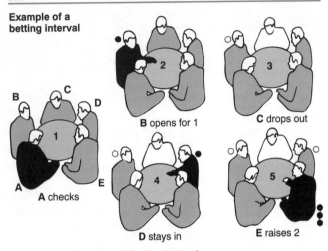

Example of a betting interval

Player bet	Bet	Action	Total bet
A	0	checks	0
B	1	opens for 1	1
C	0	drops out	(0)
D	1	stays in	1
E	3	raises 2	3
A	3	stays in	3
B	3	raises 1	4
D	0	drops out	(1)
E	1	stays in	4
A	1	stays in	4

The betting interval ends. The only three players still active have bet equal amounts; B may not raise the betting again.

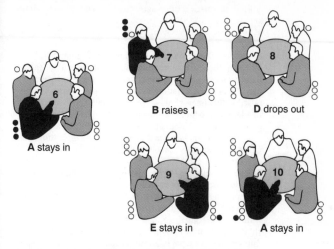

6

A stays in

7

B raises 1

8

D drops out

9

E stays in

10

A stays in

him. (A player shows that he is dropping out by discarding his hand.)

Games in which no checking is allowed are referred to as "pass and out" (or "pass out" or "bet or drop").

Sandbagging is poker slang for either:

a checking to disguise a good hand – this is sometimes considered unethical, but is better accepted as a regular part of bluffing; or

b constant raising and reraising by two players, forcing a third along with them if he wishes to stay in play.

Raising to force out other players is an essential part of poker, but beyond a certain point it can spoil the game's character.

Two optional rulings can keep it in check: limiting raises, and freezing raises.

A limit on raises is often agreed beforehand. Possible limits are:

a three (or sometimes two) by one player in one betting interval;

b a total of three by all players in one betting interval.

Freezing the raise is becoming accepted procedure. If there have been two or more raises (whether by one or several players) in a single betting interval, any player who has not raised in that interval may "freeze the raise."

In addition to betting sufficient to stay in, he bets a previously agreed amount, usually two to five times the normal maximum bet (see the section below on betting.) Other active players must then drop out or stay in by equalling his bet.

The action only freezes the raise for that betting interval.

Side bets are sometimes made between players. For example, in a "high card bet" in stud poker, players bet on who will have the highest first upcard.

Bonuses It is sometimes agreed before play that, on showdown, a player holding a royal flush, straight flush, or four will receive a payment from each player, whether active or not. The amount agreed is usually three to five times the maximum bet.

Betting prohibitions A player may not:

a bet for another player;

b borrow money or chips from another player during play;

c take back a bet after it has been placed in the pool and the bettor's hand been removed. An inadequate bet must be added to, otherwise it is lost and the player's cards are dead.

Betting limits The system to be used must be decided upon before play. The betting limits are also the raise limits. Note that a player forced to bet, for example, the maximum amount to stay in, may still in that turn raise by the maximum (or by any lesser amount).

Specified limits: fixed Minimum and maximum amounts are specified before play starts. Sometimes it is agreed that either:

a any amount between the limits is acceptable as a bet or raise;

b only specified amounts between the limits are acceptable as a bet or raise; or

c no amount between the limits is acceptable as a bet or raise.

Specified limits: varying The minimum and maximum limits change during a play; for example, limits for the final betting interval are always twice the earlier limits.

Last bet limit The opening bet is governed by agreed limits. Thereafter, the maximum bet or raise is the amount put in the pool by the previous bettor's action.

Players must decide that either:

a each betting interval recommences at the original limits; or

b continuous growth is allowed over a single play.

Pot limit The opening bet is governed by agreed limits. Thereafter, the maximum bet or raise is the total amount in the pool at that time. To calculate this, a player wishing to raise may include in the pool total the sum needed for him to stay in. Agreement on an absolute maximum is still necessary.

Table stakes Before the session, each player puts any amount of money he wishes onto the table, or buys chips to that amount.

(A minimum is agreed beforehand, and sometimes a maximum too).

Any amount a player wins is added to his table amount. He may also, from his own pocket, increase his table amount – but not during play, and only by at least the agreed minimum.

During a play, a player may not:

borrow from, or owe money to, the pool;

decrease his table amount or withdraw chips from it;

sell chips back to the bank until he withdraws from the game.

The maximum betting limit for a player is his table amount at the time (the minimum is the amount agreed beforehand). If a player's table amount is used up in a play, he has the right to remain in for the main pool showdown. Any amounts bet by other players, above the amount he has bet, are put into a side pool.

No limit A player can bet or raise any amount. He may borrow during a play, if he can, but he may not put IOUs in the pool.

To stay in, he must equal the highest bet.

In the old no limit games, a player had 24 hours to raise money for a bet. No limit games have now virtually disappeared.

Freeze out This can be played with any limits system except table stakes.

Before the session, each player puts an equal number of chips on the table in front of him. Winnings are added to this amount, but no players may add new chips, lend chips, or remove chips from the game.

As soon as a player has lost all his chips, he drops out. The session continues until one player has won all the chips.

Jackpot This ruling can be played with any limits system. It applies if all other players drop out in a play, after one player has opened the betting. In the next play and before the deal, the others must each "ante" (put) into the pool an amount equal to a single bet made in the previous play.

The new maximum limit (for this play only) is the total amount now in the pool before play starts (providing that this is higher than the normal maximum).

The minimum is as usual.

Whangdoodle This ruling can be played with any limit system.

After the appearance of any very good hand (eg full house or better), the usual or opening limits are doubled for the next play.

Sometimes the special limits hold for the next round of play, ie one deal by each player.

Example of table stakes

In the example shown overleaf: of three active players,
player B has only 30 units left on the table.

a Player A bet 40 units: 30 go into the main pool; 10 start a side pool.

b Player B bets his 30 units, if he wants to stay in the main pool.

c Player C bets 50 units: 30 go into the main pool, the rest into the side pool.

Betting between A and C then continues until their side pool bets have been equalized.

B makes no further bets, and there are no further payments into the main pool, on this or any further betting intervals in this play.

At the showdown, B wins the main pool if he has the best hand.

The side pool can only be won by A or C.

Example of table stakes

a

b

c

Arrangements

Banker poker is not a banking game. Bets are made as contributions to a pool. The "banker" simply supervises the supply of betting chips. He records how many have been issued to each player, including himself, and keeps the payments and the unissued stock to one side.

Players must not make exchanges or transactions among themselves. A player needing more chips must purchase them from the banker's stock; a player with surplus chips may sell them back into stock.

The banker is either the host or any player chosen by lot (eg high cut) or agreement.

The kitty is a fund for buying new cards or refreshments, set up by agreement before the game starts.

Usually, one betting unit is contributed to it from any pot in which there has been more than one raise or, alternatively, where the winner holds a hand of a specified rank or better. The banker arranges all this.

Any chips in the kitty at the end of the game are divided equally among those still playing. (A player who leaves before the end loses the right to any part of the kitty.)

Betting chips are almost always used rather than cash. Usually different colors represent different values; for example: white, one unit; red, five units; blue, 10 units; yellow, 25 units.

A game with seven or more players needs about 200 chips. The best value distribution depends on the maximum betting limit.

At the start of play each player buys chips to the same total value, for example 50 units.

A player's stock of chips must always be kept in full view of the other players, and not be taken from the table except for cashing.

Two decks of cards with contrasting backs are usually used in club play. At the end of one play, one deck is collected and shuffled by the player who dealt last, while the other is dealt into play by the new dealer.

New deck(s) may be called for by any player at any time.

Seating at the start of a session is random, unless a player demands a reseating after the first dealer has been chosen but before play begins.

On reseating, the first dealer has first choice of a seat. He then shuffles the deck, has it cut by the player to his right, and deals one card face up to each player in rotation, beginning with the player to his left.

The player with the lowest ranking card sits to the dealer's left, the player with the next lowest card to that player's left, and so on. Of two cards of the same denomination, that dealt first ranks higher.

The dealer then gathers the cards and has them shuffled and cut for play.

After play starts, or after a reseating, no one may demand a reseating for at least half an hour, provided no one joins or leaves the game.

If a player joins the game after it starts and someone questions the seat he takes, the dealer, between plays, deals a card to each existing player, and the new player takes his seat to the left of the player with the lowest card. This is done separately for each player joining.

If a player replaces another player, he must take the seat vacated, provided no one objects.

Two players may exchange seats just before any play, provided no one objects.

Time limit The time at which the game will end should be
agreed before play starts, and be strictly observed.
Any player who then wishes to continue can do so, but
should set a new time limit.

Time limit for a decision by a player during play (eg how
many cards to draw, how to bet) is five minutes. This is
important in a high-limit game. If a player fails to act within
this time, his hand is dead.

Rules to be agreed before the start of the game (best
written down) are:

a the form of game to be played;
b wild cards and their use;
c any special hands and rulings;
d the value of chips;
e betting limits and checking;
f limits on raises and/or payment for freezing a raise;
g bonus payments and payments to the kitty.

Club and casino poker The management supplies table,
chips, cards, dealer and/or inspector. It takes a cut – usually a
direct charge on the winner of each pool, but sometimes an
hourly charge for tables and officials.

Irregularities Because poker can be played for very high
stakes, innumerable rules govern irregularities of play, both
accidental and deliberate. It is impossible to treat all of these
here. The reader who wishes to play poker for high stakes
should consult an advanced book on the subject.

Pattern of play

Rotation of play is clockwise. No player acts until the active
player nearest to his right has acted.

Choice of first dealer is by deal: the first jack to appear.

Shuffle and cut See p 14.

The deal is clockwise to active players only, beginning with
the active player nearest the dealer's left.

Play varies from one form of poker to another.

Showdown After the final betting interval, players still
active expose their hands (in draw poker) or hole card(s) (in

stud poker), beginning with the player being called, and in a clockwise direction.

Each player announces the rank of hand he is claiming. In any discrepancy the cards "speak for themselves" – this includes giving the hand a higher rating than claimed, except if there are wild cards (when the player's announcement cannot be improved on).

The tied hand of highest rank wins.

Tied hands divide the pool equally.

Change of dealer After each play, the deal passes one player to the left of the previous dealer.

Play rotates clockwise

Deal passes to left

Forms of poker

Closed and open poker are the two main forms.

1 Closed poker, usually played in the form of draw poker.
Players receive their cards face down. After a betting
interval, they discard the cards they do not want, and receive
replacements from the deck.

A second betting interval is followed by a showdown if more
than one player is still active.

2 Open poker, known as stud poker. This is a faster game
than draw poker and allows for more skill. As there is no
exchange of cards, the average rank of winning hands is
lower than in draw poker.

Players receive some cards face down, some face up. Betting
intervals interupt the deal. After the deal, players cannot
receive replacements, but (in versions where more than five
cards per player are dealt) each chooses only five cards to
form his final hand.

A final betting interval is followed by a showdown if more
than one player is still active.

Choice of form The form to be played may be decided by
the host or by club rules; but if a decision has to be made,
two factors should be taken into account.

1 Numbers of players. The best games for a particular
number of players are as follows:

four or under, stud poker;

five to eight, any form of poker;

nine or ten, five card stud;

more than ten any variant with fewer than five cards per
player – or split into two tables.

2 Relative experience If some players are considerably more
experienced than others, it is best to choose one of the less
common variants in which the element of skill is lower.

Dealer's choice If it is agreed to play "dealer's choice," the
dealer chooses the game to be played: a standard form, a
known variant, or any new and easily explained variant he
can devise.

He designates any wild cards. He may not, however, alter the
betting limits, add cards to or remove them from the deck, or
alter basic poker rules.

His choice of game holds by agreement, either:

a for his deal only; or

b for a complete round of dealing. The next dealer in turn
then chooses for the next complete round.

Sometimes, a play or round of dealer's choice is played
whenever a very good hand appears (eg full house or better).

STUD POKER: STANDARD GAME (FIVE-CARD)

Players Up to ten may play.

Ante Usually, a small compulsory bet is made by all players.

Opening deal One card is dealt face down to each player
(the "hole" card), then one card face up. Each player
examines his hand.

First betting interval The player with the highest ranking
face-up card must open or drop. A wild card is considered
higher than an ace. If two players hold equal-ranking cards,
the player nearest the dealer's left opens.

After the opener, each player drops, stays in, bets, raises or
reraises in the normal way until betting is equalized.

Continuing play Further rounds of dealing one card face up
to each player alternate with betting intervals, until the end
of the fourth interval (when each player has one face down
and four face-up cards). On these deals, the dealer leaves the
deck resting on the table and takes cards one at a time from
the top. On the betting intervals, the player with the right to
open is the one with the highest ranking completed hand in
exposed cards – the dealer announces that player and also
announces exposed hands, possible flushes and straights, and
the last deal.

The showdown follows the fourth betting interval; all active
players expose their hole cards.

Additional rules

1 If all the players check, the betting interval ends and the
play continues.

2 If a player drops out, he turns all his cards face down and does not reveal his hole card.

3 If on any betting interval only one active player is left, he wins and the play ends. He need not show his hole card.

4 A "four flush" is often ruled a ranking hand in stud poker, ie four cards of the same suit plus one other. At showdown (and in deciding the start of a betting interval) it beats a pair but loses to two pairs.

Five-card stud:
end of betting

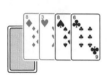

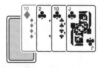

Player 3
dropped out

STUD POKER: VARIANTS

Six-card stud This is like five-card stud, except that after the fourth betting interval each player receives a sixth card face down. This is followed by a fifth (final) betting interval.

At the showdown, each active player chooses five cards from his six to form his final hand.

Seven-card stud (or seven-toed Pete or down the river). This game is for two to eight players.

The opening deal is of three cards: two hole cards, then one face up. Betting intervals and rounds of dealing face-up cards then alternate as usual, until active players have seven cards (including the two hole cards).

After a final betting interval, each active player chooses five cards from his seven to form his showdown hand.

Seven-card stud: low hole card wild As above, but each player's lower ranking hole card is wild – as, for him, is any other card of that denomination. Sometimes players are allowed to choose either one of their hole cards (and its denomination) as wild.

Seven-card stud: end of betting

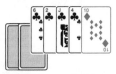

Player 3 dropped out

Mexican stud is like five-card stud, except that all cards are dealt face down.

After the second and each subsequent betting round, each player turns up any one of his face-down cards, leaving one chosen card as hole card.

Sometimes a player's final hole card is ruled wild, together with any other cards of that denomination that he holds.

Other five-card stud variants

1 Last card down: the last card is dealt face down, giving two hole cards.

2 Last card optionally down: a player may turn up his hole card before the last dealing round and receive his fifth card face down.

Low-hand stud The lowest hand wins the pool. The lowest exposed hand begins each betting interval. Other rules are as for the form of stud being played.

DRAW POKER

The basic pattern of the game is as follows:

1 Ante: a small compulsory bet is made by all players.

2 Deal: five face-down cards are dealt to each player in the normal way. Players count their cards, then look at them.

3 First betting interval: the player to the dealer's left has the right to bet first: if he does not bet, the other players may bet in turn.

4 Draw: each active player in turn may discard one or more cards and receive from the dealer the same number, face down, from the undealt part of the deck. A player need not draw – he may "stand pat."

5 Second betting interval: the player who made the first bet in the first interval has the right to bet first. If he has dropped out, the first active player to his left may bet.

6 Showdown takes place if more than one active player is left at the end of the second betting interval.

DRAW POKER: STANDARD GAME

Players Up to ten may play. No more than six should play in high-betting games, since with more players it may be necessary to use discards to complete the draw.

Ante Either:

a each player puts an equal agreed amount into the pool; or

b only the dealer antes ("dealer's edge").

The ante amount is usually the same as the minimum bet.

First betting interval There are two forms:

1 "Jacks or better." A player may not open the betting unless he holds a pair of jacks or any better hand. (Before betting is opened, players may check.) After betting has opened, a player may bet on any hand, and must bet or drop out. At the end of the play, the opener must show the cards he opened on.

2 "Pass and out" (or "pass out" or "bet or drop"). A player may open the betting on any hand. Each player must bet or drop out; no one may check. In either case, the player to the dealer's left is the first to "speak."

Once the betting has opened, it proceeds in the normal way. If no one opens, all players ante again, and the next dealer deals for the next play.

The draw occurs if more than one player is still active after the first betting interval. The dealer offers the draw to each player in turn in normal rotation, beginning with the player to his left and ending with himself.

Each player in his turn either:

a states the number of cards he requires and places that number from his hand face down on the table in full view – the dealer then gives him the same number from the undealt part of the deck; or

b says "I stand pat," or knocks on the table, to indicate that he wishes to keep the hand that he has.

In his turn, the dealer also either states the number of cards he has drawn (exchanged), or indicates that he is "standing pat." Normally it is ruled that a player may draw one, two, or three cards at his discretion.

With four or fewer players, four and five card draws are sometimes allowed.

A player may use the draw to bluff in any way he wishes about the value of his hand.

The dealer must answer truthfully how many cards he himself drew. No other question need be answered truthfully by anyone.

Draw poker: sequence of play

Deal

Betting

The draw

The bottom card of the deck is not used. If further cards are required, the bottom card and the cards discarded so far are shuffled together and cut to allow the draw to continue. The usual rules apply, but the player due to draw next cuts last. No other shuffling or cutting on the draw is allowed.

Sometimes, in "jack or better," the opening bettor discards one of his "openers" (ie one of the cards that gave him the right to open). If he does so, he must state this, and the discarded opener is kept to one side to be inspected at the end of the play. It is not used if the discards are reshuffled.

Second betting interval This follows the usual rules. All players may check, even if "pass and out" was enforced for the first interval. If all the players check, the interval ends. If all players except one drop out, that player wins without showing his hand (except for showing his openers in "jacks or better," if he opened the betting).

Showdown Each active player in turn must place all his five cards face up on the table, to be seen by all players (active or otherwise). At the same time he announces the value of his hand – he must do this even if he sees he is beaten.

If all players checked in the second betting interval, the opener shows his hand first, but if bets were placed in the second betting interval, the player who was called shows first. In either case, other active players then follow in normal rotation.

Betting   Showdown

Dropping out In draw poker a player indicates that he is
dropping out by placing his cards face down on the table
when his turn in the betting interval arrives.

As long as a player wishes to remain in the game he must
keep his cards in his hands, above table height, unless he is
forced to put down the cards temporarily for some reason, in
which case he must state this.

DRAW POKER: VARIANTS

"Jacks or better" variants

1 Progressive openers: if no one opens on a play, two queens or better are required to open on the next play. If again no one opens, two kings or better are required on the next play; then two aces or better; then back down to two kings or better, two queens or better, and two jacks or better. Each time, players must ante again; and sometimes the limits are doubled. Once a player opens, the next play reverts to jacks or better (and limits go back to normal).

2 "Jack or bobtail" to open. This is like "jacks or better" but a player may also open on a "bobtail" (four cards of the same suit plus one other card) or a "bobtail straight" (four cards in sequence plus one other card – but the sequence may not be: a,k,q,j, or 4,3,2,a).

These hands have no showdown value.

Blind opening (or "blind tiger" or "blind and straddle"). In this variation, players bet "blind," ie before receiving their hands. Before the deal:

1 the dealer antes only one chip;

2 the player to his left bets one chip blind ("edge");

3 the next player raises him, betting two chips blind ("straddle").

After the deal, the next player after the blind raiser has the first voluntary bet. He may call (two chip), drop out, or raise (three chips). The betting interval then proceeds as normal. The maximum raise before the draw is one chip. (Note that the dealer's ante does not count toward staying in, but the two players' blind bets do.)

In the second betting interval, the bet and raise limit is two chips. Betting begins with the first blind bettor or the (still active) player nearest his left. Players may check until a bet is made.

Sometimes, in the predeal betting, up to three voluntary blind bets – each doubling the last bet – are allowed after the blind raise. These bets count toward staying in the game in the first interval.

Shotgun Play as in the standard game, except for an additional (first) betting interval during the deal, after each player has received three cards.

Any hand can open. There is no checking.

Stormy weather Each player receives four cards. Three face-down cards are dealt to the table, one each after the second, third, and fourth dealing rounds.

There is then a betting interval. A player may open on any hand. There is no checking.

In the draw, each player may change up to four cards. After the draw, the dealer turns up the table cards one at a time, with a betting interval as each one is turned up.

At the showdown, a player uses any one of the table cards as his fifth card. None of the table cards is wild.

Stormy weather: deal

player 2

player 1

player 3

Dealer

Lowball is often played during "jacks or better" sessions.
When no one has openers for "jacks or better," lowball is
played for that play only.
In lowball the lowest hand wins. Rules as for the standard
game, with the following exceptions.
1 Ante: the dealer and the player to his left (sometimes also
the second player to his left) ante.
2 First betting interval: the player to the left of the last
player to ante must open or drop out. No checking is
allowed. The limit is the ante amount. Antes count toward
staying in.
3 Draw: before the draw the dealer "burns" (exposes and
then discards) the top deck card.
4 Second betting interval: this begins with the active player
nearest the dealer's left. Checking is allowed, but a player
who checks cannot later raise on that play.
Limits are agreed beforehand.
5 Showdown is won by the lowest hand.
Ace always counts low, and straights and flushes do not
count. Therefore 1,2,3,4,5 (known as a "bicycle") counts as
five low cards and is the lowest hand – regardless of suits.
The joker can be used for any card not in the player's hand.

**Lowball:
lowest hand**

Spit in the ocean There are many versions of this; some are
given in the section on closed poker games, p 310.
1 Basic game: each player receives four cards. The next card
is dealt face up to the center. The game proceeds as usual,
but at showdown each active player must count this table
card as the fifth card in his hand.

2 Pig in the poke: as above, but the face-up card and all the others of the same denomination are wild (or sometimes only cards of the same denomination as the face-up card, but not the face-up card itself).

**Spit in the ocean:
deal**

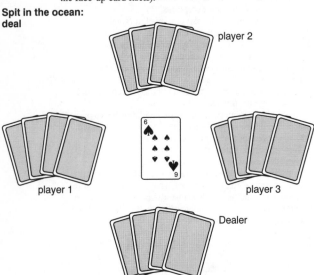

CLOSED POKER GAMES
These are variants in which there is no draw.
Showdown straight poker (or cold hand poker) There is one betting interval before the deal. The deal is normal, but the cards are dealt face up and the best hand dealt wins.
Double barred shotgun Each player receives five face-down cards. Beginning with the player to the dealer's left, all the players then expose any one of their cards.

Betting intervals then alternate with further rounds of exposing one card each. On the fifth and final round of exposure, the best hand wins.

Spit in the ocean variants

1 Crisscross (or X marks the spot): each player receives four cards. Five cards are then dealt face down to the center of the table in the shape of a cross.

Players examine their hands. The dealer then turns up any one of the table cards except the one at the center of the cross. A betting interval follows.

Exposure of the cards in the cross alternates with betting intevals until all but the center card of the cross have been exposed.

After the fourth betting interval the center card is exposed; showdown follows immediately.

The center card of the cross is wild, as are all the other cards of the same denomination.

Each player mentally selects his final five-card hand from any cards in his hand and the table cards. (Sometimes, he is only allowed to choose table cards from any three that form a straight line in the cross.)

2 Cincinnati: five cards are dealt to each player, and the next five cards are dealt face down to the center of the table.

The game is the same as crisscross, but without the cross pattern. None of the table cards is wild; a player may use any of the table cards in his final hand.

3 Lame-brain Pete: this is played like Cincinnati, but the lowest-ranking table card is wild, as are all the other cards of that denomination.

Three-card poker Each player receives three face-down cards, and there is a betting interval after each round of cards is dealt. Showdown follows immediately after the third interval.

The rank of hands (with the highest given first) is: three's; three-card straight flush; three-card flush; three-card straight; pair; high card.

Two-card poker (usually played with wild cards) comprises: a deal of two face-down cards to each player; a single betting interval; and a showdown. Pairs and high cards are the only hands.

HIGH-LOW POKER

Almost any standard game or variant, draw or stud, can also be played as a high-low game. Especially popular is seven-card high-low stud.

At showdown, the highest and lowest hands split the pool. Usually a player must declare, just before showdown, whether he is competing for the highest hand, lowest hand, or both.

It is possible to declare for both in any game where a player has more than five cards from which to select his final hand, for he is then allowed to select two different hands.

Rank of cards is as usual.

If a player is competing for the lowest hand, ace ranks low; if competing for the highest hand, ace is high or low, as he wishes; if competing for the highest and lowest hands, ace can be both high and low as he wishes.

Rank of hands is as usual. Hence the lowest possible hand without wild cards, is 6,4,3,2,a in different suits (5,4,3,2,a would be a straight).

The usual rules for comparing hands apply – highest card first, then the next highest, until a difference is found. Thus 9,7,6,5,4 ranks lower than 9,8,4,3,2.

High-low:
lowest hand

Wild cards A wild card can only be given one denomination and a suit at showdown.

If declaring for the lowest hand, a wild card ranks the same as a low ace, without pairing any ace in the hand. Thus 4,3,2, a, wild card becomes the lowest possible hand.

Declaring follows the last betting interval. There are two methods.

a Beginning with the player to the dealer's left, each active player in turn declares himself as competing for the highest hand or lowest or both.

b Each player takes one of his chips in his hand, without revealing its color. He takes a white one if declaring low, a red one if declaring high, or a blue one if declaring both.

When all the players have decided, they show their chips. The highest hand and lowest hand divide the pool equally (if an exact division is impossible, the highest hand receives any odd chips).

A player can only win the part of the pool for which he has declared. If more than one player has declared the same way, the player with the best hand wins that part of the pool.

If all the players have declared the same way, the player with the best hand wins the whole pool.

If a player has declared for both high and low, he must at least tie each way at showdown, or his hand is dead and he receives nothing.

2-10   Polish red dog

Also known as *stitch* and *Polish pachuk*, this game was
played by Polish immigrants to the United States.

Equipment:
1 one standard deck of 52 cards;
2 betting chips (or cash).
Players The game is for two to ten players.
Rank of cards is normal, with ace high. The suits are not
ranked.
Objective Players aim to hold a card in the same suit but of
a higher rank than the banker's card.
Choice of first banker is by deal: the first ace to appear.
(See p 13).
Shuffle and cut are normal (see p 14).
Bank The banker places in the center of the table the amount
he wishes to put at risk. A minimum is usually agreed before
the game.
Deal The banker deals three face-down cards to each player
except himself, dealing one card at a time.

Deal

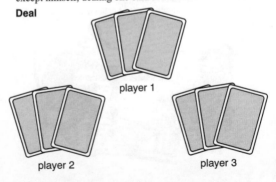

player 1

player 2   player 3

Play Players bet wihout looking at their cards. Play begins with the player to the banker's left. He places his bet in front of him: this may be any amount up to half the total of the bank. The banker then "burns" the top card of the deck, ie he turns it face up, shows it to all players, and places it face up at the bottom of the deck. He then turns up the next card and this becomes the banker's card.

Play

Banker's card

player 1 wins

player 2 loses

player 3 wins

The first player then turns his own cards face up. If he holds
a higher ranking card of the same suit as the banker's card,
he wins; if not, he loses.

If he has won, he receives back his bet and twice that amount
from the bank.

If he has lost, his bet is added to the bank.

His cards are then placed face up at the bottom of the deck.
Bet and play then pass one player to the left. After the player
has bet, the banker burns one card before exposing a new
banker's card.

Change of banker If the bank is emptied at any time, the
bank and deal immediately pass one player to the left and a

new round is begun.

If the bank is not emptied at the end of a round, the same banker continues to deal.

If, at the end of any round, the bank has increased to three or more times the size it was when the present banker began, then the banker declares a "stitch round." He deals one more round, and, at the end of this, collects anything left in the bank. Bank and deal then pass one player to the left.

A player must continue to act as banker until the bank is emptied or a stitch round has been completed.

2+   **Red and black**

This is a private banking game derived from the casino game of trente et quarante.

Equipment:
1 two standard decks of 52 playing cards;
2 betting chips.
Players Two or more.
Objective Each player tries to forecast correctly whether he will hold more red or more black cards in his hand.
Choice of first banker is by high cut (see p 13).
Shuffle and cut are standard (see p 14) – with the two decks shuffled together to form a single deck.
Betting limits are agreed beforehand.
Betting Each player bets on red or black. He bets any amount within the limits. A player bets on black by placing his bet in front of him to his left; he bets on red by placing it in front of him to his right.
(Alternatively each player may be given two colored tokens: one red and one black. He places one of these beside his bet.)

Play The banker deals five cards, one at a time, face up, to the player to his left. He deals them directly in front of the player, so that it is clear whether the player's bet lies to the right or left. If the first four cards consist of two red and two black cards, the player may double his bet before he receives his fifth card. After the first player's bet is settled, the banker deals to the next player to the left. He continues dealing until all players but himself have received a hand.

Settlement of bets A player wins from the banker if he is dealt three or more cards of the color bet on. If he has three of that color, he wins the amount of his bet. If he has four, he doubles his bet. If he has five, he wins four times his bet. A player loses to the banker if he is dealt three or more cards of the color not bet on. If he has three, he loses his bet. If he has four, he pays the banker twice his bet (his original bet and a further payment equal to it). If he has five cards, he pays four times his bet (his original bet plus a payment equal to three times his bet).

Change of banker After the banker has dealt a hand to all the other players, the bank and deal pass one player to the left.

2-10 **Red dog**

This fast betting game, also known as high-card pool, is very popular among American news reporters. It needs little skill and is usually played for low stakes.

Equipment:
1 one standard deck of 52 cards;
2 betting chips (or cash).
Players From two to ten.
Rank of cards is normal (ace high). Suits are not ranked.
Objective Players aim to hold a card in the same suit but of higher rank than a card dealt from the deck.
Choice of first dealer is by deal: first ace to appear. (See p 13).
Shuffle and cut are normal (see p 14).
Ante Before each deal, each player, including the dealer, puts an equal amount (known as the "ante") into the pool.
Deal The dealer deals five face-down cards to each player including himself, beginning with the player to his left and going clockwise.
(Four cards each are dealt if players prefer or if more than eight are playing.)

Deal

player 2

player 1

player 3

Dealer

Betting All players look at their cards. Play begins with the player to the dealer's left. He must bet if he wants to stay in the game. To bet he places his stake in front of him, near the pool. The minimum bet is equal to the ante. The maximum bet is equal to the total in the pool at the time. The dealer must keep note of all bets.

If a player does not wish to stay in the game, he must pay a forfeit equal to the minimum bet but may then place his hand face down on the table without showing it.

Play The dealer deals the top card from the deck face up onto the table in front of the bettor.

If the player holds a card of higher rank in the same suit, he wins; if not, he loses. If he has won, he shows the winning card only (**a**), and receives back his bet and an equal amount from the pool. If he has lost, he shows all his hand (**b**), and his bet is added to the pool.

In either case, his hand is then placed face down in front of him.

Play

a

b

Bet and play then pass one player to the left.

When all players including the dealer have had a turn of play, the deal passes to the next player to the left. Any money in the pool remains, but all players ante again before the next deal.

Empty pool If the pool is emptied during a round, all players ante again to allow the round to continue. They must still ante again before the next round begins.

Division of the pool Sometimes the pool becomes too large for the level of betting. It is best if a limit for the pool is agreed beforehand. If the pool passes that limit, it is divided among the players at the end of that round.

Irregularities

1 If a player receives no hand, or too many cards in his hand, he may not take part in the round. The dealer is not penalized.

2 If a player receives too few cards in his hand, he may bet if he wishes, or he may discard his hand without showing it and without betting or paying a forfeit. The dealer is not penalized.

3 If the top card of the deck is accidentally exposed, it is discarded.

4 Once a player has stated his bet, he cannot alter it. A bet paid into the pool in error cannot be returned. A bet received from the pool in error cannot be taken back once the top card for the next player has been dealt.

VARIANTS OF RED DOG

Burning card version The dealer "burns" a card from the top of the deck before each card that he exposes to settle a bet. That is, at each bettor's turn, the dealer discards the topmost card after turning it face up and showing it to all the players. The next card is then turned up to decide whether the bettor has won or lost.

Banking version Red dog can also be played as a banking game. The current dealer acts as banker. He does not deal to himself. Before the hand, the dealer places in front of him

the money or chips he wishes to put at risk. This can be any
amount he wishes. The players do not ante.

Each player in turn, excluding the banker, bets any amount
he wishes up to the total then in the bank.

Any amount left in the bank at the end of the hand is
returned to the banker. The bank and deal then pass on to the
left. If the bank is emptied before all players have had a turn,
the hand ends and the bank and deal pass at once.

SIX-SPOT RED DOG: POOL VERSION

In this version there is no banker; players ante into a pool.

Equipment:

1 one standard deck of 52 cards;

2 betting chips or cash.

Players The game is for two to 15 players.

Rank of cards is normal (ace high).

Objective Players aim to hold a card in the same suit but of higher rank than the pool card.

Choice of first dealer is by deal: first ace to appear (see p 14).

Shuffle and cut are normal (see p 14).

Ante Before each deal, each player including the dealer puts an agreed equal amount into the pool.

Deal The dealer deals three face down cards to each player including himself, beginning with the player to his left and going clockwise.

The dealer then deals one card fron the top of the deck face up to the center of the table. If it is a 6 or lower (6,5,4,3 or 2) it becomes the pool card. If it is a 7 or higher, it is discarded and the next card from the top of the deck is dealt face up onto the table. This procedure is repeated until a 6 or lower card is dealt to become the pool card. If there is no such card left in the deck, the hand is redealt.

Betting All players including the dealer bet immediately without looking at their cards. The minimum bet is one chip (or a previously agreed sum of money); the maximum is the amount in the pool. More than one player may bet the maximum.

Play Players then turn their hands face up. (See diagram overleaf.) If a player has a card of the same suit but ranking higher than the pool card, he has won. If not, he has lost.

Settlement of bets is supervised by the dealer. He first adds to the pool the bets of all players who have lost. Then he pays out to those players who have won, beginning with the player to his left and going clockwise. Winning bets are returned together with an equal amount from the pool.

Deal

If the pool is emptied before all winning players have been paid, the remaining players receive back only their bets. If anything remains in the pool after all bets have been settled, this amount is carried over to the next round.

The deal then passes one player to the left, and all players ante again to begin the next round.

Play

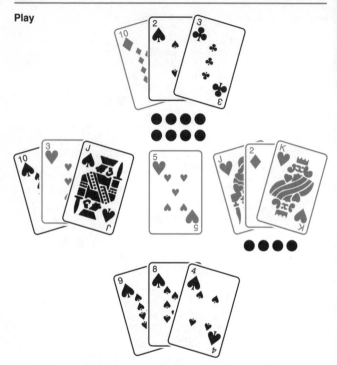

SIX-SPOT RED DOG: BANKING VERSION

In this version the dealer acts as banker, he does not bet.

Bank Before the hand, the banker places in front of him any amount he wishes to put at risk. The players do not ante.

Deal The banker deals to the players as usual but excludes himself. He then deals one card at a time to the table in the usual way, until a 6 or lower card is dealt. This is now referred to as the banker's card.

Betting begins with the player to the banker's left. He may bet ("cover" any amount up to the total of the bank. Subsequent players may only bet against any amount of the bank that has not yet been "covered." The total of bets against the bank cannot therefore exceed the amount in the bank.

If all the bank has been covered before all players have bet, the remaining players are not allowed to bet on that hand. Any part of the bank that is not covered when all players have bet is not at risk in that hand.

Play and settlement of bets takes place in the usual way. When all bets have been settled, any amount left in the bank is returned to the banker. The bank and deal then pass one player to the left.

3+ Skinball

Skinball is a very fast action game played in gaming houses in the American South and Midwest. It is very similar to ziginette and seems originally to have been a black American version of that game. It is also called skin or skinning.

Equipment:
1 one standard deck of 52 cards;
2 a card box that allows only one card to be removed at a time.

Players The game is played by three or more people. One person is banker.

There is also a house official who keeps a watch on proceedings, transfers dead cards to the discard pile, collects and pays bets for the banker, and takes the house's percentage cut. (The house never banks the game.)

The objective is for a player not to have his card matched before the banker's card has been matched. Also, if the player has made side bets, he aims not to have his card matched before the card of any player that he has bet against has been matched.

A card is "matched" when another card of the same denomination is dealt from the card box.

Choice of first banker is by deal – the first ace to appear.

Shuffle and cut (see p 14). After the cut, the banker places the deck face down in the card box.

Betting limits are decided by the banker and can be altered by him at will.

Opening play The banker slides the top card from the card box and deals it face up to the first player to his right.

The player may accept the card or refuse it for any reason. If a player refuses a card he is out of the game until the next turn of play. The card that has been refused is offered to the next player to his right.

As soon as a player accepts this first card, the banker deals a second face up card from the box to himself: this is the banker's card.

Opening bet The player who has accepted the card states his bet. This may be for any amount within the betting limits. Even if the bet is within the limits, however, the banker need not accept it. He may reduce it to any amount he chooses. If the banker does this, the player must accept the decision; he cannot withdraw.

Whichever bet the banker accepts, he places the corresponding amount of money in the center of the player's card.

The player then makes his bet by literally "covering" the banker's money with his own.

Next card in play The banker deals a third card from the box.

If this card's denomination matches either the banker's or the player's card, then the bet involved is settled.

If the card matches the banker's card, the amount on the player's card is won by the player.

If the card matches the player's card, the amount on his card is won by the banker.

If the third card does not match either of the earlier cards, it is dealt to the next player in turn. He may accept or refuse it. If he refuses it, it is offered to the next player in turn. Once the card is accepted, a bet is placed against the banker in the usual way.

Bets between players When more than one player has a card, bets may be made between them.

A player bets that the other player's card will be matched before his own.

Either of the two players may suggest the bet; the other player must be in agreement for the bet to take place.

Money involved in bets between players is stacked to one side.

Matched cards Each time a card is matched, the houseman takes both cards and puts them in a discard pile. The other two cards of the same denomination still in the deck are not allowed to enter play. When one appears it is put directly into the discard pile and a further card is dealt.

Continuation of play As long as the banker's card is not matched, the deal and betting continue as above until each player has been offered a card.

The banker then continues to deal further cards (one at a time and face up) to the table. Any card that appears that does not match either a player's card, a discarded card, or the banker's card is called a "fresh" card.

If there is a player without a card – either because he refused an earlier card or because his card has been matched – he is offered the first fresh card to appear.

If there is more than one player without a card, the fresh card is offered first to the player without a card who is nearest the banker's right.

If he refuses it, it is offered to the next player to his right without a card.

Any fresh cards that appear when every player is holding a
card are placed face up in the center of the table. A player
may accept any one of them as soon as the card he holds has
been matched.

Each time a player accepts a card, he makes a bet against the
banker in the usual way. A player with a card will often have
side bets against every other player, but he must bet against
the banker first.

Banker's card matched Whenever the banker's card is
matched, all the players betting against him at the time win
the amounts on their cards.

If there are no unsettled side bets, the bank passes to the next
player to the right. All cards are collected and shuffled for
the next deal.

If there are unsettled side bets, the banker chooses either:

a to continue to deal for the betting players only – he does
not enter into any further bets himself and does not give out
any fresh cards; or

b to take the first fresh card dealt from the deck as his new
banker's card.

Any player's cards that are matched while the banker has no
card become dead without the players losing their bets.

After the banker has a new card, players without cards may
take fresh cards as they appear, and place new bets.

Although players with outstanding side bets may make new
bets against the banker, they are not obliged to do so.

When the bank is exhausted, the bank must pass.

House percentage The house takes either:

a 25% of the last winning bet of each deal; or

b 2% from each bet won by a player against the banker, plus
2% of the banker's winnings, if any, at the end of his deal.

2-8   Slippery Sam

This is a private banking game related to red dog. It is
popular in parts of America's Midwest.

Equipment:
1 one standard deck of 52 cards;
2 betting chips or cash.
Players Ideally six to eight, but two or more can play.
Rank of cards is normal (ace high). Suits are not ranked.
Objective Players aim to hold a card in the same suit but of
a higher rank that the banker's card.
Choice of first banker is by high cut (see p 13).
Shuffle and cut are normal (see p 14).
Bank The banker places in the center of the table the amount
he wishes to put at risk. This is any amount above an agreed
minimum.
Deal The banker deals three cards to each player, dealing
them one at a time and face down. He then deals one card
face up to himself.
Play Players bet without looking at their hands. Play begins
with the player to the banker's left. He may agree or refuse
to bet against the exposed banker's card.
1 If he agrees, he bets any amount he chooses, above an
agreed minimum, up to the total amount in the bank. He then
looks at his cards. If he holds a card in the same suit but of
higher rank than the banker's card, he wins; if not, he loses.
2 Alternatively, he refuses to bet against the exposed
banker's card. In this case he says "Deal me another card."
For this privilege he may pay into the bank an amount equal
to one fifth of the bank (or, under alternative rules, he pays a
previously agreed amount).
The exposed banker's card is then discarded and another
card dealt from the top of the deck face up onto the table.
This becomes the new banker's card. The player either bets

Deal

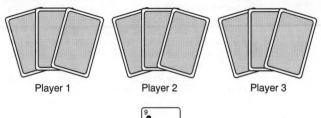

Player 1   Player 2   Player 3

Banker

Play

Player 1 wins

Player 2 loses

Banker's new card

Player 3 wins

against this card in the usual way, or pays again for a new banker's card to be dealt.

A player may reject the banker's card up to three times on a single hand, paying the same amount each time.

After the third rejection, the player may either bet in the usual way against the banker's card now exposed, or he may pass his turn without betting.

3 If the player has bet and won, he shows his winning card only. His bet is returned, plus an equal amount from the bank.

If he has bet and lost, he shows all his hand and his bet is added to the bank.

Whether he has won or lost, his hand is then added face down to a discard pile.

4 Bet and play then pass one player to the left, and continue in the same way. Each player's turn begins with the banker's card on which the last player bet or passed: a new banker's card is dealt only when paid for.

When all players except the banker have had a turn, the banker collects whatever amount is now in the bank. Bank and deal then pass one player to the left.

If the bank is emptied ("bust") before each player has had a turn, the bank and deal pass immediately.

Stuss

Stuss is a simplified form of faro with a larger percentage in the gambling house's favor.

Equipment:
1 a table with the stuss layout, usually made up of the entire spades suit;
2 a dealing box allowing one card to be removed at a time, but with a recess ("pocket") at the bottom of the box that prevents the last four cards of the deck appearing in play;
3 a standard 52-card deck;
4 betting chips of various colors.

Players Up to ten can play. House officials are a dealer and a lookout who supervises betting.

The objective is for a player to bet on a denomination that subsequently appears as a winning card before it appears as a losing card.

Cards appear in play two at a time. The first in each pair is always the losing card, the second is the winning card.

Shuffle, cut, and bet The house dealer shuffles the cards, cuts the deck, and puts it face down in the box.

Bets are then placed on the layout.

Betting A player may place as many bets as he wishes, but each bet is on one denomination only. A bet is always for a denomination to win – ie that the next card of that denomination to appear will be the second (winning) card in a turn.

A turn
1 The dealer removes the top card from the box and places it face up to the right.
2 Any bets on the denomination of this (losing) card are collected by the house.
3 The dealer removes the next card from the box and places it face up to the left.

4 Any bets on the denomination of this card are won by the bettors. Their bet is returned together with an equal payment by the house.

Between turns Other bets may be changed and new bets placed.

Continuing play Play continues in this way through the deck. The two cards in play in each turn are added to those played previously, to form a winning and a losing pile.

Eventually no more cards can be dealt. There will then have been 24 two-card turns, and four cards will still remain in the pocket of the box.

Pocket cards The dealer opens the box and shows the four remaining cards. If any bets have been placed on their denominations, they are all won by the house.

Splits If two cards of the same denomination appear on a turn (a "split'), any bets on that denomination are won by the house.

Second bets are bets on a denomination of which one card has already been dealt; usually they are bet on in the normal way. Some casinos, however, do not allow second bets. In this case, the last four cards are not "pocketed" but appear for play and for betting in the normal way.

Variants

1 In a very simple form of stuss, the cards are dealt from the hand.

2 Stuss is sometimes played as a private banking game; the role of banker is taken by the player willing to put up the largest bank.

2-5   Thirty-five

Thirty-five is a modern version of the Italian game of
trentacinque. Bets are placed in a central pool; there is no
banker.

Equipment:
1 one standard deck of 52 cards;
2 betting chips or cash.
Players The game is for two to five players.
Rank of cards Face cards count 10 points; others count their
numerical face value.

Card values

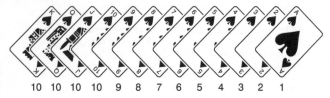

10 10 10 10   9   8   7   6   5   4   3   2   1

Objective Each player aims to hold a total of 35 points or
more in one suit.
Choice of first dealer is by high cut (see p 13).
Shuffle and deal are normal (see p 14).
Ante Before each hand, each player including the dealer
places an agreed equal amount in the center of the table to
constitute the pool.
Deal
1 The dealer deals one card face down to each player
including himself and then one card face down to the center
of the table. He continues in this way until each hand,
including the hand on the table, contains four cards. He then
deals no further cards to the center of the table, but continues

dealing to each player, including himself, until each has a further five cards. Thus the hand at the center of the table contains four cards and the other hands nine cards each.

2 The remaining cards of the deck are placed to one side and do not enter subsequent play.

3 The players then examine their cards. A player who holds cards in any one suit to the value of 35 or over announces this and takes the pool. If two or more players have 35 or more, the pool is divided between them.

4 If no player claims the pool, bidding begins.

Deal

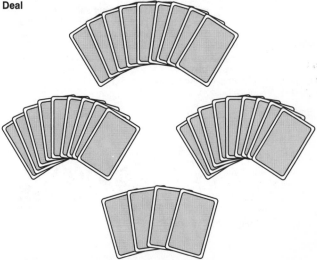

Bidding for the "buy" Betting takes the form of bidding for the table hand – the "buy."

Bidding begins with the player to the dealer's left. His opening bid may be any amount up to the total in the pool.

(If he does not wish to bid, he throws in his cards.) Thereafter, each player may raise the bid or throw in his cards until only one player is left prepared to bid. He then takes the table hand and adds it to the nine cards he already holds.

Settlement involves only the pool and the player who has taken the table hand. If the player now holds cards to the value of 35 or over in any one suit, he declares this, shows his cards, and takes an amount from the pool equal to his bid. If his bid exceeded the amount of the pool, he takes all the pool but has no further claim.

If the player does not hold cards in one suit to the value of 35 or more, he pays into the pool an amount equal to his bid.

Division of the pool Sometimes the pool becomes too large for the level of betting. It is best if a limit for the pool is agreed beforehand. If the pool passes that limit, it is divided among the players.

Change of dealer The deal passes one player to the left after each hand.

End of play

Making 35 – in hearts

Thirty-one

3-15

The name thirty-one comes from the number of points awarded to the highest scoring hand (ace, queen, 10 of the same suit) in this pool betting game. An alternative name is schnautz.

Equipment:
1 one standard deck of 52 cards;
2 betting chips or cash.
Players From 3 to 15.
Value of cards Aces count 11, face cards 10, and all other cards their numerical face value.

Card values

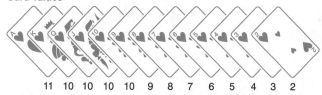

11 10 10 10 10 9 8 7 6 5 4 3 2

Rank of cards is normal, ace high. Thus although face cards all count 10, king beats queen, and queen beats jack.
Objective Players aim to obtain the highest points count from three cards of the same suit or rank.
Choice of first dealer is by low cut (see p 13).
Shuffle and cut are normal (see p 14).
Ante Before each hand, each player including the dealer puts an agreed amount into a pool.
Deal The dealer deals one card face down to each player including himself, beginning with the player to this left and going clockwise; and then one card face up to the center. This continues until all players and the table hand (the "widow") each have three cards.

Deal

"Widow"

Play Each player examines his cards and announces immediately if he holds:
a three cards of one suit – with a points total of 31 ("31 points");
b any three cards of the same rank ("three cards");
c three cards of one suit – with a points total that he feels is high enough to win ("x points").
If a player announces immediately, all players show their hands and the highest point count wins.
If a player announces immediately, the player to the dealer's left must exchange one of his cards with any face up card on the table. (Sometimes it is agreed that two or even three cards may be exchanged in one turn). He is not allowed to pass. The next player then does the same. Cards that have been put out by a player may subsequently be picked up.

Play continues around the table in this way until one player
has 31 points or is satisfied with his cards.

If a player has 31 points he must announce it immediately,
and all exchanging ends. All players then show their hands.

If a player is satisfied with his hand, he knocks on the table
instead of exchanging a card in his next turn. In this case,
hands are not shown until each of the other players in turn
has had the option of exchanging one more card.

The pool is won by the player who shows the best hand.
The deal then passes to the next player to the left.

Scoring of hands A hand with three cards of the same rank
scores 30 ½; all others score their points count.

Where two or more players have hands scoring the same
number of points, the hand containing the higher ranking
card wins. For example: ace, king, queen beats ace, queen,
jack. (Note that a score of 25 or 26 points often wins.)

Play

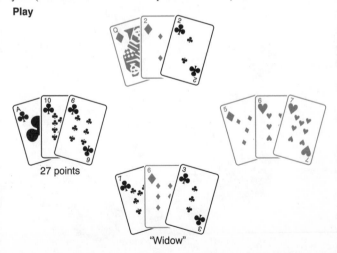

27 points

"Widow"

Trente et quarante

Trente et quarante is one of the most popular games in
French and Italian casinos, although it is rarely found
elsewhere. It originated in seventeenth-century Europe and is
also known as rouge et noir.

Equipment:
1 regulation table with trente et quarante double layout;
2 six standard 52-card decks shuffled together to form a
single deck of 312 cards;
3 an indicator card for cutting the deck.
Players Any number of people can play up to the limit that
the table will accommodate.

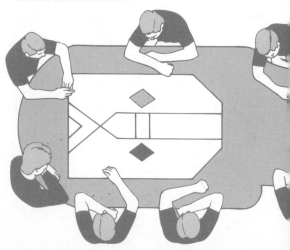

Five croupiers operate the game: four control the bank and one acts as dealer ("tailleur"). A supervisor sits on a stand overlooking the table.

Value of cards Court cards count 10. All other cards count their face value, with aces counting one.

Card values

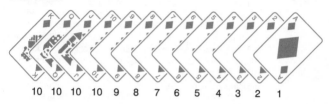

10   10   10   10   9   8   7   6   5   4   3   2   1

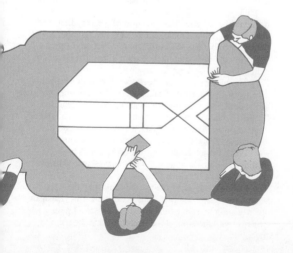

The objective is to bet which of two rows of cards will give a total points count near 31.

Shuffle and cut At the start of a round of play the dealing croupier spreads all six decks on the table. (If it is not the first round of play, the cards must first be taken from the discard receiver and sorted until they are all face down.) All croupiers and players each take a group of cards and shuffle them. The croupier then gathers all the cards and gives them a further shuffle. He offers one player the whole deck to cut. The player iserts the indicator card at the point at which he wants the cards cut. The dealer cuts the deck at this point and the indicator card and all cards above it go to the bottom of the deck.

Betting All bets are placed against the bank. Before the play, players bet in one or both of the following ways, placing their bets on the layout.

a Players bet which row will win, either black (N for "noir" on the layout) or red (R for "rouge").

b Players bet whether the suit color of the very first card dealt will or will not match the color of the winning row. If they want to bet that it will match, they bet on C for "couleur" on the layout. If they want to bet that it will not match, they bet on I for "inverse."

Play The players place their bets (see the section on betting). The dealing croupier then takes about 50 cards from the top of the deck and deals one card face up onto the table. He then deals further cards face up, placing them alternately to the right and left of the first card. After each card he announces the total number of points now contained in the row. When the total equals or passes 31 points he stops dealing. This first row is called the "black" row, whatever the suit color of the cards it contains.

The dealing croupier in exactly the same way then deals a second row below the first. This is the "red" row. He again stops dealing when the total equals or passes 31 points. The row with the points total nearer to 31 is the winning row.

Sample betting and play

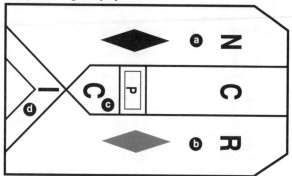

a bets black row to win
b bets red row
c bets first card will match winning row
d bets first card will not match winning row

Black row

    33 points

Red row

    37 points

The black row is nearer to 31, and so wins

a wins
b loses
c wins
d loses

The winning total will always be in the range 31 to 39 inclusive – ie between 30 and 40. It is from this that the game takes its name.

Settlement of bets After the deal the dealing croupier announces the result.

Traditionally he calls the results for red and color only, ie "Rouge gagne" (red wins) or "Rouge perd" (red loses), and "Couleur gagne" (color wins) or "Couleur perd" (color loses). The croupiers collect all losing bets. All winning bets are paid off at even money (1 to 1). If both rows tie at more than 31 (a "refait"), all bets are returned.

If both rows tie at 31 ("refait de trente et un") the bank takes half of all bets and returns the remainder, or, rather than lose half his bet, a player may decide to leave his bet in "prison" (P on the layout) for the next deal. If his original bet is successful in this next deal, his bet is returned but earns no money. If it is unsuccessful he now loses all his bet. (Sometimes with a bet in prison the player may choose whether to maintain his original bet or transfer it to its opposite.)

Insurance bet Before a hand is dealt, a player can indicate that he wishes to insure against a tie at 31. The charge for this is 5% of his wager.

Yablon

2-8

This game is also called in between and ace-deuce. It is most commonly played as a pool game.

Equipment:
1 one standard deck of 52 cards;
2 betting chips or cash.
Players From two to eight.
Rank of cards is normal, ace high. Suits have no significance.
Objective Each player hopes to draw a card ranking between his first two cards.
Choice of first dealer is by deal: first ace to appear (see p 13).
Shuffle and cut are normal (see p 14).
Ante Before each deal each player including the dealer puts an equal agreed amount into the pool.
Deal The dealer deals two face down cards one at a time to each player including himself.
Play Begins with the player to the dealer's left.
1 He examines his cards and decides whether to bet.
2 If he does not wish to bet he says "No bet," and returns his cards to the dealer to be placed on a discard pile. Play then passes to the left.
If the next player does not wish to bet, he places his bet in front of him near the pool. The minimum bet is the same amount as a player's ante; the maximum is the total then in the pool.
3 The dealer deals him the top card from the deck, face up. This is called the player's draw card.
4 The player turns his two original cards face up.
5 If his draw card ranks between his original two cards, the player wins. For example, if he has a 5 and a 9 he must draw a 6, 7 or 8 to win; if he has a 2 and an ace he can draw any

card except a 2 or an ace to win. Note that if a player holds
two identical cards (eg two 6s) or two consecutive cards (eg
10 and jack), he cannot win and will not bet.
6 If the player has won, he retains his bet and takes from the
pool a similar sum. If he has lost, his bet goes to the pool.
7 Each player including the dealer has a turn of play, with
turns passing to the left.
Continuing play After each player has had a turn, the deal
passes to the player to the dealer's left. He collects all the
cards, shuffles them and has them cut for the next hand.
Any money left in the pool remains for the next hand, but
players also ante again.
Division of pool If the pool passes a limit agreed beforehand
it is immediately divided among the players.

Deal

Play

Player wins

Consecutive cards: no bet

Player loses

BANKING VERSION

Yablon can also be played as a banking game. The dealer acts as banker and does not deal himself a hand.

Before the hand, the dealer places in front of him the money or chips he wishes to put at risk. This can be any amount he wishes. The players do not ante.

Each player in turn bets any amount he wishes, up to the amount then in the bank. The dealer does not have a turn. Any amount left in the bank at the end of the hand is returned to the banker. The bank and deal then pass one player to the left.

If the bank is emptied before all players have had a turn, the hand ends and the bank and deal pass at once.

2+ Ziginette

Ziginette is the Italians' favorite way of seeing money
change hands at cards. The rules given here are those played
in American gaming houses.

Equipment:
1 one standard 52-card deck from which all the 8s, 9s, and
10s have been removed, leaving 40 cards;
2 a metal card box that allows only one card to be removed
at a time.

Cards used

Players Two or more people can play. One person is the banker. There are also two house officials. One, the "cutter," collects and pays bets for the banker and takes the house percentage cut. (The house never banks the game). The other, the "lookout," keeps a watch on proceedings and transfers dead cards to the discard pile.

The objective is for a player to bet on a table card that is not matched by the time the banker's card has been matched. A card is "matched" when another card of the same denomination becomes visible at the top of the card box.

Choice of first bank is by deal – the first ace to appear. The cutter carries out the deal after he has shuffled the cards and has them cut by any player.

Shuffle and cut See p 14.

Any player other than the banker cuts the cards. The banker places the deck face up in the card box.

Deal The banker deals two cards from the box face up onto the table. The next card in the box is now visible: this is the banker's card.

If all three cards are of different denominations, players may now bet; if they are not, special rules govern further procedure (see the section on "playette," p 356).

Opening bet Any player other than the banker may place a bet on one or both of the table cards.

Betting limits The banker decides the minimum and maximum allowable bets and can alter them at will between stages of play.

Opening play The banker takes the banker's card from the box and places it so that one end rests beneath the card box but most of it is visible. It stays in this position for the rest of the deal.

This action exposes the next card in the box. If this card matches any card on the table (including the banker's card), any bets involved are settled. But if it does not match any card on the table, there is no further action in this turn, unless any player wishes to place a further bet.

Opening play

Banker's card matches

Table card matches

Settlement of bets If at any time a card exposed in the box matches the banker's card, the banker loses all unsettled bets, ie he pays all outstanding bets by players on all table cards. Settlement is at even money – a winning player gets back his stake plus an equal amount from the bank. Play on this deal then ceases and the bank and the deck pass one player to the right. If a card exposed in the box matches a table card on which bets have been placed, these bets are won by the banker and he continues to operate the bank.

The house cutter pays out the banker's loses and collects his winnings for him. He takes a 10% house cut from each bet won by the bank.

Next turn of play If the banker's card has not been matched, then any settlement of bets and placing of new bets ends the turn of play.

The exposed card is taken from the card box.

1 If the exposed card has matched a table card, then the exposed card and the table card it matched are now dead (even if the table card had no bets placed on it).

The cutter takes both cards and places them to one side out of play. They are dead for the remainder of the deal, as are the other two cards of the same denomination still in the card box. If cards appearing in the box are the same denomination as cards already matched, they are removed and added to the discard pile. The discard pile is kept fanned out so that the denominations of dead cards can be seen.

2 If the exposed card has not matched the table card, then it is placed face up on the table alongside the other table cards. It is now available for players to bet on in the usual way at the end of a turn of play, provided it is not immediately matched by the new exposed card in the box. If it is immediately matched, both it and the matching card are transferred to the discard pile in the usual way and the other cards of the same denomination are also dead.

Summary of continuation play After the opening play, turns are as follows.

1 The top card is removed from the card box. If, on the previous turn, this card matched the table card, both are placed on the discard pile. If the top card was the same denomination as a card already matched, the top card is added to the discard pile. If the top card matched neither a table card nor a dead card, it is added to the table cards.

2 If the card now exposed in the box matches a table card, any bets involved are settled. If it matches the banker's card, the banker collects all bets and the deal ends.

3 If the banker's card has not been matched, players can bet on any card now on the table. This includes any card just added to the table, providing that this card has not been immediately matched by the new card exposed in the box.

Playette This is the term used when two cards of the same denomination appear in the opening deal. It is usually ruled "no deal." The cards are removed from the box and reshuffled. Sometimes the rule is that duplicate cards are "doubled up."

Doubling up – opening deal If two table cards match they are placed together, and the top card from the box is dealt to fill the empty table position.

If a table card and a box card match, the box card is added to the table card's position. In either case, the next card in the box becomes the banker's card.

Doubling up

Doubling up – settlement of bets When any two cards have been doubled up, whatever the denomination, no bets are settled until three cards of that denomination have appeared. For example, the bank does not win the bet on the 6s until a further 6 has been exposed;

the bank does not win the bet on the queen of hearts until two further queens have been exposed;

the bank does not lose until two further 10s have been exposed.

Tripling If all three cards of the opening deal are of the same denomination, then (providing "doubling up" is allowed) they are all placed together on one of the table hand positions. No decision is reached on any bet, or on the bank, until four cards of a denomination have been exposed.

Change of banker A banker may pass the bank at any time when there are no unsettled bets on the table.

When the banker's card is matched he must pass the bank. All cards are collected, shuffled, and cut before the new game begins.

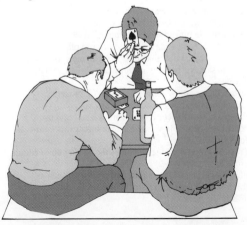

Section 3
SOLITAIRE CARD GAMES

PROCEDURE AND TERMS

Patience and solitaire are general names for any card game for one player. The exact origin of such games is obscure, but they have probably existed for centuries and several hundred different games exist today. Although the outcome of many of these games depends mainly on the luck of the shuffle, others involve real skill and judgment. In addition to games for one player, this section also includes two games for two players: Russian bank and spite and malice, which share many of the features of games devised for one.

Cards Some games are played with a standard 52-card deck, others with two decks shuffled together.

Yet others are played with a "stripped" deck, from which certain cards have been discarded prior to play.

Special cards, smaller than ordinary playing cards, may be used; these are especially useful when playing in a confined space.

Certain games allow for the inclusion of a joker.

Ace, unless otherwise specified, ranks low.

Objective The object of many games is to build up sequences of cards in their suits onto base cards known as "foundations."

A second group of games involves the pairing up of certain cards.

Other games have quite a different objective, such as rebuilding the deck into a single pile, or discarding all the cards in the deck.

3

If a game is successful, ie if the game's objective is exactly achieved, it is said to "come out" or to "go through."

If a game is "blocked" this means that the cards are such that the game cannot possibly be won.

Layout At the start of most games, cards are laid out in a prescribed formation that varies from game to game. This formation or "tableau," together with any other cards dealt out at the beginning of play, forms the "layout."

Foundation cards are the first cards of certain piles onto which sequences of cards are built (the objective of many games).

In some games they form part of the layout and are set out at the beginning of a game. More often, they are not included in the layout, but are put out as they come into play.

They are usually cards of a specified rank – often aces. With rare exceptions (such as in King Albert) a card cannot be removed once it has been placed in a foundation.

Spaces (sometimes called vacancies) are gaps in the layout into which cards may legitimately be played, or places from which the cards have been removed and which may or may not be reoccupied, depending on the rules of the game.

Reserve In some games the layout includes one or more cards that may be brought into play as appropriate. This "reserve" of cards may not, however, be built onto – unlike the cards in the tableau.

The stock comprises those cards that remain after the layout has been dealt.

The stock is invariably kept face down, and may be brought into play in different ways according to the rules for particular games.

Waste pile or heap Cards from the stock that cannot immediately be played onto the layout are sometimes placed face up in one or more waste piles, to be brought back into the game as appropriate.

The discard pile is made up of any cards that have been set aside during the course of play and that are not brought back into the game.

The objective of some games is to discard all or most of the deck.

Available cards Any card that can, in accordance with the rules, be played onto the tableau, foundations, or spaces is termed "available."

Sometimes the removal of a card "releases" the card next to it; for example when the top card of a waste pile is removed and makes the next card in the pile available for play.

Building

Exposed cards A card is usually only available for play if it is fully exposed, ie if no other card covers it either wholly or partially.

Building is the term used for placing a card onto the tableau, foundations, or a space in its correct sequence. This may be done numerically, by suit or by color.

a Cards may be "built down" numerically (eg a 7 is built onto an 8, a 6 onto the 7, etc).

b Cards may be "built up" numerically (eg a 3 is built onto a 2, a 4 onto the 3, etc).

c Sometimes the numerical sequence may be continuous or "round the corner" (eg 3,2,a,k,q), or in twos (eg 7,9,j,k,2,4, etc).

d A card may only be built onto another card of the same suit (eg all hearts). Or, in other games, a card may only be built onto a card of a suit other than its own.

e A card may only be built onto a card of the same color (eg all red cards).

f A card may only be built onto a card of the other color (eg red, black, red, black).

 **d**

 **e**

 **f**

Accordion

Accordion, also called Tower of Babel, idle year, or
Methuselah, is one of the most difficult single-deck games to
get out. It is unusual in that there is no formal layout at the
start of the game: the cards are merely dealt in a single row.

Cards One standard 52-card deck is used.
Objective The player aims to rebuild the deck into a single pile.
Play The cards are dealt out face up in a row, as many at a
time as space allows.
Any card may be moved onto the card immediately to the
left, or onto the third card to the left, provided it is of the
same suit or has the same rank.
A pile of two or more cards, identified by its top card, can be
similarly moved.
If a card matches both its neighbor and the card three to the
left, the player may choose either move, taking into account
the various possibilities.

Beleaguered castle

Beleaguered castle is also known by the names of sham
battle and laying siege.

Cards One standard deck of 52 cards is used.
Layout Set out the four aces in a column as foundation
cards. Then deal out the rest of the deck face up to form
wings of six overlapping cards to the left and right of each
ace; it is usual to deal columns of four cards alternately to
the left and to the right of the aces.
The objective is to build up each suit in ascending numerical
order, from ace through to king, on its correct foundation
card.
Play Only the fully exposed cards at the ends of the rows in
each wing are available for play (one card only being moved
at a time). Available cards can either be moved onto one of
the foundations, building suits numerically upward, or be
transferred to the end of another wing, building numerically
downward with no regard to suit. Spaces, created by removal
of an entire row, may be filled by transferring any exposed
card.

Layout

Foundations

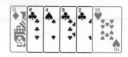

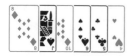

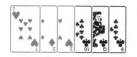

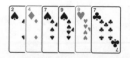

Bisley

Kings as well as aces come into play as foundation cards in this single-deck game.

Cards A standard 52-deck is used.
Layout Set out the four aces at the beginning of the top row of the tableau. Deal nine cards to the right of the aces; then deal the rest of the deck to complete a layout of four rows of 13 cards each. In the course of play, as they become available, the four kings are put out in a row above their aces (king of hearts above ace of hearts, etc).

Layout

Foundations

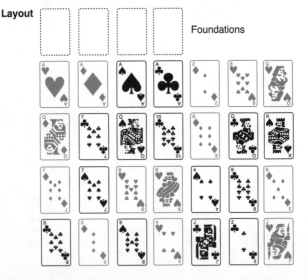

Objective The aces and the kings are foundation cards, and the aim is to complete entire suits, by building up in suit sequence on the aces and building down in suit sequence on the kings. When the two sequences meet they are put together (it does not matter at which point they meet).

Play The bottom card of each column of the tableau is available for play, either onto a foundation or onto the bottom card of another column.

Building onto the bottom cards of the columns is in ascending or descending suit sequence as the player wishes, and he may at any time reverse the order.

Spaces created in the tableau are not filled.

It is evidently important to free the kings as soon as possible, and to use every opportunity of building onto the foundations.

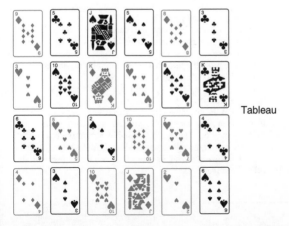

Tableau

Braid

Braid, or plait, is a straightforward game that gets its name from its particularly attractive layout.

Cards Two standard 52-card decks are used.
Layout Twenty cards are dealt face up in the form of a braid: the cards are laid out diagonally, and alternately pointing to right and left – each card partially covering the card beneath it (as illustrated).
Columns of six face up cards are dealt to either side of the braid; the braid and the columns together form the reserve. The next (33rd) card is placed to the right of the reserve. It determines the rank of the other seven foundations, which are set out as they become available to make two rows of four cards.
Objective The player tries to build ascending "round the corner" suit sequences on the eight foundations (ace following king and preceding 2).
Play The bottom (fully exposed) card of the braid and all the cards in the two columns are available for play onto the foundations.
The stock is dealt one card at a time, and if the card is unplayable it is placed on a waste heap.
Any number of redeals is permitted, until the game either becomes blocked or goes through.
A space in the columns must be filled as soon as it occurs. If the top or bottom card of a column has been removed, the vacancy may be filled by the available card of the braid, or from the top of the waste heap (which is always available). If the vacancy is anywhere else in the column, it may only be filled from the stock.

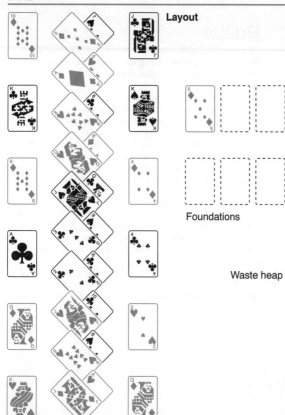

Layout

Foundations

Waste heap

Reserve   Reserve

Bristol

In this game, eight fans and three waste heaps provide the
cards to be transferred onto four foundations.

Cards One standard 52-card deck is used.
Layout Deal 24 cards, face up, in eight fans each of three
cards. Any kings that turn up in the deal are placed at the
bottom of their respective fans.
Next to this tableau, deal three more cards face up in a row
to form the start of the waste heaps or reserve.
Objective The foundation cards are aces, which are set out
in a row above the tableau as they occur in play. The aim is
to build four ascending sequences, ace through king,
regardless of suit or color.
Play The top cards of the fans and the three waste heaps are
available for play, but only one card may be moved at a time
– either to a foundation or in descending sequence,
regardless of suit or color, onto the exposed card of another
fan.
The stock is dealt three cards at a time, one card to each of
the three waste heaps.
Spaces in the waste heaps are filled only in the deal. Spaces
in the tableau (caused by the removal of an entire fan)
remain unfilled. Only one deal is permitted.

Layout

Foundations

Tableau

Waste heaps

Calculation

Calculation is an aptly named game, for it involves a
considerable amount of thinking ahead. (It is sometimes
called broken intervals.)

Cards One standard 52-card deck is used.
Layout Set out in a row any ace, 2, 3, and 4 as the
foundation cards.
The objective is to build up the rest of the deck on these
base cards regardless of suit or color, but strictly in
accordance with the following order:
On the ace: 2,3,4,5,6,7,8,9,10,j,q,k.
On the 2: 4,6,8,10,q,a,3,5,7,9,j,k.
On the 3: 6,9,q,2,5,8,j,a,4,7,10,k.
On the 4: 8,q,3,7,j,2,6,10,a,5,9,k.
Play Cards are turned up one at a time and either built onto
the appropriate base card or placed on one of the four waste
heaps immediately beside these.
Only the top card on each waste heap is available and cards
cannot be moved from one waste heap to another.
Any space in the waste heaps is filled with the top card of
the stock.
Much of the skill of the game lies in playing the cards to the
various heaps in such a way that they are later readily
available for transfer to foundations.
For example, it is best to keep kings in one waste heap or, if
they come out early, at the bottom of the waste heaps. Cards
of the same rank should be dispersed among the waste heaps
rather than concentrated in any single heap.
Whenever possible, cards should be played to the waste
heaps in reverse order to their build-up on the foundations.

Layout

Foundations   Waste heaps

Order of building

   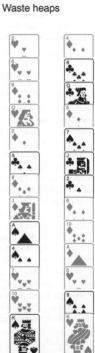

Canfield

Canfield is named for the nineteenth-century American gambler and art collector Richard A. Canfield; this game is one of the most popular single-deck games. It is sometimes known as demon in the United Kingdom. (Another game sometimes known as Canfield in the United Kingdom is described here as Klondike.)

Cards One standard 52-card deck is used.

Layout Deal out a reserve pile of 13 cards face down, then turn the pile over to expose one card. Deal four more face up cards to the right of the reserve to form a tableau.

Above the first card of the tableau place the next card face up; this is the first of the four foundation cards and its rank determines the other three cards (which are laid out as they come into play).

Should one of the tableau cards have the same rank as the foundation, move it up into position and deal another card into the space left in the tableau.

The objective of the game is to build up the four suits on the foundation cards.

The cards rank continuously, ie if the foundation cards are kings, the next cards in the sequence must be aces.

Play The stock is turned over three cards at a time, only the exposed card of each three being in play (although cards below it can be played as they become available).

If there are only one or two cards at the end of the stock, they are dealt singly.

Cards are built up by suit on the foundations, and in descending alternate-color sequence regardless of suit on the columns of the tableau.

Provided the correct color and numerical sequences are maintained, an entire column of tableau can be transferred to another column.

Spaces in the tableau are filled immediately from the reserve. If the reserve is exhausted, the player may fill the space from the top of the waste heap, but he need not do so immediately.

Redeal The stock may be redealt, without shuffling, as many times as necessary until the game either blocks or is won.

Layout

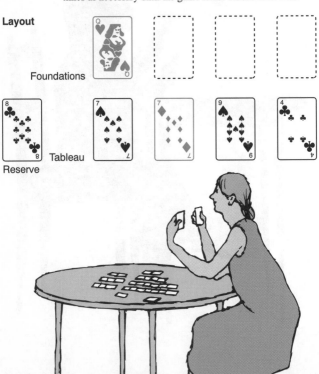

Foundations

Tableau

Reserve

Play

Reserve

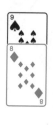

Waste heap

Clock

Although the chances of winning this game are slight, it is fun to play and very fast-moving. The name clock comes from the layout, which takes the form of a clock dial. Other names by which this game is known are sun dial, travelers, hidden cards, and four of a kind.

Layout

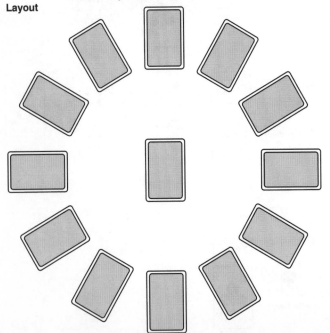

Cards One standard 52-card deck is used.

Layout The deck is dealt face down into 13 piles of four cards each. The cards may be dealt singly or in fours. The piles are arranged to represent a clock dial, one pile corresponding to each hour. The thirteenth pile is placed in the center.

Objective By rearranging the cards, the player hopes to end up with thirteen piles of like-numbered cards in their correct "time" position: the four aces at one o'clock, the four 2s at two o'clock, and so on around the dial.

The jacks represent 11 o'clock and the queens 12 o'clock. The four kings make up the thirteenth, center pile.

Play The player takes the card at the top of the center pile and places it face up at the bottom of the pile of the same number or "time." For example, if the card is a 7, it is put face up underneath the seven o'clock pile.

The player then takes the top card of the seven o'clock pile and puts it under its matching pile.

In this way the player works his way from pile to pile, always removing the top card of the pile under which he has just put its matching card.

If the player turns a card that happens to be on its correct pile (eg a 3 is turned up from the three o'clock pile), it is still placed at the bottom of the pile in the usual way, and the next face down card is taken from the top of the pile.

The outcome depends on the order in which the kings are turned up. If the fourth king is turned up before all the other cards are face up, then the game is blocked. This means in effect that the game can only be won if the last card to be turned up is the fourth king. As the chance of this happening is very small, the king may be exchanged for any one face down card in the layout. Only one exchange is allowed, and if the fourth king is again turned up before the other cards are in the correct piles, then the game is lost.

Crazy quilt

Crazy quilt is an unusual and interesting solitaire that gets its name from its layout of interwoven cards. It is also known as Indian carpet or Japanese rug.

Cards Two standard 52-card decks are used.
Layout Take an ace and a king of each suit and set them out face up in a row. These are the eight foundations.
Above them, deal out a reserve or "quilt" of eight rows of eight face up cards each, laying the cards vertically and horizontally in turn. Any card in the quilt that has one or both of its narrow sides free is available for play. For example, at the start of play four projecting cards at each side of the quilt are available.
Objective The aim is to build ascending suit sequences on the aces, and descending suit sequences on the kings.
Play Study the reserve to see if any available cards can be built onto the foundations. The removal of the reserve card releases one or more other reserve cards for play.
Spaces in the reserve remain unfilled.
Then turn up the stock one card at a time, putting the card in a waste heap if it cannot be played to a foundation. (The top card of the waste heap is always available.)
In order to release a useful card in the quilt, an available card may be played from the quilt to the top of the waste heap in either ascending or descending suit sequence.
The stock may be redealt once.

Waste heap

Layout

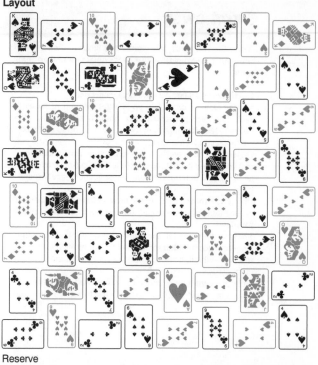

Reserve

Foundations

Eight away

Also called eight off, this game has a tableau of eight
columns, none of which must ever contain more than eight
cards.

Cards One standard 52-card deck is needed.
Layout Deal 48 cards face up in eight columns of six cards
each. The cards in each column should overlap so that all are
visible. Deal the remaining four cards face up in a row below
the tableau to form the start of the reserve.
Objective The player's aim is to free the aces (which are
moved as they become available to form a row above the
tableau), and to build on them suit sequences, ace through
king.
Play The exposed cards in the tableau (those at the bottoms
of the eight columns) and all the reserve cards are available
for play.
They can be moved to the foundations, built in descending
suit sequence on other exposed cards, or moved to the
reserve – which, however, must never contain more than
eight cards.
Only one card may be moved at a time. Any space that
occurs in the tableau can be filled only by an available king.

Layout

Foundations

Tableau

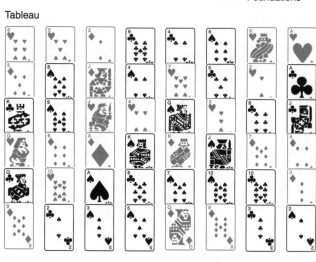

Reserve

Florentine

Features of this game are a tableau in the form of a five-card
cross, and four foundations of which the bases are
determined by the sixth card to be dealt.

Cards One standard deck is used.
Layout Deal five cards face up to form a cross. Deal a sixth
card face up at the top left-hand corner. The rank of this card
denotes the foundations; the other three cards of that rank
being placed at the other corners as they come into play.
The objective is to build up ascending suit sequences on the
four foundation cards.
Aces follow kings.

Layout

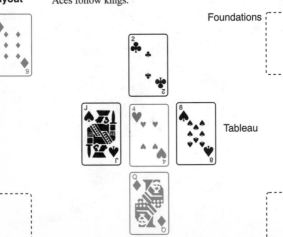

Foundations

Tableau

Play Cards from the stock are dealt one at a time. They can be played on the foundations if eligible, or packed in downward sequences regardless of suit on the four outer cards of the cross. The center card of the cross is at all times kept clear.

If one of the outer cards is transferred to a foundation card or packed on another outer card, the vacancy thus created is filled by a card from the waste heap, or by the center card of the cross (which is then replaced by a card from the waste heap).

The waste heap can be turned over and relayed once without shuffling.

Flower garden

In this game cards from fans, called flower beds, and cards
from the hand, or bouquet, are built onto foundation cards.
The flower beds are collectively called the flower garden.

Cards One standard deck is needed.
Layout Deal out 36 cards into six fans to form the flower
garden. The remaining cards form the bouquet, and may be
held in the hand or spread out on the table.
The objective is to free the aces, which are set out below the
garden as they become available, and to build onto them suit
sequences in ascending order, aces through king.

Layout

Tableau

Foundations

Play The exposed cards of each bed and all the bouquet cards are available for play. They may be played onto a foundation, or added to a bed in downward numerical sequence, regardless of suit.

A sequence may be transferred from one bed to another, provided that the correct numerical order is preserved. If a space is created by the removal of an entire bed, it may be filled by any available card, or by a sequence from another bed.

Friday the thirteenth

This game requires the player to establish and build upon 13 foundations, each based on a card of a different rank.

Cards One standard deck is used.

Layout Set out in a row from left to right any jack, queen, king, and ace – regardless of suit. Leave enough space to the right of them for a further nine cards to be added to the row.

The objective is to establish a total of 13 foundation cards – the jack, queen, king, and ace and then any 2 through 10 as they come up in play – onto which the remaining cards (the stock) are built up four to a pile in ascending numerical order, regardless of suit or color.

Play Work through the stock, turning one card at a time face upward and building it onto one of the foundations (eg a queen onto the jack), or putting it out as the next foundation card. The foundations must be set out in their correct order: for example, a 3 cannot be laid out before the 2 has been established.

If a card cannot be played immediately, it is put face up on a waste heap.

Where there is a choice, it is usually better to establish a new base card rather than to build onto an existing pile. For example, if the first card turned up were a 2, it would be wiser to use it as the next base card rather than building it onto the ace.

Foundations

Layout

The waste heap Any exposed card on the waste heap is available for play. When the stock is exhausted, the waste heap is turned over and may be replayed once without shuffling.

Frog

This two deck game is also called toad in the hole. There are eight foundations based on aces, and five waste heaps.

Cards Two standard decks are used.

Layout Deal a reserve pile of 13 cards face up. If any of these cards are aces, set them out to the right of the reserve as foundations.

If no aces are turned up, take one ace of any suit from the stock to begin the foundation row.

The other aces are added to the row as they turn up in play, to give a complete row of eight foundations.

The objective is to build on the aces, ascending sequences from ace to king, regardless of suit or color.

Layout

Reserve   Foundations

Play Cards are turned up from the stock one at a time and
played either onto the foundations or onto any one of five
waste heaps.

The waste heaps are set out below the foundations, and cards
may be added to them in any order the player chooses.

The top card of the reserve and the top cards of the waste
heaps are available at all times for playing onto the
foundations.

If a space occurs in the waste heaps it is filled from the
stock; if the reserve is exhausted it is not replaced.

It is sound strategy to keep one waste heap for high-value
cards such as kings and queens, and – if at all possible – to
add cards to the waste heaps in descending numerical order
so as to avoid burying low-ranking cards.

Waste heaps

King Albert

This game is named for King Albert I of the Belgians, who during World War I led his country's army against the Germans. Cards from the tableau and from the "Belgian Reserve" are built onto four foundation cards.

Cards One standard deck is used.
Layout Forty-five cards are dealt face up in rows from left to right, to form a tableau of nine columns.
The first column has one card, the second column two, and so on – the last column comprising nine cards.
The cards in each column should overlap so that all are visible.

Layout

Tableau

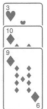

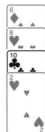

Reserve

The remaining seven cards, known as the "Belgian Reserve," may either be held in the hand or fanned out next to the tableau.

The objective is to free the four aces (the foundations), which are placed above the tableau as they come into play. Cards are built onto them in ascending suit sequence, from ace through king.

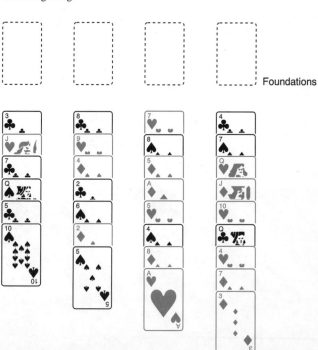

Foundations

Play All cards in the reserve are available, as are the exposed cards of the tableau.

Only one card may be moved at a time, either onto a foundation pile or in descending, alternate-color sequence on the columns of the tableau.

If an entire column becomes vacant, the space may be filled by any available card.

If the player wishes, he may transfer cards from the foundations to the tableau, provided that they fit into the correct numerical and color sequence.

Klondike

Klondike probably owes its great popularity to its combination of judgment, luck, attractive layout, and fast-moving tempo – all ingredients of a good patience game. (In the United Kingdom this game is sometimes called Canfield.)

Cards One standard 52-card deck is used.
Layout Deal a row of seven cards, with only the first card face up. Add another row of six cards, with the first card face up on the second card of the first row, and the others face down. Deal five more rows in the same way, each row

Layout

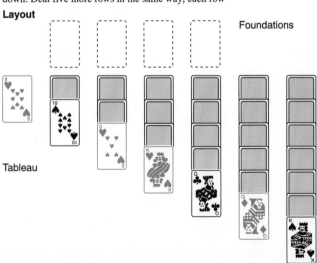

Foundations

Tableau

having one card fewer than the row beneath it and having
only its first card face up.

Objective The four aces are the foundation cards, and they
are set out above the tableau as they become available. The
object is to build up the four suits on their respective aces in
correct ascending order.

Play The hand is played one card at a time and once only.
Cards that are not immediately playable are put face up in a
waste heap, the top card of which is always available.

Cards are built up in their correct suits on the foundations, or
added to the columns of the tableau in descending, alternate-
color order (regardless of suit).

The top (fully exposed) card of each tableau column is
always available for play onto a foundation or another
column.

By removing an exposed card, the face down card beneath it
is turned up and becomes available.

Sequences in the tableau may be transferred from one
column to another, but only as a complete unit.

Spaces created in the tableau can only be filled by kings.
These may be taken (together with any cards built onto
them) either from the stock or from anywhere in the tableau.

La belle Lucie

This game has an attractive layout in which cards are
arranged initially in fans of three cards each. Cards are then
moved from fan to fan to free cards to be built onto four
foundation piles.

Cards One standard deck is used.
Layout The deck is dealt out into 17 fans of three cards each
and one single card.
Objective The aces are the foundation cards, and they
are set out in a row above the tableau as they come
into play. Cards are built onto the foundations
in ascending suit sequence, from ace through king.

Layout

Foundations

Tableau

Play The top card of each fan and the single card are
available for play. One card at a time may be moved onto a
foundation, or built onto another fan in downward suit
sequence.

Cards may always safely be built onto the foundations, but
any building down on the fans should be carefully
considered, as any cards to the left of the built-down cards
consequently become immobilized.

Any spaces caused by the removal of a fan are left unfilled.

Redealing Two redeals are permitted. When no further play
is possible, all cards other than those on the foundation piles
are gathered up, thoroughly shuffled, and redealt into fans of
three cards (any one or two remaining cards forming a
separate fan). After the second redeal, the player may pick
out and play one card from any fan of his choice.

Leapfrog

Moving cards leapfrog fashion about the tableau makes for
an unusual and interesting game.

Cards One standard deck is required.
Layout Deal out 20 cards face up into four rows of five
cards each.
The objective is to deal out all the remaining cards onto the
table, and to end with as many spaces as possible in the
layout.

Layout

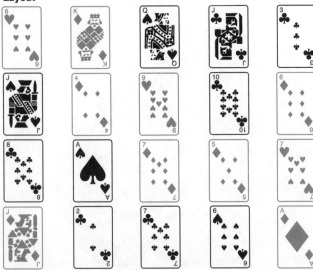

Play Moves in leapfrog are very like the "jumping" moves in a game of checkers.

A card in the layout may be "leapfrogged" over an adjoining card (either horizontally, vertically, or diagonally), provided that the card onto which it lands is of the same suit or rank.

A card so played now becomes the top and identifying card of a pile, and in any subsequent leapfrogging the whole pile is moved.

A move is not limited to a single leapfrog: a succession of leapfrogs is sometimes possible.

Any card leapfrogged by another card is removed to a waste heap.

Empty spaces are filled by cards dealt from the hand whenever the player wishes. (It is better to fill the gaps as soon as they occur, in order to provide a wider choice of moves.)

Maze

Although maze is not one of the better known patience
games, it is particularly satisfying and requires time and
ingenuity to succeed.

Cards One standard 52-card deck is used.
Layout The entire deck is dealt face up into two rows of
eight cards and four rows of nine cards.
The four kings are then discarded, leaving a total of six
spaces.
Objective By rearranging the cards one at a time, the player
aims to get the four suits into their correct ascending
sequence, ace through queen – one suit following the next.
(The order of the suits is immaterial.)
The cards must run from left to right and from the end of one
row to the beginning of the next. During play the top row is
counted as following on from the bottom row.
In the final sequence, the first card must be an ace and the
last card a queen.
For example, in a successful game the order might be:
ace of hearts through queen of hearts, ace of spades through
queen of spades, ace of clubs through queen of clubs, ace of
diamonds through queen of diamonds.
Play A card may be moved into any of the six spaces
provided it is in the same suit as the card to the left or the
right side of the space and that it is either:
lower than the card to the right of the space; or
higher than the card to the left of the space.
(For example, a 2 of diamonds may be moved into a space
that either has an ace of diamonds to its left or a 3 of
diamonds to its right.)
Whenever there is a space to the right of a queen, it may be
filled with any of the four aces (even if there is no matching
2 on the right of the space).

Layout

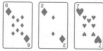

Miss Milligan

In this two-deck game, cards are dealt eight at a time onto
the tableau for transference onto eight foundations based on
aces.

Cards Two standard decks are required.
Objective With the eight aces as the foundations, the player
aims to build up the cards into ascending suit sequences.
Play Deal out eight cards face up in a row. If any of these is
an ace, set it out above the row as a foundation. Also move
any cards that can be built up on the ace in correct suit
sequence, or arrranged in descending alternate-color
sequence on other cards in the row.
Now deal out another row of eight cards, overlapping cards
already in position or filling in any spaces as appropriate.
Once again, study the layout to see which cards may be built
onto the foundations or transferred to other columns.
(Several cards may be transferred together, provided they are
in correct sequence.)
If at this stage a space occurs, it may only be filled by a king
(plus any cards built onto it).
Continue in this way until the entire stock has been dealt –
always completing all possible moves before dealing out the
next batch of cards.
Weaving When no cards remain in the stock, the player may
lift up any one available card or build from the tableau, and
set it aside as a reserve.
Each of these reserve cards is available, and the player tries
to rebuild them onto the tableau or foundations.
If he fails in rebuilding the reserve, the game is lost. If he
succeeds, however, he may repeat the "weaving" process
until the game goes through or is blocked.

Start of play

Foundations

First row of cards

Foundations

Cards moved into
appropriate columns

Monte Carlo

Monte Carlo, also called weddings or double and quits, is a
straightforward pairing game.

Layout   Cards One standard deck of 52 cards is used.

Layout Twenty cards are dealt out into four rows of five cards each. (Some players may prefer to deal out 25 cards in five rows of five cards each.)

Objective At the end of a successful game the player will have dealt out the entire deck and paired up all the cards, leaving an empty layout.

Play Any two cards of the same rank that touch each other top to bottom, side to side, or corner to corner are discarded. The spaces thus made are filled by closing up the remaining cards of the layout from right to left, moving up cards from row to row as necessary, but preserving their order as originally laid out.

Extra cards are added from the stock to complete the layout, and the process is repeated until further pairing is impossible, or until the game goes through.

Napoleon at St. Helena

Although Napoleon was recorded as having played patience while in exile on St. Helena, it is most unlikely that he invented or even played the many games attributed to him today. The game described here is among the most interesting of this group. Its other names are forty thieves and big forty.

Cards Two standard 52-card decks are used.
Layout Deal out forty cards into four overlapping rows of ten cards each. The bottom card in each column is available for play.

Layout

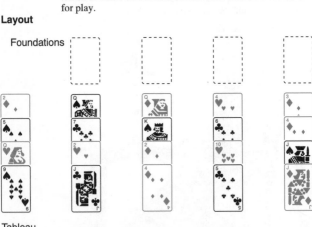

Foundations

Tableau

The objective is to build up suit sequences through to the kings on the eight aces, which are set out in a row above the tableau as they come into play.

Play The stock is turned over one card at a time and is either played onto the foundations, or built onto the tableau in downward suit sequence. If unplayable, cards are placed on a waste heap, of which the top card is always available. Available tableau cards may similarly be played one at a time onto the foundations or onto another column of the tableau.

Spaces If an entire column of the tableau is cleared away, the resulting space may be filled by any one available card from elsewhere in the tableau or from the top of the waste heap.

The player should choose this card carefully, as it may give him the opportunity of releasing useful cards.

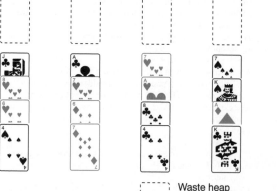

Waste heap

Poker solitaire

Poker solitaire is a very challenging game that needs a mixture of luck, judgment, and practice to score well. It is a useful game for familiarizing the beginner with the scoring combinations used in regular poker.

Cards One standard deck of 52 cards is used.
Layout The tableau for poker solitaire comprises five rows of five face up cards each.
Play The cards are dealt out one by one from a thoroughly shuffled deck. Each card may be placed anywhere within the limits of the tableau.
Once in position a card may not be moved; its placing on the tableau is therefore of great importance.
Objective Each row and each column of the tableau is the equivalent of a poker hand (ie there is a total of 10 hands). The player tries to place the cards of each "hand" to give the highest possible scoring poker combinations.
Scoring Two different scoring systems – British and American – are given in the table on p 412. A score of about 50 (British) or 150 (American) is considered good, and a score of about 60 (British) or 200 (American) excellent.
Ace can rank either high or low, but may not form part of a "round the corner" sequence (ie king, ace, 2 is not allowed).
Alternative rules
1 In order to improve his chance of a good score, the player may include a joker in the deal.
He can either:
a substitute the joker for one of the 25 cards before dealing them; or
b play all 25 cards in the usual way, exchanging the joker for any one card of his choice before totalling the score.

Sample play

One pair	Flush	One pair	Flush	Straight

Full house

Three of a kind

Straight

Four of a kind

No score

2 Another simplification of the game involves dealing out all 25 cards at the start of play in random order, and then rearranging them at will to form the best possible hands.
3 If the player wishes to make the game more taxing, he may only place a card onto the tableau if it touches a previously played card either horizontally, vertically, or diagonally (rather than placing it anywhere within the confines of the tableau).

Scoring table

Combination	British	American	Definition
Royal flush	30	100	A, k, q, j, 10 of one suit
Straight flush	30	75	Sequence of five cards in one suit
Four of a kind	16	50	Four cards of the same rank with one odd card
Full house	10	25	Three cards of one rank and two of another
Flush	5	20	Any five cards of the same suit
Straight	12	15	Five cards in sequence regardless of suit
Three of a kind	6	10	Three cards of the same rank with two odd cards
Two pairs	3	5	Two pairs with one odd card
One pair	1	2	One pair with three odd cards

Puss in the corner

This game has one of the most straightforward layouts of all single-deck games

Cards One standard deck is used.
Layout The four aces are placed face up in a square, and then during the course of play four waste heaps are established at its corners.
The object of the game is to build up ascending sequences, ace through king, according to color but irrespective of suit.
Play Cards are played from the stock one at a time, either

Layout

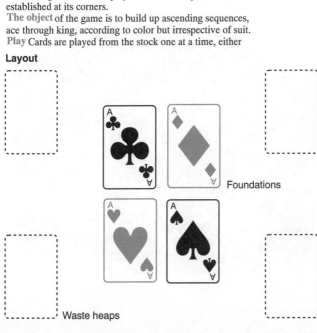

Foundations

Waste heaps

onto the aces (the foundation cards) or – if ineligible – onto one of the four waste heaps.

The top cards of the waste heaps are always available for play.

The player can choose onto which of the four waste heaps he wishes to put a card.

It is wise to reserve one heap for face cards, and if possible to avoid burying low-value cards under higher ones.

Redeal When the stock is exhausted, the cards in the waste heaps are collected in any order and redealt once without shuffling.

Pyramid

In its opening stages this game of pairing cards appears
deceptively easy, and the player may think he is well on the
way to winning. He will need a lot of lucky card
combinations, however, for the game to go through!

Cards One standard deck of 52 cards is used.

Layout Twenty-eight cards are dealt face up in seven rows
to form a pyramid. (See diagram overleaf.)
Each card is overlapped by two other cards in the row below,
except for the cards in the bottom row, which are fully
exposed. Only the fully exposed cards are available for play
(ie at the start of the game the seven cards in the bottom row).
When two cards are discarded during the course of play, the
card they were overlapping becomes exposed and available
for play.

The objective is to pair off the entire deck.

Play Any two available cards that together total 13
(regardless of color or suit) are paired off and placed in a
waste heap.
The kings are worth 13 and may be discarded singly.
Queens are worth 12, jacks 11, and aces one.
For example, a 10 can be paired with a 3, a jack with a 2, or
a 4 with a 9.
Cards in the stock are turned up one by one onto a waste
heap, of which the top card is always available.
A pair may be made up of:
two tableau cards;
one tableau card and one card from the stock; or
two stock cards (the top card from the waste pile plus the
next stock card turned up).

Redeal When the stock has been dealt once and no further
pairing is possible, the waste pile may be redealt without
shuffling.

Layout

Tableau

Waste heaps

Some players permit two redeals; others prefer not to allow any redeal.

Royal cotillion

Named for an eighteenth-century French court dance for four
couples, this two deck game uses for its foundations four
aces coupled with four 2s.

Cards Two standard decks are needed.
Layout Set out face up in two columns an ace and a 2 of
each suit.
To the left of the ace column, deal 12 cards face up in three
rows of four cards each.

Layout

To the right of the 2 column, deal 16 cards face up in four
rows of four cards each.
(Some players prefer to establish the two central columns by
putting out the aces and 2s as they come into play.)
The objective is to build suit sequences in the following
order:

on the aces, 3, 5, 7, 9, j, k, 2, 4, 6, 8, 10,q;

on the 2s, 4, 6, 8, 10, q, a, 3, 5, 7, 9, j, k.

Play Only the bottom card of each column in the left wing of
cards is available for play onto a foundation card, and the
space made by such a move is not filled.

All the cards in the right wing are available, however, and
spaces that occur must be filled immediately, with the top card
of either the waste heap or the stock.

The stock is played one card at a time. Any card that cannot
be built on a foundation or is not required for filling a space
is put on the waste heap, of which the top card is always
available. There is no redeal.

Russian bank

Also known as crapette, this patience game for two players requires a great deal of concentration. Moves are made according to a strict procedure which, if broken, may result in the player forfeiting his turn.

Cards Two standard decks are used. Each player should have his own deck with a distinctive back in order to avoid confusion.

Cards rank: k (high), q,j,10,9,8,7,6,5,4,3,2,a (low).

The objective A player's objective is to build all or as many as possible of the cards in his deck onto the foundations, the tableau, or his opponent's reserve or discard piles.

Preliminaries Each player draws a card from one of the decks: the player drawing the lower card will play first. Players then shuffle and cut their opponent's deck.

Layout To establish his reserve, each player counts out 12 cards from his deck and places them face down in a pile to his right.

Both players then deal out a column of four face up cards above their reserve: these eight cards form the tableau and are for common use.

The remaining cards in each deck are placed face down in a pile in front of each player and form his stock.

Foundations The eight aces are the foundations. They are laid out between the two columns of the tableau as they come into play. Cards are built onto the foundations in ascending suit sequence.

Building cards onto the foundations is also called building to the "center." Once a card has been built onto a foundation, it may not be removed.

Play The player who drew the lower card plays first; thereafter players take alternate turns.

Cards must be moved according to a set procedure, as follows.

Layout

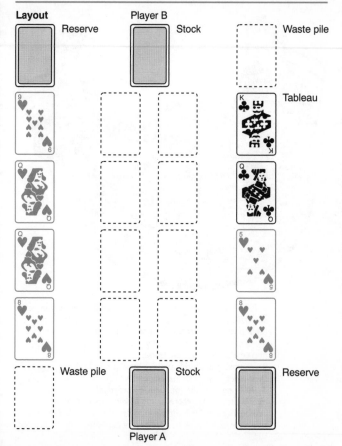

1 Both players must start their opening turns by playing any available tableau cards to the center. They must then turn up the top card of their reserve and – if possible – play that to the center. If it cannot be played to the center, it may be played elsewhere on the layout.

2 In subsequent turns, players may turn over the top card of their reserve prior to making a play.

3 Building onto the foundation always takes precedence over building elsewhere on the layout. Also, if there is a choice of cards for building onto the center, cards from the reserve must always be used before cards from the tableau or stock.

4 If no more cards can be built onto the foundation, the player may build onto the tableau in descending alternate-color sequence. He may use the top card from another tableau pile, the reserve, or the stock – there is no order of precedence.

(Players should take every opportunity of rearranging tableau cards, so as to free blocked cards for play to the center.)

Cards in the tableau piles should be built in overlapping rows, so that all the cards are visible.

5 A space in the tableau may be filled by the top card of another tableau pile, the reserve, or, once the reserve is exhausted, from the stock. (Spaces need not be filled as soon as they occur.)

6 If no cards can be built to the center and the top reserve card cannot be built onto the tableau, the player may turn up the top card in his stock. If this card can be played directly to the center or the tableau, the next card in the stock may be turned up, and so on until an unplayable stock card is turned up. As soon as this happens, the player must move the unplayable card face up onto a waste pile to his left. His turn then ends.

7 Cards in the waste pile cannot be played. If the player's stock is exhausted, he may, however, take the waste pile and turn it face down and unshuffled to form a new stock.

Loading Once all available cards have been played to the center, the player has the option of "loading" cards onto his opponent's reserve or waste piles in up or down suit sequence. The player must use cards from the tableau, or from his own reserve and stock.

Should the opponent's top reserve card be face down, the player may ask him at any time to turn it face up.

If an opponent has used up his reserve or waste pile (ie toward the end of the game) a player cannot off-load cards onto the resultant spaces.

Stops If a player thinks that his opponent has made an error in procedure, he may call "Stop," and play must immediately be halted.

If the error is proved, the wrongly moved card is returned to its former position and the offending player forfeits the rest of that turn.

Should an error not be noticed until after further moves have been made, the offender is allowed to continue without penalty.

Result The game is won by the first person who succeeds in discarding his entire deck, ie all the cards in his reserve, stock, and waste pile.

He scores 30 points for winning, plus two points for each card left in his opponent's reserve and one point for each left in his opponent's stock and waste pile.

If neither player succeeds in winning outright, the game is considered a draw.

Alternatively, players can evaluate their remaining cards to decide who wins. Each player counts two points for each card in his reserve and one point for each card in his stock and waste pile; the player with fewer points then scores the difference between his points total and that of his opponent.

Scorpion

The unwary player may be caught out by the scorpion's "sting" at the tail end of the game – since delay in exposing the hidden cards may prevent the game going through!

Cards One standard deck of 52 cards is used.

Layout Deal three rows of seven cards each – the first four cards in each row face down and the remainder face up. Below these deal four more rows of seven cards each, all face up. This makes a total of 49 cards in the tableau, and the three cards left over are put face down as the reserve.

Objective The four kings are the foundations onto which the cards are built in descending suit sequence (king through ace). The kings are not removed to separate foundation piles, but are built onto within the tableau.

Play Cards are built on the exposed cards of the layout (ie the bottom card of each column) in correct descending order and suit.

If, as in the example illustrated, the 6 of hearts is exposed, the 5 of hearts may be moved onto it. It may be taken from anywhere within the layout, but all the cards laid on top of it must also be moved.

Nothing may be built onto an ace.

Face down cards As each face down card is reached (by the removal of the card or cards on top of it) it is turned face up. The sooner the hidden cards are uncovered, the better the player's chances of getting the game through. It is therefore advisable to plan moves that will clear the face down cards as rapidly as possible.

Spaces and reserve If an entire column is cleared away, the space may be filled by a king (and any cards laid on top of it).

A space need not be filled as soon as it occurs.

When no further moves are possible, the three reserve cards are turned up and added to the layout, one to the foot of each of the three left-hand columns.

Not all spaces need to be filled before using the reserve cards. It often helps to see the reserve before filling a space, and this may be done provided that all other moves have been exhausted.

Layout

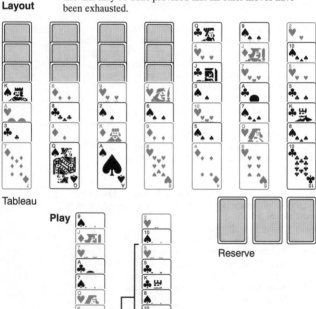

Tableau

Reserve

Play

Transferring cards

Spider

There are numerous versions of spider; the one described
here is reputed to have been the favorite solitaire of President
Franklin D. Roosevelt.

Cards Two standard 52-card decks are used.
Layout Deal out a tableau of four overlapping rows, each
row having ten cards. Deal the first three rows face down
and the fourth row face up.

Objective Cards are built onto the eight kings in descending suit sequence. Instead of setting out the kings in separate piles as they come into play, they are built onto within the tableau.

Only when a sequence is complete (ie king through ace in any one suit) is it discarded from the tableau.

If the solitaire comes out, all eight completed sequences will have been discarded.

Play The face up cards in the bottom row are all available, and may be built on any other available card in descending numerical sequence, irrespective of suit or color.

When a card is moved to another column, the player must also transfer all the cards built onto it.

Layout

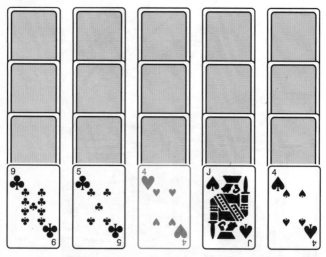

Nothing may be built onto an ace, which ranks low and can only follow a two.

When a face down card is reached, it is turned face up and becomes available for play.

A space in the tableau may be filled by any available card or build.

Stock When there are no more moves to be made in the tableau and all the spaces have been filled, ten cards are dealt face up from the stock – one to the bottom of each column. Play continues in the same way, a fresh batch of ten cards being dealt from the stock each time all possible moves in the tableau have been completed.

(The last deal will be of only four cards, one to be dealt to the bottom of the first four columns.)

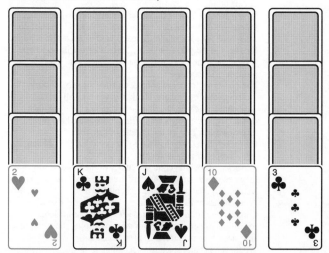

Spite and malice

Like Russian bank, this is a solitaire game for two players.
The players' objective is to be first to get rid of all the cards
from their own "payoff pile"; to achieve this end, cards are
built in sequence onto stacks at the center and sides of the
table.

Cards Two standard decks and four jokers are used. The
decks should be distinctively backed. Ace ranks low; jokers
are wild.

The objective A player aims to get rid of all the cards on his
payoff pile.

Preliminaries One of the decks is shuffled – without its
jokers – and divided into two separate "payoff" piles of 26
cards, one for each player. The top card of each pile is turned
face up and the player with the highest card will play first.
If by chance the two cards have the same value, the
procedure is repeated.

The player with the lower card shuffles the second deck,
including the four jokers. He then gives himself and his
opponent five cards, dealing them one at a time and face
down. The remaining cards form the stock and are placed
face down in a pile in the middle of the table.

Play The player who had the higher card has the opening
turn; thereafter play is alternate.

1 Aces must be played to the center of the table as soon as
they become available; they are the base cards of "center
stacks" (equivalent to foundation piles).

Available 2s must be built on the aces whenever possible.
Cards are built on the center stacks in ascending sequence
regardless of suit; a card from the payoff pile, the hand, or a
side stack (see paragraph 3) may be used.

Whenever a center stack has been built up through to the king,
it is shuffled together with the stock at the next break in play.

2 The top card of the payoff pile may be played only to the center stacks. Whenever this happens, the player may turn up the next card in the payoff pile, and so on, until an unplayable card is turned up.

Layout

Payoff pile   Player B's cards

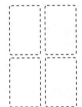
Side stacks

Center stacks

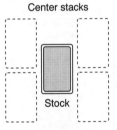
Stock

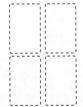
Side stacks

Player A's cards   Payoff pile

3 Each player may build up to four "side stacks" using only cards from his hand. A side stack may be started with a card of any value, and is built on regardless of suit either in descending sequence or with a card of the same value (eg 7 on a 7). Only one build onto a side stack may be made in any one turn.

4 Jokers may take the place of any card except an ace.

End of turn A player may make any number of legal plays to the center stacks, but his turn ends as soon as he plays a card from his hand to a side stack.

A player may also finish his turn by saying "End" if he cannot, or wishes not to, make further moves.

Stock At the start of their second and subsequent turns, players take as many cards from the stock as they need to replenish their hand (ie anything up to five cards).

Result The winner is the first player to have exhausted his payoff pile. Should neither player be able to make any further moves but still have cards left in his payoff pile, the game is considered drawn.

Windmill

This is a two deck game in which cards are laid out to represent the four sails of a windmill. An alternative name for the game is propeller – in which case the arms of the cross in the layout represent propeller blades.

Cards Two standard decks are used.

Layout Place any king face up at the center of the playing area. Then deal out a reserve (called the "sails") of eight face up cards: two above the king, two below it, and two to either side.

The objective is to build:

a a descending sequence of 52 cards on the central king, regardless of suit or color and with kings following aces;

b ascending sequences, ace through king and regardless of suit and color, on the first four aces that come up in play.

Play Cards are turned face up from the stock one at a time and if unplayable are put on a waste heap. The stock is only dealt once.

The first four aces to appear are put as foundation cards in the four angles of the sails.

Cards are played to the foundations from either the stock, the sails, or from the top of the waste heap (which is always available for play).

The top card of any ace foundation may be transferred to the central king foundation (building on the central pile is of prime importance if the game is to go through).

Spaces A space in the layout must be filled by the top card of either the stock or the waste heap, but it need not be filled as soon as it occurs.

This means that a space can be "saved" for a useful card – and by using his judgment in the way he fills spaces, the player can greatly increase his chances of winning.

Alternative rule Some players prefer the central foundation
card to be an ace and the other four foundations to be kings.
Should a player choose this alternative, he must build an
ascending sequence on the central ace and descending
sequences on the four kings.

Layout

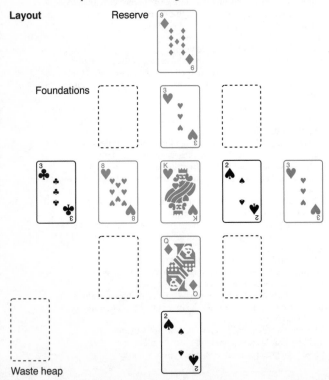

Section 4

CHILDREN'S CARD GAMES

INTRODUCTION

All the games in this section are fast-moving and fun for
children to play. The easiest among them – games such as
slapjack, snap, and beggar my neighbor – provide an
excellent first introduction to games using standard playing
cards. At the other end of the scale are games like racing
demon, cheat, and concentration, which are challenging
enough to be enjoyed by adults and children alike.

Card recognition The simplest card games using standard
playing cards involve recognizing certain cards as they
appear in play. Simplest of all is slapjack, in which only the
jacks must be picked out. Slightly more elaborate is beggar
my neighbor, in which players must recognize face cards –
kings, queens, jacks – and aces.

Matching cards by rank Many card games for children
depend on matching cards of the same rank. In snap,
menagerie, old maid, and memory, players must watch out
for pairs – for example, two 7s or two queens. In donkey
and go fish, players try to collect all four cards of the same
kind. Other easy games that involve matching cards by rank
include go boom, cheat, and snip-snap-snorem.

Following suit Another group of simple games requires
players to know the four suits – hearts, diamonds, spades,
and clubs. In my ship sails, the winner is the first player to
collect seven cards belonging to the same suit – for example
seven spades. For other games in this group, players must
also know the usual rank order of cards – from ace (low),

through 2,3,4,5,6,7,8 9, and 10, to jack, queen and king (high). It is then possible to play a whole variety of games. Some of these – like card dominoes, give away, play or pay, sequence, spit, and racing demon – involve building up sequences of cards to rank order. Others – like linger longer, knockout whist, and rolling stone – serve as a useful introduction to whist and other more complex games in which tricks must be won.

2-6   **Beggar my neighbor**

Beggar my neighbor is an easy and exciting game. No skill is required as the outcome depends on the luck of the deal.

Players There may be two to six players.

Cards Any deck of standard playing cards may be used, and it need not be complete. For more than three players it is a good idea to mix two decks together.

The objective is to win all the cards. But, as the game may go on for a very long time, the winner may be the player who has the most cards at the end of an agreed length of time.

Deal One player deals out all the cards in a clockwise direction – one at a time and face down. It does not matter if some players have one card more than the others.

Each player puts his cards into a neat pile face down in front of him.

Players are not allowed to look at their cards.

Play The player to the dealer's left turns up the top card in his pile and places it in the center of the playing area.

Each player in turn, in a clockwise direction, then places the top card from his pile face up on the central pile.

This continues until one player turns up an ace or face card (a jack, queen, or king).

Payment of cards The next player to the left then has to "pay" him by placing a certain number of cards on the central pile:

a four cards for an ace;

b three cards for a king;

c two cards for a queen;

d one card for a jack.

If, however, one of the payment cards is an ace or a face card, the payer stops turning over his cards and the player to his left then has to pay the correct number of cards.

This goes on until a player paying out cards turns over the correct number of cards with no aces or face cards.

When this happens, the last player to have turned over an ace
or a face card may take the central pile and place it at the
bottom of his own pile.

The player then starts a new round by playing his next card
face up in the center of the playing area.

As soon as a player has no more cards, he is out.

Payment

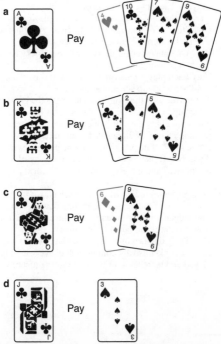

2+   **Card dominoes**

This game of luck and skill is also called sevens, parliament, and fan-tan. A player can increase his chances of winning by carefully choosing the order in which he plays his cards.

Players The game is for two or more players.

Cards One complete deck of standard playing cards is used.

Objective Each player aims to be first to play his cards onto a central pattern of cards in sequence.

Deal One player deals all the cards in a clockwise direction, one at a time and face down.

Play Each player looks at his cards and sorts them in his hand according to suit and sequence.

The player with the 7 of diamonds starts the game by putting it face up in the center. The player to his left must then try to put down either the 6 or 8 of diamonds or another 7. If he plays the 6 or 8 of diamonds he puts it respectively below or above the 7. If he plays another 7 he puts it next to the 7 of diamonds. If, however, he does not hold any of these cards he "passes" and the play then goes to the next player to the left.

Play continues in this way, with each player in turn adding a card to one of the sequences, putting down a 7, or passing. The sequences are built up from 7 through 8,9,10, jack and queen to king, and down from 6 to ace.

End The game is won by the first player to put down all his cards, but play usually continues until every card has been played and there are four complete suit sequences.

Sample play

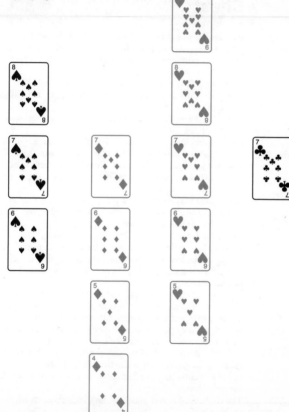

3+   **Cheat**

Also known as I doubt it, this game is great fun for those
who like taking risks and calling people's bluffs.

Players A minimum of three people is needed to play, but
the more the better.

Cards One or two decks of playing cards are used.

Objective Each player aims to be the first to get rid of all of
his cards.

Deal One player deals out all the cards. Some players may
have one extra card.

Play Players look at their cards. The player to the left of the
dealer places one to four cards of the "same" rank (eg all 7s)
face down in a pile in the center. He calls their rank as he
does so. (In fact, the cards need not be what he claims – see
cheating.)

Subsequent players must then play – or claim that they are
playing – one to four cards of the rank one higher than those
played by the preceding player.

Cheating There are at least two ways of cheating.

a instead of putting down cards of the correct rank, a player
can put down any other cards, so long as he pretends that
they are all the same, and of the next highest value to those
just played.

If a player does not have cards of the required value, he has
no alternative but to do this. It is important that a player
should avoid giving the others reason to doubt him.

b A player may put down more cards than he states. Again,
he should avoid drawing people's attention to this.

Calling a player's bluff If a player suspects another of
cheating, he can challenge him by calling "Cheat" or "I
doubt it" before the suspect's cards are covered by those of
the next player.

The challenged player must then turn over his cards for
inspection.

If the player who called "Cheat" or "I doubt it" is correct, the person who cheated picks up all the cards in the central pile and adds them to his hand.

If the player did not cheat, the challenger must pick up the central pile of cards.

The player who picks up the cards from the center starts the next round.

End The winner is the first person to succeed in playing his last card – ie either:

a he withstands a challenge from another player; or

b his cards are covered by the next player's before anyone has challenged him.

UP AND DOWN CHEAT

The only difference between this game and ordinary cheat or I doubt it is the rank of the cards that can be played. Instead of only claiming to play cards in ascending rank, a player may also claim that he is playing cards that are either of the same rank or one rank lower than the last player's cards.

2+   Concentration

This card game for any number of players is also called
pelmanism or memory. It is easy to play and is an excellent
test of memory and observation.

Cards One or two standard decks of playing cards are used,
depending on the number of players.
The cards should be clean and reasonably new, so that when
they are lying face down they cannot be identified by
creases, marks, or torn corners!
The playing area must be flat and as large as possible – the
floor or a big table is best.
The deal One player shuffles the cards and plays them face
down on the table – in all directions and so that no card is
touching another.
Objective Each player tries to collect as many cards as
possible by turning up pairs with the same rank (number or
picture).
First player The player to the left of the dealer starts the
game. He turns over two cards at random and allows the
other players to see them.
If the rank of the two cards is the same, for example two aces
or two kings, he takes them and may turn over two more
cards. He continues in this way until he turns over two cards
that do not match.
If the cards that are turned over do not match, the player
must put them face down in their original positions. His turn
then ends.
Second player The person to the first player's left now turns
over any two cards.
If the first card matches one that has already been turned
over he must try to remember where that card is. If he is
successful, he takes the pair. He continues his turn until he
fails to turn over a matching pair.

Successive players Play continues with the players taking their turns in a clockwise direction, until all the cards have been collected.

The winner is the player with most cards at the end of the game.

3+   **Donkey**

Donkey is a fast and noisy card game in which players are
penalized with letters from the game's name.

Players Three or more can play.

Cards Special cards can be bought but donkey is usually
played with sets of cards taken from an old deck of standard
playing cards.

Each set consists of four cards with the same picture or
number. The number of sets used is the same as the number
of people playing. For example, if there are five players, the
aces, kings, queens, jacks, and 10s might be used.

Spoons, buttons, or some other unbreakable objects should
be placed in the center of the table at the start of each
round.

There must be one object fewer than the number of players.

The objective is to collect a set of four cards and at the same
time to avoid being the "donkey" (ie the first player to lose
six rounds of the game).

A player is penalized with one letter from the word donkey
each time he fails to pick up an object at the end of a round.

Play Keeping his cards hidden from the other players, each
player chooses one card that he does not want and places it
face down on the table. All the players then pass their
unwanted card to the player to their left.

Each player then looks at his new card and again chooses a
card to pass to his neighbor.

He may pass the new card if he wishes.

The game continues in this way, as quickly as possible, until
one player has a set of four cards of the same value. When a
player has a set of cards, for example four 10s, he should
quietly put them face up on the table and pick up an object
from the table. As soon as any player does this, the other
players must reach for an object whether they have a set of
four cards or not.

The player who fails to pick up an object loses the round and is penalized with a letter.

Donkey The first player to be penalized with all the letters of the word donkey loses the game and must "hee-haw" three times.

PIG

Pig is a similar game to donkey. The number of players and the cards used are the same as for donkey, but in pig there is no need for any unbreakable objects.

The objective is to collect a set of four cards of the same value while also avoiding becoming the "prize pig."

Play is the same as for donkey, except that when a player has a set of cards he puts his finger to his nose. The last player to do so is pig for the round.

Prize pig The game is lost when one player becomes prize pig after losing ten rounds. As a forfeit, the prize pig must say "oink-oink" three times.

2+   Give away

Give away is a simple game that requires players to stay alert. The faster it is played the better.

Objective Each player aims to be first to get rid of all his cards.

Players Two or more can play this game.

Cards A standard deck of playing cards is used.

Deal One player deals out all the cards in a clockwise direction – face down and one at a time. It does not matter if some players have one card more than others.

Players do not look at their cards but put them in a neat face down pile in front of them.

Play The player to the left of the dealer turns over the top card of his face down pile.

If it is not an ace, he places if face up by his face down pile and ends his turn.

Play

Play to center

Play on opponent's face up card

If it is an ace, he puts it face up in the center of the table and
turns over another card. His turn continues until he turns
over a card that he is unable to play to the center – a card
may be played to the center if it is an ace or if it can be built
in rank order (a,2,3,4,5,6,7,8,9,10,j,q,k) onto a center card of
the same suit. When he turns over a card that cannot be
played to the center he places it face up by his face down
pile and ends his turn.

Each player then plays in turn. As well as playing to the
center, a player may play a card onto another player's face
up pile – provided that it is one higher or lower in rank than
the top card of that pile.

Whan a player plays his last face down card onto his face up
pile, he waits until his next turn before turning over his face
up pile to start again.

If he plays his last face down card into the center or onto
another player's pile, he turns over his face up pile
immediately and continues his turn.

End The first player to get rid of all his cards wins the game.

2+ **Go boom**

Go boom is a straightforward game for two or more players, which can be played by quite young children.

Cards A standard deck of playing cards is used.

Objective Each player aims to be the first player to get rid of all his cards.

Deal The players cut for deal; the one with the highest card (ace ranks high) deals out the cards in a clockwise direction one at a time and face down, until each player has seven cards. Spare cards are placed face down in a neat pile in the center.

Play Each player looks at his cards and sorts them in his hand. Turns pass clockwise around the players, starting with the player to the dealer's left.

The first player chooses a card from his hand and places it face up in the center. Each of the other players in turn, making a central face up pile, plays a card that is either:

a of the same suit (eg all spades); or

b of the same rank (number or picture) as the card put down by the person before him.

If a player cannot follow suit or rank, he takes cards one at a time from the top of the central face down pile until he has a card that he can play onto the central face up pile. If all the cards have been taken, the player says "Pass" and play moves on to the next player.

When each player has played a card or "passed," the cards are compared for the highest card (ace ranks high) and the player of the highest card starts the next round.

If two or more players tie for the highest card, the first one to play his card starts the next round.

End The winner is the first player to get rid of all his cards and shout "Boom."

SCORING GO BOOM
This is a variant of go boom that is made more interesting by
the introduction of a scoring system. It is played in the same
way as basic go boom, except that several rounds are played
and points are scored for going boom.

When a player goes boom, he scores points for all the
unplayed cards still in the other players' hands. Scoring is:
a 10 points for each king, queen, or jack;
b one point for each ace;
c the numerical face value of all other cards.

A game is won by the first player to score an agreed number
of points (usually 250).

10 points

1 point

CRAZY EIGHTS
Crazy eights is the same basic game as go boom except that
the 8s are wild.

A player may play any 8 after any card, and then decides
which suit should follow.

As in scoring go boom, the first player to play all his cards
scores points for the unplayed cards still in the other players'
hands.

Points are scored as follows:
a 50 points for each 8;
b 10 points for each king, queen, or jack;
c one point for each ace;
d the numerical face value of all other cards.

If the face down pile of cards is exhausted before any player plays all his cards, the game is blocked and the player with the lowest count in his remaining cards scores the difference in count betwen his own hand and the other players' hands.

50 points   10 points   1 point

Go fish

2+

To win at this popular game, players will need a a mixture of skill and luck.

Players Fish can be played by two players, but it is better with more.

Cards A standard deck of cards is normally used, but young players may prefer to use special happy families cards.

Deal One of the players deals out all the cards. As well as dealing a hand of each player, the dealer also deals a spare hand – so, for example, five hands are dealt if there are four players.

The spare hand is placed face down in the center of the table and is called the "fish pile."

Objective Each player tries to get rid of all his cards.

Play Each player looks at his cards and sorts them into groups with the same rank (number or picture). Players must take care not to let anyone else see their cards at any time. When all the players are ready, the person to the dealer's left asks any player, by name, for a particular card (eg 7 of spades). He must already possess at least one card of the same rank (eg 7 of hearts). If the person who is asked for a card has it, he must give it to the player who asked for it. The player who made the first request may then ask any player for another card, again provided he already has at least one card of the same rank.

A group of
four 7s

A player can go on asking for cards in this way until he asks someone for a card that he does not have. The person who does not have the card then tells the player who asked for it to "go fish." The player who was told to go fish must then take one card from the top of the fish pile. The player who told him to go fish then takes over asking for cards.

Once a player collects all four cards in a group, he puts them into a pile face down in front of him.

End The winner is the first player to have no cards other than his completed groups. If two players finish at the same time, the one with most completed groups of four cards is the winner.

Knockout whist

2-7

An easy-to-play member of the whist family, knockout whist is very popular with older children. It is a good way of learning about tricks and trumps. Players are eliminated until only one remains.

Rank of cards

Players Two to seven people can play.
Cards A standard deck of playing cards is used.
Objective Each player aims to win all the tricks of a hand.
A trick contains one card from each player played into the center.
Except when a trump has been played, a trick is won by the highest card belonging to the suit that was led – ie to the same suit as the first card played in that trick.
Aces are the highest cards, followed by kings, queens, jacks, and so on down from the 10s to the 2s.
A trump is a card belonging to the trump suit. The trump suit is determined before each game is played. A trump card beats any card belonging to the suit led.
Deal One player deals out the cards face down, one at a time, and in a clockwise direction until each player has seven cards. The remaining cards are put face down in a pile in the center. Each time the cards are dealt, the number dealt to each player is decreased by one.
Play The top card of the center pile is turned over and this determines the trump suit for the first hand.
The player to the dealer's left then starts the first trick by playing any card he chooses.

Each player in turn then plays a card, following suit if he can. If a player cannot follow suit, he may either play a trump or discard any other card into the center.

The trick is won by the player who played the highest trump card or, if no trump was played, by the player who played the highest card of the suit led.

When all seven tricks have been played, anyone who has not won a trick drops out of the game.

The dealer collects all the cards, shuffles them, and deals six cards to each remaining player.

The winner of the most tricks in the first round chooses the trump suit and plays the first card in the second hand.

Play continues in this way – with players without tricks dropping out at the end of each hand.

End The first player to win all the tricks in a single hand is the overall winner.

If play continues to the seventh hand, each player will have only one card. There will be only one trick, and the winner of this trick wins the game.

**Tricks
(four players)**

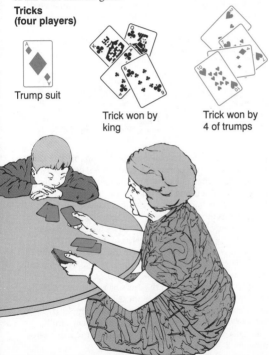

Trump suit

Trick won by
king

Trick won by
4 of trumps

3+ Linger longer

Linger longer is an ideal introduction to the principles of trump play that form the basis of many more complicated card games.

Players Three or more people can play. Four to six is best.
Cards A standard deck of playing cards is used.

Rank of cards

Objective Each player tries to be the last person with cards in his hand. Players obtain new cards by winning tricks.
A trick comprises one card from each player played into the center. Unless a trump has been played, a trick is won by the highest card belonging to the suit that was led – ie to the same suit as the first card played in that trick.
Aces are the highest cards, followed by the kings, queens, jacks, and so on down from the 10s to the 2s.
A trump is a card belonging to the trump suit. The trump suit is determined before each game is played. A trump card beats any card belonging to the suit led.
Deal One player deals out the cards in a clockwise direction, face down and one at a time, until each player has the same number of cards as there are players. For example, if there are four players, each one of them receives four cards.
The remaining cards are placed in the center in a face down pile called the stock.
The last card dealt to the dealer is shown to all the players. The suit of this card is the trump suit for the game.

Play The player to the left of the dealer plays any card he likes face up in the center.

Each player in turn then plays one card into the center. (These cards together form a trick.) If possible, players must play a card of the same suit as the first card – this is called "following suit." If a player is unable to follow suit, he may play a trump card or any other card.

A trick is won by the player who played the highest trump card, or, if no trump was played, by the player who played the highest card of the suit led. Ace ranks high for this game. A player who wins a trick places these cards face down in front of him. He then draws the top card from the stock and adds it to the cards in his hand (no other player draws). This player plays the first card of the next trick. Players continue playing tricks in this way as long as they have any

Tricks

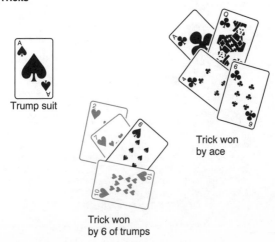

Trump suit

Trick won
by ace

Trick won
by 6 of trumps

cards in their hand – ignoring the cards in any tricks that they have won.

A player with no cards in his hand must leave the game.

End The last player left in the game wins.

Menagerie

2+

This hilarious and noisy game is similar to snap. It is sometimes called animals.

Players It can be played by two, but is better with more.
Cards One or two decks of standard playing cards are used.
Objective Players aim to win all the cards.
Choosing the animals Players first choose the name of an animal with a long and tongue-twisting name.

After checking that everyone has chosen a different animal, each player is given a small piece of paper on which he must write his animal's name. (An older person can help anyone who hasn't learned to write.)

All the pieces of paper are folded and then shaken together in a bag or hat. Each player then takes one piece of paper – and the name on that paper is his animal for the game.

Players should then learn the animal names of all the persons playing.

Deal One player deals out all the cards in a clockwise direction – one at a time and face down. It does not matter if some players have one card more than the others.

Each player puts his cards into a neat pile face down in front of him. Players are not allowed to look at their cards.

Play The player to the dealer's left turns over the top card of his pile and places it face up to start a face up pile of cards next to his face down pile. The next player to his left does the same, and so on around the players until any player sees that the cards on the top of any two face up piles have the same value.

Whenever the top card on any two players' face up piles are the same (eg two 7s), each of these two players must call out the other player's animal name three times.

The first player to do so wins the other player's face up pile and adds these cards to the bottom of his own face down pile.

Penalty If a player wrongly calls out a name, he must give all his face up cards to the player whose animal name he called.

ANIMAL NOISES

This game is played like menagerie, except that:

a players choose animals that make distinctive noises (eg dog, cat, or duck);

b players imitate their opponents' animal noises instead of repeating their animal names.

My ship sails   4-7

An easy game for beginners, my ship sails is also great fun
when played at speed by those familiar with it.

Players Four to seven people may play.
Cards A standard deck of playing cards is used.
Objective Each player aims to be the first to collect seven
cards of the same suit, for example seven spades.
Deal Each player cuts the cards and the one with the highest
card (ace high) is the dealer.
He deals out the cards in a clockwise direction, one at a time
and face down, until each player has seven cards. The
remaining cards are not used.
Play Each player sorts his cards into suits in his hand and
decides which suit he will try to collect. This will probably
be the suit for which he has most cards at the start of a
round, but he may change his mind during the course of
play.
Exchange of cards Each player takes one card that he does
not want and puts it face down on the table. When all the
players are ready, they pass these cards to the next person to
the right. The players pick up their new cards, decide on
another card to discard, and then pass it in the same way.
End Players continue to exchange cards until one person
collects seven cards of the same suit. He then calls "My ship
sails," and wins the game. If two players call together, the
first to start calling is the winner.

My ship sails

3+   Old maid

Old maid is a simple card game that is a great favorite with young children. Another name for this game is pass the lady.

Players This is a game for three or more players.

Cards One of the queens is removed from a standard deck to leave an odd queen – the "old maid."

Deal One player deals all the cards face down, one at a time, to all players. It does not matter if some players have one card more than the others.

Objective Each player aims to get rid of all his cards by discarding pairs of equal value. The player who is left with the old maid card when play ends is the loser. There are no winners in this game.

Play Each player looks at his cards, making sure that none of the other players can see them.

If he has any pairs – two matching character cards or two playing cards with the same value – eg two 9s or two kings – he lays them face down on the table.

A player with three cards of the same value may only put down two of them and must keep the third, but a player with four cards of the same value may put down all four in two pairs.

The players to the dealer's left fans out his cards, keeping their faces toward him, and offers them to the player to his left.

The player who is offered the cards must take any one of them. He then looks to see whether the new card pairs up with any of the cards already in his hand. If it does, he lays the pair face down on the table. If not, he adds the new card to the cards in his hand. He then fans out his cards and offers them to the player to his left.

Play continues in this way until all cards but the "old maid" have been played. The player holding the "old maid" is the

loser, and all the other players call him "old maid" before a
new game is started.

Old maid

One queen removed   Pair of queens   The old maid

Variation To make the game last longer, cards may be
considered as pairs only if their color matches as well as
their number, for example, two red 7s or two black aces.

Pairs

LE VIEUX GARÇON

This French game is similar to old maid.

It is played with a standard deck of playing cards, with the jacks of hearts, diamonds, and clubs removed.

The game is lost by the player left with the jack of spades – called "le vieux garçon" or "old boy."

Le vieux garçon

Play or pay

3+

This easy game, sometimes called round the corner, is fun
for players learning about the rank and sequence of playing
cards.

Players Three or more can play.
Cards A standard deck of playing cards is used.

Cards in sequence

Counters Each player starts with 20 counters.
Objective Each player aims to be first to get rid of all his
cards.
Deal One player is chosen as dealer. He deals out all the
cards in a clockwise direction, one at a time and face down.
It does not matter if some players have one card more than
others.
Play the player to the left of the dealer chooses any one of
his cards and places it face up in the center.
The next player to his left then looks at his cards to see if he
has the next card "in sequence."
A card is in sequence if it belongs to the same suit as the last
card that was played and follows the order a,2,3,4,5,6,
7,8,9,10,j,q,k. If the last card was a king, the next card in
sequence for this game is the ace of the same suit. (This is
called a "round the corner" sequence.)
If the player has the next card in sequence he plays it face up
onto the card in the center.
If he does not have this card, he must pay one counter into
the center.

Play continues with each player in turn either playing the next card in sequence or paying a counter.

When all the cards of a suit have been played, the player who put down the last card has an extra turn and may play any card that he chooses.

End The first player to get rid of all his cards is the winner of the round and takes all the counters from the center. Each loser must also pay him one counter for every card left in his hand. The winner of the game is the player with most counters after an agreed number of rounds.

Racing demon 2+

Racing demon is a fast and noisy game in which players race to get rid of all their cards.

Players Any number can play.
Cards One complete deck of standard playing cards is needed for each player. Old decks with different backs are recommended.
Playing area This game requires a lot of space.
Deal Each player shuffles and deals his own deck.
After shuffling, each player first deals out 13 cards, face down in a pile in front of him.
This pile is then turned over so that only the top card is visible. He then deals four cards face up, in a row alongside his pile of 13 cards.
His spare cards should be held face down in one hand.
Objective Each player aims:
a to get rid of his pile of 13 cards;
b to play as many cards as possible into the center.
Start of play One of the players is chosen to be the starter.
When all the players have dealt out their cards, he starts play by shouting "Go!"
Play All the players play at the same time: there is no waiting to play in turn. Players may either play cards into the center or onto their own face up cards.
Play into the center If a player has an ace among his face up cards, he should place it face up in the center.
Once an ace has been played into the center, anyone with a face up 2 of the same suit can play this onto the ace. A face up 3 of the same suit can then be added by any player, and so on through to the 10, jack, queen, and king.
Playing on face up cards As well as building up the piles in the center, a player can build piles of cards on the four cards alongside his original pile of 13.

Cards added to these piles must be in descending order and alternately black and red (for example a black 6 can be added to a red 7 and then a red 5 added to the black 6).
Cards added to these piles may be:
a the top card from the player's original pile of 13;
b a card, or a correct sequence of cards, from one of the player's other face up piles.
Any space left by the removal of one of the four face up piles should be filled with the top card from the player's original pile of 13.

Play

Play to center

Play on face up cards

Spare card If a player is unable to play a face up card into the center or to move any of his face up cards, he turns to the cards that were spare after he first dealt out his cards.
These spare cards are turned over, three at a time, onto a separate pile, until one of them can be played into the center or onto a face up pile.
When all the spare cards have been turned over, the player picks up the pile, turns it face down, and continues play.

End As soon as any player uses up all his cards from his original pile of 13, he shouts "Out" and play ends.

Scoring The cards in the center are sorted into their separate decks.

A player's final score is the difference between the number of his cards in the center and the number of cards left in his original face up piles.

The winner is the player with the highest score.

4-6 Rolling stone

This popular game is highly unpredictable in its outcome.
Just as a player is on the verge of winning he can get a new
handful of cards to play. It is also known as enflay or
schwellen.

Players Four, five, or six people can play.
Cards A standard deck of playing cards is used, but with
cards removed so that there are eight cards per player.
The following cards should be removed before play:
a for four players, the 2s,3s,4s,5s and 6s;
b for five players, the 2s,3s, and 4s;
c for six players, the 2s.

Rank of cards

Objective Each player aims to be the first to get rid of all his
cards.
Deal Each player cuts the cards and the one with the highest
card (ace high) is the dealer. He deals out all the cards in a
clockwise direction, one at a time and face down.
Play Each player looks at his cards and sorts them into suits
in his hand.
The player to the dealer's left starts play by choosing a card
from his hand and placing it, face up, in the center.
The other players, in turn, then try to play one card of the
same suit.
If all the players are able to "follow suit," these cards (called
a "trick") are put to one side and are out of play for the rest

of the game. The player who played the highest card (with ace high) then starts the next trick by playing the next card into the center.

If any player is unable to follow suit, he must pick up the cards already played for that trick and add them to his own hand.

He then plays the first card of the next trick, but must not use any of the cards that he has just picked up.

End The winner is the first person to play all his cards.

2+ Sequence

This game is easily learned but calls for a little skill in choosing which card to play when starting a sequence.

Players Two or more can play sequence but it is best with four or five players.
Cards A standard deck of playing cards is used.

A sequence

Objective Each player aims to be first to get rid of all his cards.
Deal One player is chosen as dealer. He deals out all the cards in a clockwise direction, one at a time and face down. It does not matter if some players have one card more than others.
Play The player to the left of the dealer starts by putting his lowest cards of any suit face up in the center. (2s count as the lowest cards and aces as the highest.)
The player with the next card in sequence then plays it face up onto the card in the center. A card is in sequence if it is of the same suit as the last card that was played and follows the order 2, 3, 4, 5, 6, 7, 8, 9, 10, j, q, k, a.
Play continues in this way until the ace is played and the sequence ends.
A player who ends a sequence starts another by playing any card from his hand.

When part of a suit has already been played, a sequence ends
with the highest card yet to play. The following sequence is
then started by the player who played the highest card.

End The first player to get rid of all his cards is the winner.

Scoring If more than one round is to be played, players may
each start with 10 counters or beans.

At the end of every round each loser pays the winner one
bean for every card still in his hand.

The winner is the player with most counters or beans after an
agreed number of rounds.

2+   Slapjack

This is an exciting game that needs no skill. It can be
enjoyed by the very young as the only requirement is that
players can recognize a jack.

Players Two or more can play.
Cards Standard playing cards are used. If there are more
than three players it is a good idea to mix two decks
together. It does not matter if a few cards are missing.
Objective Players aim to win all the cards.
Deal One player deals out all the cards in a clockwise
direction – one at a time and face down. It does not matter if
some players have one card more than others.
Each player puts his card into a neat pile face down in front
of him. Players are not allowed to look at their cards.
Play The player to the dealer's left turns over the top card of
his pile and places it face up in the center.
Turns then pass around to the left, with each player placing
his card on top of the previous player's card.
Slapping a jack When a jack is turned up, each player tries
to be the first to put his hand on the card – ie to "slap the
jack."

Slapping a jack

The successful player wins the central pile of cards and shufffles them with his own cards to form his new face down pile.

The player to the winner's left starts the next round, placing a card face up in the center.

If more than one player puts his hand on the jack, the winner is the player whose hand is underneath.

If possible it is a good idea to appoint a referee to settle arguments.

If a player loses all his cards, he can stay in the game if he is first to slap the next jack.

If he fails to slap the next jack he must retire from the game.

Penalty If a player slaps a card that is not a jack, he must give his top card to the player whose card he slapped in error.

End The winner of the game is either:

a the first person to collect all the cards; or

b the player with the most cards at the end of the game.

2+   Snap

Amusing and noisy, snap is among the most familiar of all
children's card games.

Players Two or more can play.
Cards Special snap cards can be bought, but the game is just
as much fun with standard playing cards.
It is best to use old cards in case of damage, and it does not
matter if any of the cards are missing.
If there are more than three players it is a good idea to use
two decks of cards.
Objective Players aim to win all the cards.
Deal One player deals out all the cards in a clockwise
direction – one at a time and face down. It does not matter if
some players have one card more than the others.
Each player puts his cards into a neat pile face down in front
of him.
Players are not allowed to look at their cards.
Play The player to the dealer's left turns over the top card of
his pile and places it face up to start a face up pile of cards
next to his face down pile.

The next player to his left does the same, and so on around the players until any player sees that the cards on top of any two face up piles have the same value (eg two 10s).

Snap The first player to shout "Snap," when there are matching cards on top of two face up piles, collects both these piles of cards and puts them at the bottom of his own face down pile.

Players now continue turning cards over as before, beginning with the player to the left of the last player who turned over a card.

Snap!

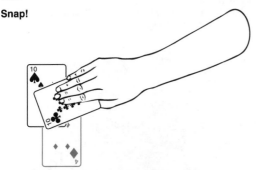

Snap pool If two players shout "Snap" together, the matching face up piles are put face up in a pool in the center. Players then continue to turn over cards, and the pool is won by the first player to shout "Snap pool" when the top card of any player's face up pile matches the top card of the pool.

No more cards When a player runs out of face down cards, he simply turns over his face up cards when it is next his turn to play.

Penalty There are diferent rules for when a player calls "Snap" in error:

a the player gives one card from his face down pile to each of the other players;

b the player's own face up pile is put into a central pool to be won like an ordinary snap pool.

End The game ends when only one player has any cards.

EASY SNAP

This version is particularly suitable for very young children. Instead of having individual face up piles, each player plays his cards onto a central face up pile. Players shout "Snap" when the top two cards are of the same value.

SPEED SNAP

In this faster version of snap, players still turn their cards up one at a time, but all players do so together.

Snip-snap-snorem

3+

A game with funny words to say, snip-snap-snorem is noisy, fast-moving, and fun to play.

Players It is a game for three or more players.
Cards A standard deck of playing cards is used.
Objective Each player aims to be the first to get rid of all his cards.
Deal Each player cuts the cards and the one with the highest card (ace high) is the dealer.
He deals out all the cards in a clockwise direction, one at a time, and face down.
It does not matter if some players have one card more than the others.
Play Each player looks at his cards without letting any other player see them, and sorts them in his hand.
Turns pass clockwise around the players, starting with the player to the dealer's left.
The first player places any one of his cards face up in the center.
If the next player has a card of the same rank (eg another queen, if the first player played a queen), he places this face up in the center of the table and shouts "Snip" as he plays it.
If he has another card of the same rank he keeps it until his next turn.
If he does not have a card of the same rank, he says "Pass" and play moves on around the players.
The next player with a card of the same rank shouts "Snap" when he plays it, and the player of the fourth card shouts "Snorem!"
The player of the fourth card starts the next round.
End The winner is the first player to play all his cards.
Variation If a player has more than one card of the same rank, he must play them all in the same turn, saying the appropriate words.

Sample play

Snap

Snip

Snorem!

JIG

This is played exactly like snip-snap-snorem except that
instead of playing four cards of the same rank, a sequence of
four cards is played.

For example, if the first player puts down a 5, this is
followed by a 6, then a 7, and finally an 8.

The cards can be from different suits.

Players call out "Jiggety, joggety, jig" when playing the
cards.

2   Spit

Spit is an excellent game that calls for alertness and speed.

Players Two people can play.

Cards A complete deck of standard cards is used.

Deal All the cards are dealt out equally between the two players.

Before play starts, each player lays out a row of cards in front of him as follows:

1 starting from the left, he places three cards face down followed by a fourth card face up;

2 he places a second face down card on each of the first two face down cards and a face down and a face up card on the third;

3 he places a face down card on the first pile and a face up card on the second;

4 he places a face up card on the first pile.

Each player then places the rest of his cards face down in a pile to the left of his row.

Objective Each player aims to be the first to get rid of all his cards.

Start of play When both players are ready, either one of them calls "Spit!"

Immediately both players take the top card from their piles of spare cards and place them face up, side by side, in the center.

Playing into the center Each player then quickly plays as many cards as possible from his row of face up cards onto either of the face up cards in the center of the table.

A card may be played into the center if it has a numerical value either one higher or one lower than a central face up card. (For example, a 9 or a jack can be played onto a 10. Either a king or 2 can be played onto an ace.) If playing a face up card into the center exposes a face down card in a player's row, this card should be turned face up.

Play to center

Players continue to play cards onto the central piles in this manner until neither player can put out any more of his cards.

Spit If neither player can play any card from his row of face up cards, one of the players shouts "Spit!."

Both players take the top card from the piles of spare cards and place them face up on their central piles.

If possible, players then resume playing cards into the center from their face up piles.

If players still cannot add any cards from their face up rows, the other player calls "Spit!" and both players again play the top card of their spare piles. They continue in this way until either player can play a card from his row.

If a player wishes to call "Spit!" and the player's spare piles have been used up, each player takes his own central pile and turns it face down to form a new spare pile. The player then calls "Spit!" and play continues as before.

End of a round When a player has played all the cards from his face up row into the center, he shouts "Out!" and wins the round. He then picks up his spare pile.

The other player then collects both central face up piles, picks up the cards left in his row, and adds all these cards to the bottom of his spare pile.

Starting a new round Players lay out their cards as for the first round.

New rounds are played in the same way as the first round, except that if one player does not have enough cards for a spare pile he does without and both players play onto a single central pile.

End of game A game is won by the first player to get rid of all his cards.

Stealing bundles

2-4

As soon as a player can spot that two cards have the same rank (face value), he is old enough to play stealing bundles. Other names for this game are old man's bundle and stealing the old man's bundle.

Players Two or four people can play.
Cards A standard deck of playing cards is used.
Objective Each player tries to collect as many cards as possible.
Deal One person is chosen as dealer. He deals the cards in a clockwise direction, one at a time and face down, until each player has four cards.
The dealer then places four cards face up in a row in the center.
Play The player to the left of the dealer begins.
If he has a card of the same rank as one of the cards in the center, he captures that card. He places the captured card and his matching card face up in a pile in front of him. This is the beginning of his "bundle."
If two or three center cards have the same rank as one of the player's cards he may capture them all in the same turn.
If none of the player's cards matches a center card, he must place one of his own cards face up in the center. This is called "trailing."
Each player then plays one card in turn. In place of or in addition to capturing cards from the center, he may steal another player's bundle if his card matches the top card of that bundle.
Every time a player captures cards he places them in his bundle with the matching card face up.
If none of his cards matches any face up card he must "trail" one of his cards.

Extra deals When all players have played each of the four cards in their hands, the dealer deals out four more cards to each player. No cards are dealt to the center. Play then continues as before.

End The game ends when all the cards have been dealt and played.

The winner is the player with the most cards in his bundle when play ends.

War 2

An easy game, war is a good way of introducing young children to card playing.

Players This game is for two people.
Cards A complete deck of standard playing cards is used.

Rank of cards

Objective Each player aims to win all the cards.
Deal One player deals all the cards.
Each player puts his cards into a neat pile face down in front of him. Players are not allowed to look at their cards.
Play Both players turn over the top card of their piles, and place them face up, side by side, in the center.
The player who has played the higher card, regardless of suit, wins both cards and places them face down at the bottom of his pile.
Aces are the highest cards, followed by kings, queens, jacks, and so on down from the 10s to the 2s.
The "war" If the two cards turned up have the same value, the war is on.
Each player puts one card face down on top of his first card in the center. He then puts another card face up on top of this.
The two new face up cards are compared, and the highest card wins all six cards in the center.
If the face up cards match again, the war continues. Each player puts out another face down card with a face up card

on top. Play continues in this way until someone plays a card higher than the other.

End The winner of the game is either:

a the first player to win all the cards; or

b the player with the most cards at the end of a time limit set at the start of the game.

"War"

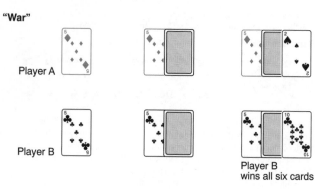

Player A

Player B

Player B
wins all six cards

WAR FOR THE THREE PLAYERS

This version of war is for three players.

Deal The cards are dealt out as for war for two, except that the last card is not dealt out. (In this way, all three players begin with the same number of cards.)

Play is the same as in war for two, except that:

a when two cards of the same value are turned up, all three players engage in war;

b when three cards of the same value are turned up, the players engage in double war.

In double war each player puts out two cards face down and then one card face up. If the cards still match, the three players then continue with single war.

PERSIAN PASHA

Persian pasha, also called pisha pasha, is a similiar game to war.

Players It is a game for two players.

Cards A complete deck of standard playing cards is used.

Objective Each player aims to win all the cards.

Deal Cards are dealt as for war.

Play Each player turns over his top card and places it on a face up pile next to his face down pile.

Players continue turning over cards until their top face up cards are of the same suit.

The player with the higher card then takes all the other player's face up pile and puts these cards at the bottom of his face down pile.

Section 5
FINDING A GAME

5

How many players?

This section of the book shows at a glance which games are suitable for different numbers of players. It begins with lists of games for specific numbers and ends with games for groups of two or more (p 500) and three or more (p 502) players.

GAMES FOR ONE PLAYER

With the exception of two double solitaire games (Russian bank, and Spite and malice), all the games in Section 3 of this book are for one player.

GAMES FOR TWO PLAYERS
Also see games for two or more players (p 500).

General games

All fives	Euchre, two-handed	Piquet
Auction pinochle	Five hundred, two-handed	Royal casino
Auction piquet		Rubicon bezique
Bezique	Forty-five	Russian bank
California Jack	Gin rummy	Rummy
Casino	Hearts, two-handed	Seven up
Cribbage	Imperial	Spade casino
Draw casino	Kalabriasz	Spite and malice
Ecarte	Pinochle	

Gambling games

Brag, nine-card
Fifteen
Thirty-five

Children's games

Persian pasha	Stealing bundles
Spit	War

GAMES FOR THREE PLAYERS
Also see games for two or more (p 500) and three or more (p 502) players.

General games

All fives	Draw casino	Rummy
Auction pinochle	Euchre, three-handed	Seven up
Bezique, three-handed	Five hundred	Skat
Calabrasella	Kalabriasz,	Solo, three-handed
California Jack	three-handed	Spade casino
Casino	Knaves	
Cribbage, three-handed	Preference	
	Royal casino	

Gambling games

Brag, nine-card
Thirty-five

Children's games

Animal noises
Menagerie
War, for three players

GAMES FOR FOUR PLAYERS
Also see games for two or more (p 500) and three or more (p 502) players.

General games

Auction bridge
Auction forty-five
Bezique, four-handed
Boston
California jack
Call-ace euchre
Canasta
Casino
Contract bridge
Cribbage, four-handed
Draw casino

Duplicate contract
 bridge
Euchre, four-handed
Five hundred,
 four-handed
Forty-five
Gin rummy,
 partnership
Grand
Kalabriasz,
 partnership

Polignac
Railroad euchre
Royal casino
Rummy
Seven up, four-handed
Skat
Solo whist
Spade casino
Vint
Whist

Gambling games

Brag, nine-card
Thirty-five

Children's games

Animal noises
Menagerie
My ship sails

Rolling stone
Stealing bundles

GAMES FOR FIVE PLAYERS
Also see games for two or more (p 500) and three or more (p 502) players.

General games

Call-ace euchre
Polignac

Children's games

My ship sails
Rolling stone

GAMES FOR SIX PLAYERS
Also see games for two or more (p 500) and three or more (p 502) players.

General games

Auction forty-five	Gin rummy,	Rummy
Call-ace euchre	partnership	Skat
Forty-five	Polignac	

Gambling games

Brag, nine-card
Thirty-five

Children's games

My ship sails
Rolling stone

GAMES FOR TWO OR MORE PLAYERS
*Note that many of these games become impracticable for groups of more
than seven or eight players.*
Also see games for three or more players (p 502).

General games

Auction pitch	Nap, seven-card	Spoil five
Auction pitch, with joker	Napoleon	
	Purchase nap	

Gambling games

Ace-deuce-jack	Farmer	Red dog
Banker and broker	Faro	Seven and a half
Baccarat/Chemin de fer	Hoggenheimer	Six-spot red dog
Blackjack	Injun	Slippery sam
Brag, nine-card	Lansquenet	Stop the bus
Brag, seven-card	Macao	Stuss
Card craps	Monte bank	Tom and a half
Card put-and-take	Poker	Trente et quarante
Chinese fan-tan	Polish red dog	Yablon
	Red and black	Ziginette

Children's games

Beggar my neighbor	Go boom	Scoring go boom
Card dominoes	Go fish	Sequence
Concentration	Knockout whist	Slapjack
Crazy eights	Menagerie	Snap
Give away	Racing demon	

GAMES FOR THREE OR MORE PLAYERS
Note that many of these games become impracticable for groups of more than seven or eight players.

General games

Black lady hearts	Heartsette	Oh hell
Black Maria	Irish loo	Pope Joan
Domino hearts	Joker hearts	Spot hearts
Greek hearts	Loo	
Hearts	Michigan	

Gambling games

Bango	Brag, three-card	Skinball
Blücher	Horse race	Thirty-one
Brag, seven-card	Kentucky derby	

Children's games

Cheat	Linger longer	Snip-snap-snorem
Donkey	Old maid	Up and down cheat
Jig	Pig	
Le vieux garçon	Play or pay	

Card game variations and alternative names

VARIATIONS

The following games are included in this book as sub-sections or variations of a game with a different name (here given in color).

Animal noises Menagerie
Black lady Hearts
Black Maria Hearts
Blind and straddle Poker
Blind opening Poker
Blind tiger Poker
California jack Seven up
Call-ace Euchre
Chemin de fer Baccarat
Cincinnati Poker
Crazy eights Go boom
Crisscross Poker
Down the river Poker
Easy go Card put-and-take
Farmer Blackjack
Fifteen Blackjack
Gin Rummy
Heartsette Hearts
Jacks or better Poker
Jig Snip-snap-snorem
Lame-brain Pete Poker

Le vieux garçon Old maid
Lowball Poker
Macao Blackjack
Mexican stud Poker
Persian pasha War
Pig Donkey
Pig in the poke Poker
Polignac Knaves
Railroad Euchre
Rubicon Bezique
Seven and a half Blackjack
Seven-toed Pete Poker
Shotgun Poker
Six spot Red dog
Spit in the ocean Poker
Stop the bus Brag
Stormy weather Poker
Ten and a half Blackjack
Up-and-down river Card put-and-take

ALTERNATIVE NAMES

The following games appear in this book under an alternative name (given here in color).

Ace-deuce Yablon
Ace low Fifteen
All fours Seven up
Animals Menagerie
Belote Kalabriasz
Big forty Napoleon at St. Helena
BJ Blackjack
Blackout Oh hell
Blind hooker Banker and broker
Boodle Michigan
Broken intervals Calculation
California loo California jack
Cans Fifteen
Chicago Michigan
Chinese bezique Six-deck bezique
Chip hearts Spot hearts
Club Kalabriasz
Clobber Kalabriasz
Crapette Russian bank
Cutthroat euchre Three-hundred euchre
Demon Canfield
Double and quits Monte Carlo
Draw seven California jack
Dutch bank Banker and broker
Eight off Eight away
Enflay Rolling stone
Fan-tan Card dominoes
Fan-tan Chinese fan-tan
Farobank Faro
Forty thieves Napoleon at St. Helena
Four of a kind Clock

Hidden cards Clock
High-card pool Red dog
High-low-jack Seven up
I doubt it Cheat
Idle year Accordion
In between Yablon
Indian carpet Crazy quilt
Japanese rug Crazy quilt
Klaberjass Kalabriasz
Lanterloo Loo
Laying siege Beleaguered castle
Memory Concentration
Methuselah Accordion
Monte Monte bank
Nap Napoleon
Newmarket Michigan
Old man's bundle Stealing bundles
Old sledge Seven up
Parliament Card dominoes
Pass the lady Old maid
Pasteboard derby Kentucky derby
Pelmanism Concentration
Penuchle Pinochle
Pisha pasha Persian pasha
Plait Braid
Polish pachuk Polish red dog
Pontoon Blackjack
Propeller Windmill
Put-and-take Card put-and-take
Quince Fifteen
Rauber skat Skat
Rouge et noir Trente et quarante

Round the corner Play or pay
Saratoga Michigan
Saton pong Ten and a half
Schnautz Thirty-one
Schwellen Rolling stone
Setback Auction pitch
Sevens Card dominoes
Sham battle Beleaguered castle
Skin Skinball
Skinning Skinball
Slippery Anne Black Maria

Spanish monte Monte bank
Stitch Polish red dog
Sun dial Clock
Three naturals Macao
Toad in the hole Frog
Tower of Babel Accordion
Travelers Clock
Twenty-one Blackjack
Vanjohn Blackjack
Vingt-et-un Blackjack
Weddings Monte Carlo

Index

A

Accordion 362
Ace-deuce (see Yablon) 349
Ace-deuce-jack 172
Ace low (see Fifteen) 214
All fives 18
All fours (see Seven up) 143
Animal noises 462
Animals (see Menagerie) 461
Auction bridge 46
Auction forty-five 82
Auction pinochle 120
Auction pitch 20
Auction pitch, with joker 21

B

Baccarat 175
Baccarat banque 183
Baccarat-chemin de fer 175
Bango 188
Banker and broker 191
Beggar my neighbor 438
Beleaguered castle 364
Belote (see Kalabriasz) 98
Bezique 22
Bezique, eight-deck 28
Bezique, four-handed 29
Bezique, rubicon 25
Bezique, six-deck 27
Bezique, three-handed 25
Bezique, two-handed 22
Big forty (see Napoleon at
    St. Helena) 408

Bisley 366
BJ (see Blackjack) 194
Black lady hearts 89
Black Maria 92
Blackjack 194
Blackout (see Oh hell) 114
Blind and straddle (see Blind
    opening) 307
Blind hooker (see Banker and
    broker) 191
Blind opening 307
Blind tiger (see Blind opening) 307
Blücher 219
Boodle (see Michigan) 109
Boston 31
Brag 222
Brag, nine-card 228
Brag, seven-card 227
Brag, three-card 225
Braid 368
Bridge, auction 46
Bridge, contract 34
Bridge, duplicate contract 44
Bristol 370
Broken intervals (see Calculation)
    372

C

Calabrasella 48
Calculation 372
California jack 144
California loo (see California jack)
    144

Call-ace euchre 75
Canasta 50
Canfield (see also Klondike) 374
Cans (see Fifteen) 214
Card craps 230
Card dominoes 440
Card put-and-take 238
Casino 56
Casino, draw 60
Casino, royal 60
Casino, spade 61
Cheat 442
Cheat, up and down 443
Chemin de fer 177
Chicago (see Michigan) 109
Chinese bezique (see Six-deck bezique) 27
Chinese fan-tan 241
Chip hearts (see Spot hearts) 89
Cincinnati (see Poker, closed games) 310
Clab (see Kalabriasz) 98
Clobber (see Kalabriasz) 98
Clock 378
Concentration 444
Crapette (see Russian bank) 420
Contract bridge 34
Crazy eights 451
Crazy quilt 380
Cribbage 62
Cribbage, five-card 68
Cribbage, four-handed 69
Cribbage, seven-card 68
Cribbage, six-card 63
Cribbage, three-handed 68
Crisscross poker (see Poker, closed games) 310

Cutthroat euchre (see Euchre, three-handed) 74

D
Demon (see Canfield) 374
Domino hearts 90
Donkey 446
Double and quits (see Monte Carlo) 406
Down the river (see Seven-card stud poker) 301
Draw casino 60
Draw poker 303
Draw poker, variants 307
Draw seven (see California jack) 144
Duplicate contract bridge 44
Dutch bank (see Banker and broker) 191

E
Easy snap 480
Ecarté 70
Eight away 382
Eight off (see Eight away) 382
Enflay (see Rolling stone) 472
Euchre 72
Euchre, call-ace 75
Euchre, cut-throat (see Euchre, three-handed) 74
Eurchre, four-handed 72
Euchre, railroad 74
Euchre, three-handed 74
Euchre, two-handed 74

F
Fan-tan (see Card dominoes) 440

Fan-tan (see Chinese fan-tan) 241
Farmer 215
Faro 244
Farobank (see Faro) 244
Fifteen 214
Five hundred 76
Five hundred, four-handed 78
Five hundred, three-handed 76
Five hundred, two-handed 78
Florentine 384
Flower garden 386
Forty-five 79
Forty-five, auction 82
Forty thieves (see Napoleon at St. Helena) 408
Four of a kind (see Clock) 378
Friday the thirteenth 388
Frog 390

G

Gin rummy 140
Give away 448
Go boom 450
Go boom, scoring 451
Go fish 453
Grand 84
Greek hearts 89

H

Hearts 88
Hearts, black lady 89
Hearts, domino 90
Hearts, Greek 89
Hearts, joker 91
Hearts, spot 89
Hearts, two-handed 91
Heartsette 91

Hidden cards (see Clock) 378
High-card pool (see Red dog) 320
High-low jack (see Seven up) 143
High-low poker 312
Hoggenheimer 252
Horse race 255

I

I doubt it (see Cheat) 442
Idle year (see Accordion) 362
Imperial 94
In between (see Yablon) 349
Indian carpet (see Crazy quilt) 380
Injun 258
Irish loo 108

J

Jacks or better 307
Japanese rug (see Crazy quilt) 380
Jig 482
Joker hearts 91

K

Kalabriasz 98
Kalabriasz, partnership 102
Kalabriasz, three-handed 102
Kentucky derby 261
King Albert 392
Klaberjass (see Kalabriasz) 98
Klondike 395
Knaves 104
Knockout whist 455

L

La belle Lucie 397
Lame-brain Pete (see Poker, closed games) 310

Lansquenet 266
Lanterloo (see Loo) 106
Laying siege (see Beleaguered
  castle) 364
Le vieux garçon 466
Leapfrog 400
Linger longer 458
Loo 106
Loo, five-card 107
Loo, Irish 108
Loo, three-card 106
Low-hand stud 302
Lowball poker 309

M

Macao 214
Maze 402
Memory (see Concentration) 444
Menagerie 461
Methuselah (see Accordion) 362
Mexican stud poker 302
Michigan 109
Miss Milligan 404
Monte (see Monte bank) 269
Monte bank 269
Monte bank, casino 269
Monte bank, private 277
Monte Carlo 406
My ship sails 463

N

Nap (see Napoleon) 112
Nap, purchase 113
Nap, seven-card 113
Napoleon 112
Napoleon at St. Helena 408
Newmarket (see Michigan) 109

O

Oh hell 114
Old maid 464
Old man's bundle (see Stealing
  bundles) 487
Old sledge (see Seven up) 143

P

Parliament (see Card dominoes) 440
Pass the lady (see Old maid) 464
Pasteboard derby (see Kentucky
  derby) 261
Pelmanism (see Concentration) 444
Penuchle (see Pinochle) 116
Persian Pasha 491
Pig 447
Pig in the poke (see Spit in the
  ocean) 309
Pinochle 116
Pinochle, auction 120
Piquet 122
Piquet au cent 128
Piquet, auction 128
Pisha pasha (see Persian pasha) 491
Plait (see Braid) 368
Play or pay 467
Poker 279
Poker, closed games 310
Poker, draw 303
Poker, draw variants 307
Poker, high-low 312
Poker, stud 300
Poker, stud variants 301
Poker solitaire 410
Polignac 104
Polish Pachuk (see Polish red dog)
  314

Polish red dog 314
Pontoon (see Blackjack) 194
Pope Joan 130
Preference 136
Propeller (see Windmill) 433
Purchase nap 113
Puss in the corner 413
Put-and-take (see Card put-and-take) 238
Pyramid 415

Q

Quince (see Fifteen) 214

R

Racing demon 469
Railroad euchre 74
Rauber skat (see Skat) 146
Red and black 318
Red dog 320
Red dog, Polish 314
Red dog, six-spot 324
Rolling stone 472
Rouge et noir (see Trente et quarante) 344
Round the corner (see Play or pay) 467
Royal casino 60
Royal cotillion 418
Rubicon bezique 25
Rummy 138
Russian bank 420

S

Saratoga (see Michigan) 109
Saton pong (see Ten and a half) 213
Schnautz (see Thirty-one) 341

Schwellen (see Rolling stone) 472
Scoring go boom 451
Scorpion 425
Sequence 474
Set back (see Auction pitch) 20
Seven and a half 211
Seven-card stud poker 301
Seven-toed Pete (see Seven-card stud poker) 301
Seven up 143
Seven up, four-handed 144
Sevens (see Card dominoes) 440
Sham battle (see Beleaguered castle) 364
Shotgun 308
Six-card stud poker 301
Six-spot red dog 324
Skat 146
Skin (see Skinball) 328
Skinball 328
Skinning (see Skinball) 328
Slapjack 476
Slippery Anne (see Black Maria) 92
Slippery Sam 332
Snap 478
Snap, easy 480
Snap, speed 480
Snip-snap-snorem 481
Solo (see Solo whist) 154
Solo, three-handed 156
Solo whist 154
Spade casino 61
Spanish monte (see Monte bank) 269
Speed snap 480
Spider 427
Spit 484
Spit in the ocean 309

Spite and malice 430
Spoil five 157
Spot hearts 89
Stealing bundles 487
Stitch (see Polish red dog) 314
Stop the bus 229
Stormy weather 308
Stud poker 300
Stuss 335
Sun dial (see Clock) 378

T

Ten and a half 213
Thirty-five 338
Thirty-one 341
Three naturals (see Macao) 214
Toad in the hole (see Frog) 390
Tower of Babel (see Accordion) 362
Travelers (see Clock) 378
Trente et quarante 344
Twenty-one (see Blackjack) 194

U

Up and down cheat 443
Up and down the river 240

V

Vanjohn (see Blackjack) 194
Ving-et-un (see Blackjack) 194
Vint 161

W

War 489
War, for three players 490
Weddings (see Monte Carlo) 406
Whist 164

Whist, knockout 455
Whist, solo 154
Windmill 433

Y

Yablon 349

Z

Ziginette 352